The Spiritual Wisdom of the Gospels for Christian Preachers and Teachers

Year C

The Relentless Widow

John Shea

LITURGICAL PRESS
Collegeville, Minnesota

www.litpress.org

Cover design by James Rhoades

ISBN-13: 978-0-8146-2913-0	(Year A)
ISBN-10: 0-8146-2913-X	(Year A)
ISBN-13: 978-0-8146-2914-7	(Year B)
ISBN-10: 0-8146-2914-8	(Year B)
ISBN-13: 978-0-8146-2915-4	(Year C)
ISBN-10: 0-8146-2915-6	(Year C)
ISBN-13: 978-0-8146-2916-1	(Feasts, Funerals, & Weddings) Publication Date: Fall 2007
ISBN-10: 0-8146-2916-4	(Feasts, Funerals, & Weddings) Publication Date: Fall 2007
ISBN-13: 978-08146-2917-8	(set)
ISBN-10: 0-8146-2917-2	(set)

1   2   3   4   5   6   7   8

Library of Congress Cataloging-in-Publication Data

Shea, John, 1941–
   The spiritual wisdom of the Gospels for Christian preachers and teachers / John Shea.
      p. cm.
   Includes bibliographical references and index.
   ISBN 0-8146-2913-X (Year A : pbk. : alk. paper)
   1. Bible. N.T. Gospels—Criticism, interpretation, etc.   2. Bible.
N.T. Gospels—Homiletical use. 3. Lectionary preaching. I. Title.

BS2555.52.S54 2004
251'.6—dc22   2003025635

Contents

First Sunday of Advent

Luke 21:25-28, 34-36 _LM_ • Luke 21:25-36 _RCL_

❧

Engaging Collapse

A Spiritual Commentary

There will be signs in the sun, the moon, and the stars, and on the earth distress among nations confused by the roaring of the sea and the waves. People will faint from fear and foreboding of what is coming upon the world, for the powers of the heavens will be shaken. Then they will see "the Son of Man coming in a cloud" with power and great glory. Now when these things begin to take place, stand up and raise your heads, because your redemption is drawing near.

Creation is falling apart. Genesis is being reversed. The lamps that God hung in the sky to light the earth—the sun, moon, and stars—are now sending out alarm signals. The waters that once covered everything and that God siphoned off into containers called seas are making a comeback. God had raised up the earth in the midst of the seas, giving people a place to stand secure. But now the seas are seething and roaring, threatening the order of creation with a return to primordial chaos. This noise frightens people, reminding them of Noah's time and the flood that buried the earth and its unrepentant inhabitants. But what of the rainbow at the end of Noah's story? What of the pledge that God would never again drown creation?

The rainbow is the Son of Man, the Full Human Being. This one appears as things are falling apart, arriving from a space that transcends collapse. His advent banishes fear and allows his followers to stand up straight. The Son of Man is the new earth, the new place to stand. The waters cannot cover him. He is the redemption that is offered in the midst of a perishing world.

Be on guard so that your hearts are not weighed down with dissipation and drunkenness and the worries of this life, and that day catch you unexpectedly, like a trap. For it will come upon all who live on the face of the whole earth. Be alert at

all times, praying that you may have the strength to escape all these things that will take place, and to stand before the Son of Man.

Surviving and engaging collapse depends on knowing where to stand, on finding higher ground. If we give ourselves over to the physical and social world that is collapsing, we will go down with it. We must guard our spirit against triviality, against allowing it to become drunk and bloated with cares so that "neither moth nor rust consumes" (Matt 6:20). These cares weigh us down, do not allow us to move, and make us inattentive to subtle reality. If we do not do this, the collapse will appear to us as a trap, completely capturing us, threatening the total reality of who we are. We will not be aware of our transcendent self. We will have identified with those aspects of ourselves that are vulnerable to breakdown.

Therefore, our task is prayer and vigilance. These disciplines heighten awareness of our spiritual nature, that dimension of ourselves that withstands destruction. Standing secure in this space, we know ourselves as companions of the Son of Man, the Full Human Being. With this new identity, there emerges the courage not only to survive collapse but to engage it. When our worlds fall apart and the prediction is that everyone's will ("The day I speak of will come upon all who dwell on the face of the earth"), the Son of Man is the name we give to the fearless endeavor of rescue and redemption. It is the name that belongs to all people who, following Jesus, stay vigilant in prayer. Far from shrinking from destruction, we lean into it. We hold one another through and beyond the terrible collapses of life.

But what exactly is falling apart? What are these terrible collapses?

Some take the cosmic symbolism literally. They wait for the end of the space-time world, and buy binoculars to catch the first glimpse of the cloud-riding Son of Man. Their vigil continues.

Some take the cosmic symbolism to express political anarchy, the breakdown of the social order that puts everything at risk. Those who have endured this type of collapse know the truth of this symbolism in their hearts. Their world does fall apart, and the only images that do it justice are pictures of universal, cosmic destruction.

Some take the cosmic symbolism to refer to individual death, the vulnerability of the mind-body organism. We have all seen this collapse in others, and, despite a voracious appetite for self-deception, we cannot convince ourselves we will be spared.

Some take the cosmic symbolism to point to our personally constructed worlds of meaning, the way we put things together, the plans we have formulated and are eagerly implementing. Then our children move away, our job is downsized, our real estate taxes are raised beyond our means, our spouse turns moody and silent—the world we inhabited and hoped would continue is in shambles. The house has fallen. These collapses can be complete or partial. But is there anyone who has not experienced the tentative nature of their personal constructions of meaning?

However we interpret what is collapsing—cosmos, society, mind-body organism, or personal world of meaning—one thing is certain. In human life breakdown is inevitable.

Teaching

Spiritual traditions often characterize people as border walkers. We live at the intersection of the created and the Uncreated, time and eternity, space and infinity, matter and spirit. Evelyn Underhill, a spiritual writer in the Anglican tradition, calls this the two-sided or double reality of human life.

> We are, then, faced by two concepts, both needful if we are to make any sense of our crude experience; the historical, natural, and contingent; the timeless, supernatural, and absolute. They must be welded together, if we are to provide a frame for all the possibilities of human life; and that life, whether social or individual, must have both its historically flowing and its changelessly absolute side. (Evelyn Underhill, "Our Two-Fold Relation to Reality" in *Evelyn Underhill: Modern Guide to the Ancient Quest for the Holy* [New York: SUNY Press, 1988] 164–5)

Although this is the truth of the human condition, Underhill does not think most people are consistently conscious of this situation.

> Doubtless for the mass of men such consciousness is still in the rudimentary and sporadic stage. Here and there it does appear among us, though in very unequal degrees. And in so far as we are aware of these two aspects in ourselves and in the universe, we have to strike a working balance between them, if we would rightly harmonize the elements of life and achieve a stable relation with reality. (Ibid.)

Therefore, people face two tasks. The first is to become conscious of the full, two-sided reality of who they are. The second is to learn to "weld" these together, to find a "working balance" between them, to "harmonize" their elements.

But the apocalyptic text for the first Sunday of Advent does not talk in generalities about harmony, welding, and balance. The "historically flowing" and "changelessly absolute" sides are being ripped apart. The hope that is held out is to learn to identify with the "changelessly absolute" side. Grounded in this identity, we are able to relate to the historical flowing. Ancient spirituality valued "harmony, welding, and balance," but it was also clear-headed about the priority of the spiritual. It held pride of place for the simple reason that it survived historical passage. It did not go down into the dust. A classic statement of this emphasis comes from Vedanta philosophy.

> Two birds of golden plumage sat on the same tree. The one above, serene, majestic, immersed in his own glory; the one below restless and eating the fruits of the tree, now sweet, now bitter. Once he ate an exceptionally bitter fruit, then he paused and looked up at the majestic bird above; but he soon forgot about the other bird and went on eating the fruits of the tree as before. Again he ate a bitter fruit, and this time he hopped up a few boughs nearer to the bird at the top. This happened many times until at last the lower bird came to the place of the upper bird and lost himself. He found all at once that there had never been two birds, but that he was all the time that upper bird, serene, majestic, and immersed in his own glory. (Lucinda Vardey, ed., *God in All Worlds: An Anthology of Contemporary Spiritual Writing* [New York: Pantheon Books, 1995] 475)

We do not have to accept the dualism and negative assessment of historical life implied in this text to appreciate the spiritual instinct at its core. How the historically flowing and changelessly absolute sides come together in negative times is that we move closer to the changelessly absolute.

In the most threatening moments of our lives, the Son of Man appears as a protecting nearness that does not permit final destruction. It seems to me this truth entails more than the survival of the soul. It means we have the freedom to engage collapse, to relate to it from the transcendent center of our being. For me the image of the Full Human Being coming on the clouds with power and glory is a magnificent imaginative picture of this possibility that God graciously offers. It has all the flavor and excitement of last-minute rescue. However, another picture, more realistic but no less dramatic, haunts me. It is the earthly Son of Man swallowing the world of collapse with his voice. "Then Jesus gave a loud cry and breathed his last" (Mark 15:37).

Second Sunday of Advent
Luke 3:1-6

ᴧ

Going Beyond the Mind

A Spiritual Commentary

In the fifteenth year of the reign of Emperor Tiberius, when Pontius Pilate was governor of Judea, and Herod was ruler of Galilee, and his brother Philip ruler of the region of Ituraea and Trachonitis, and Lysanias ruler of Abilene, during the high priesthood of Annas and Caiaphas, the word of God came to John son of Zechariah in the wilderness.

This clever, opening sentence cuts two ways. On one level, it is the proper way to historically date an event. It names the ruling parties, beginning with Roman overlords, proceeding to Jewish rulers, and finally acknowledging Temple authorities. Hierarchical protocol is correctly followed. We know the time and place of John the Baptist by situating him in the context of the major players of the day.

On another level, it is a scathing theological judgment on the Roman and Jewish political leadership and the religious establishment. The Word of God has bypassed them all. The political and religious leaders are meant to be mediations of divine power. Earthly thrones mirror the divine throne; earthly authority participates in divine authority. But the Word of God does not stop at palaces or the temple. Instead, it searches out a priest's son who is also a prophet and finds him in the desert. The desert is a place of purification and inner scrutiny, far from the machinations of power.

He went into all the region around the Jordan, proclaiming a baptism of repentance for the forgiveness of sins, as it is written in the book of the words of the prophet Isaiah, "The voice of one crying out in the wilderness:

**'Prepare the way of the Lord, make his paths straight.
Every valley shall be filled,
and every mountain and hill shall be made low,
and the crooked shall be made straight,**

and the rough ways made smooth;
and all flesh shall see the salvation of God.'"

John's baptism is an outer ritual meant to express and facilitate an inner process. A standard interpretation is: as dirt is washed off by water, so sin is washed away by baptism. Another interpretation sees the submerged person dying to their previous life, returning to the waters of the womb, and emerging from the waters into a new life. Neither of these interpretations names the intricacies of inner process. Instead, they stress change, a transition from one state to another.

The intricacies of the inner change process are captured in the phrase a "baptism of repentance for the forgiveness of sins." "Repentance" is a translation of the Greek word *metanoia*. Metanoia literally means "going beyond the mind." When we are able to go beyond the mind, forgiveness of sins follows. This is an enigmatic connection. It assumes there is something about the mind that holds onto sins; and there is something about going beyond the mind that lets go of sins.

This going beyond the mind to let go of sins is not an end in itself. For John the Baptist it is the necessary work of preparation. Borrowing the language of Isaiah, he sees himself as a construction worker. He is building a highway for the arrival of the Lord. Whatever is an obstacle will be eliminated. If the road is winding, it will be straightened. If it is rough, it will be smoothed. If a mountain is in the way, it will be flattened. If a valley slows travel time, it will be lifted into a flat surface. The effect of these multiple images is a sense of determination. Whatever is needed to ease the Lord's arrival will be done. This is a man on a mission.

But what is this "going beyond the mind to let go of sins" preparation for?

The account of Jesus' baptism gives a symbolic answer. In the Gospel of Luke, when Jesus comes out of the water, he prays. In prayer the sky opens, the Spirit as a dove descends, and the heavenly voice affirms, "You are my Son, the Beloved; with you I am well pleased" (Luke 3:22). This is the goal of the going beyond the mind and forgiving sins. It readies the baptized person to hear the transcendent word of love. Without forgiveness of sins, people are blind and deaf to the descent of the dove and the voice from the sky. The full process entails going beyond the mind to let go of sins and receive the Holy Spirit. This is what happens to Jesus, and this is what can happen to his followers. John's highway is ultimately a path to let God get close, to make it possible to welcome Jesus as the Giver of the Spirit.

Teaching

The mind has a mind of its own. Thoughts think themselves, seemingly undirected by the thinker. The discovery of this simple and undeniable facet of our makeup can be quite startling. We fantasize we are in complete control of mental processes. However, the actual situation seems to be quite different. When we concentrate, we can focus thinking along a certain path. But if we relax attention, certain automatic mental processes kick in. The automatic process that concerns John the Baptist is how we deal with the wounds that have been inflicted on us and the wounds we have inflicted on others. In religious language, his focus is on how the mind seduces us into identifying with sin.

There is an adhesive quality about sinful experiences. They stick. We remember the beatings, the humiliations, the hateful glances, and the mocking words. The wrongs done to us are available to memory in a way neutral and even positive experiences are not. Although the experience of sin begins with being sinned against, we are quick learners in this way of being human. We soon learn to wound others. We engage in hitting, lying, cheating, betraying, etc. We need to protect and promote ourselves at all costs. Any behavior that appears to further this narrow and intense self-preoccupation we embrace. Soon we can tell our life story in term of blows received and blows given. It is a tale of sin; and even if we repress it, it secretly shapes our sense of who we are.

This attraction of the mind to the negative has a cumulative effect. As the mind simultaneously nurtures a sense of victimhood and wallows in guilt over its own mistakes, sin rises to a new status in the interior life. We gradually begin to identity with the sinful dimension of our lives. In our own eyes, we become, above all else, one who has been sinned against and one who sins in turn. We are the receiver and giver of blows, and the highest compliment is, "He gave as good as he got." The mind is convinced this is the "real us," and it defends this identity by citing facts and providing rationalizations. Nothing can disprove this obvious truth.

However, there is an important distinction to be made in telling this inner story of sin. The distinction is between what has happened and what the mind does with what has happened. We *really* have been maltreated, victims of the wrongdoing of others; and we *really* have maltreated others, making them victims of our wrongdoing. Not to acknowledge this active participation in the sin of the world is to be either incredibly dense or in chronic denial.

But the point is not the sheer factuality of moral evil. The point is what the mind does with these experiences. It enthrones them as the secret and irreversible truth about the human person. Sinner becomes the depth identity, the loudest interior noise that blocks out any refuting voices. The result is an ever-deepening connection of who we are with the wrongs done to us and by us.

This inner escalation of sin raises the gospel question: "Are grapes gathered from thorns or figs from thistles?" (Matt 7:16). If we think we are unredeemed sinners, we will not bear fruit. We will not ripen and blossom with compassion, justice, love, and respect. Most importantly, we will not be able to hear the real name that Jesus calls us. Our identification with sin becomes a serious roadblock—a mountain in the way, a winding and rough path that means slow travel, a valley that delays arrival. Jesus cannot get to us with his radical address that we are the light of the world, the salt of the earth, and a blessedness that is always present no matter what external circumstances prevail. When we cling to our identity as sinner, his words cannot penetrate the armor of our hardened self-evaluation. He is not the One Who Is to Come, but the One Sin Keeps Away. That is why John the Baptist is needed as preparation for Christ. He enables people to go beyond the mind and let go of sins.

This repentance that leads to the forgiveness of sins is a subtle process, but it is not an impossible one. Two key insights often help us. The first insight involves our awareness of the nature of the mind. When we become aware of the powerful tendency of the mind to hold onto sin, we are already beyond it. We see what it is doing, and so we are more than it. We transcend the mind by noticing how it works. When this happens, a sense of spaciousness replaces the sense of restriction and a sense of freedom replaces the sense of compulsion. We feel we have walked through a door into a hidden room that feels like home. We are closer to who we really are.

The second insight involves an implication of the basic Christian conviction of the unconditional forgiveness of God. God is ultimate reality and, therefore, if God holds the sin, the sin transcends the flow of time and remains permanently present. But if God has let go of the sin, then who is holding on? The forgiveness of God clears the way for us to see where the real action is. The real action is the mind and how it clings to negative evaluations. The question changes from "Will God forgive me?" to "How can I go beyond the mind that clings to sin, even though God has forgiven me?"

Before we can hear the words that Jesus heard, "You are my beloved child. In you I am well pleased," we will have to undergo John's baptism which entails a repentance that leads to the forgiveness of sins. If we do this, the path is cleared.

Third Sunday of Advent

Luke 3:10-18 *LM* • **Luke 3:7-18** *RCL*

❧

Repenting Forever

A Spiritual Commentary

The crowds asked John the Baptist, "What then should we do?"

In reply he said to them, "Whoever has two coats must share with anyone who has none; and whoever has food must do likewise."

Even tax collectors came to be baptized and they asked him, "Teacher, what should we do?"

He said to them, "Collect no more than the amount prescribed for you."

Soldiers also asked him, "And we, what should we do?"

He said to them, "Do not extort money from anyone by threats or false accusation, and be satisfied with your wages."

Spiritual development always entails both understanding and action, mental realization and behavioral integration, interior illumination and outer righteousness. In the life of any individual these two aspects are always interacting, coming together and breaking apart in myriad ways. The standard connection is the logical movement from understanding to action. For example, if people love their neighbors, they will share their resources with them. The interior love manifests itself in handing over the second coat. Although thinking like this abounds in moral theology, things are never quite this simple.

A different connection is established when the seekers ask for an action plan, "What are we to do?" and the teacher is willing to provide one. Then the seekers try to implement the action plan. In doing this, they have to return again and again to their interior consciousness. When action is abstractly conceived, it always unfolds without a hitch. But when action is concretely engaged, it hesitates and stumbles. Although there are always exterior factors to take into account and reevaluate, seekers invariably discover mental blocks. Their desire to do an action is undercut by their own mental conditioning. Therefore, they are thrown back into the reciprocal flow between understanding and action, mental realization and behavioral integration, inner illumination and outer righteousness.

We can imagine the spiritual paths of these groups of people who made the mistake of asking John what they should do. The crowds would find themselves holding onto their second coat and extra bread and old sandals, etc. "What is enough?" they might ask themselves. "Do I jeopardize myself for someone who hasn't worked as hard as I have?" The tax collectors have done well with their thumb on the scale. "Can we take a cutback in revenue? Is not this the expected way of doing things? Will I lose my position if I go against the common practice?" Soldiers, by definition, push people around. After all, they don't teach dancing. Who would know they were soldiers if they stopped bullying people, threatening to denounce them falsely, and making a little on the side? Their pay is meant to be supplemented in this way. When we attempt to change morally, we have to work on the inside to sustain different behavior on the outside.

The spiritual teacher knows any outer action will inevitably lead to the discovery of inner reluctances and obstacles. John the Baptist is about removing obstacles. The first step toward removing obstacles is discovering them. There is no better way to uncover inner blocks than trying to do something that entails a change in the way we have previously worked. What seems like simple advice from John the Baptist becomes a journey of self-discovery.

> **As the people were filled with expectation, and all were questioning in their heart concerning John, whether he might be the Messiah. John answered all of them by saying, "I baptize you with water; but one who is more powerful than I is coming. I am not worthy to untie the thong of his sandals. He will baptize you with the Holy Spirit and fire. His winnowing fork is in his hand to clear his threshing floor and gather the wheat into his granary, but the chaff he will burn with unquenchable fire." So, with many other exhortations, he proclaimed the good news to the people.**

There is poignancy in the character of John the Baptist. He correctly understands that he is not the Messiah but the forerunner of one mightier than himself. He must learn from that one, for he is not fit to loosen his sandal strap. This attitude of learning from the One Who Is to Come will be important, for what John envisions will not be what will come about.

John foresees a baptism in "the Holy Spirit and fire." But he mistakenly assumes this Holy Spirit and fire means judgment and destruction. The Holy Spirit becomes a rough wind that separates the wheat and the chaff when the winnowing fan lifts it into the air, and fire awaits the combustible chaff. Wind (Holy Spirit) and fire work together to separate the good from the bad and to reward the good and punish the bad.

However, when Jesus comes, he will be the source of the Holy Spirit and fire in a quite different way. He will connect people to God so that the Holy Spirit can work through them to such a degree that people will see their "good works and give glory to your Father in heaven" (Matt 5:16). This Holy Spirit will inspire and direct their lives, providing the commitment to carry out John's agenda of reform. The Holy Spirit is the spiritual energy to share with others and not oppress them. This is the fire that both purifies every moral effort and provides the passion to persevere. It is a fire that burns without burning out, the fire of the bush that energized Moses in his relentless efforts to free the people from slavery (Exod 3:2).

Teaching

The crowds asked him, "What should we do?"

Glad you asked.

Pick a value. It must be a transcendent value, one that is grounded in God. Not one of those contemporary whims that pass as values, like "keeping in touch."

I mean a real value, like compassion or forgiveness or reconciliation or peace or justice. Something that has some bite in it and will be around long after you're gone. Something moths and rust cannot consume and thieves cannot break in and steal. For example, let's take compassion.

Now take ten minutes a day in the morning and meditate on it. Clear your mind of other thoughts and distractions. If they continue to intrude, just notice them and let them go. Return to compassion.

It is good to have a phrase to repeat silently and mindfully. Some Buddhists think equality is the path to compassion, and they suggest a phrase like "Everyone wants to be happy and doesn't want to suffer." As you slowly and silently repeat this phrase that makes you equal with everyone else, pictures of people you know may enter your mind. Simply use their name in the next phrase, "Joan wants to be happy and doesn't want to suffer . . . Frank wants to be happy and doesn't want to suffer," and every so often say, "I want to be happy and don't want to suffer." Now you are in the human mess with everyone else.

When you have done this for about ten minutes, get on with the day. Don't evaluate how the meditation is going. Dismiss all questions like "Did I do it right? Why am I doing this? Did I waste my time?" Just continue to do it.

Also you should read some stuff on compassion. Meditation is not enough. Over the long haul it will heighten your awareness of opportunities for compassionate action. But, in itself, it won't make you much smarter about compassion. You need to read and ponder, to reflect on what you are reading.

Try this little story from Parker Palmer.

> At Pendle Hill, the Quaker community where I lived and worked for eleven years, our lives were so intertwined that people could quickly become attached to each other and just as quickly become alienated. But *alienated* is a mild word to describe my relation to one woman who lived there. She was, in my mind, the devil's spawn, sent here directly from the pits of hell to destroy all that is green and good about life on earth.
>
> The people at Pendle Hill gather every morning in a "meeting for worship," forty-five minutes of communal silence, occasionally broken by words spoken spontaneously from the heart. One morning, I arrived late for worship, and the only seat available was next to *her*. Agitated, I came close to turning around and walking out. But I managed somehow to sit down, close my eyes, and start to meditate, slowly forgetting that I was sitting next to a creature from the dark side.
>
> About half an hour later, head still bowed, I opened my eyes and found myself staring at the upturned hand this woman had rested on her knee. There, spotlighted by a shaft of sunlight, I saw the faint but steady throb of an artery in her wrist, the elemental beat of her very human heart. In that moment, I knew beyond words that here was a person just like me, with strengths and weaknesses, hopes and disappointments, joys and despairs. In that moment, my sense of who she was, and of who I was to her, underwent some sort of transformation.
>
> I never became close to this woman. In truth, I never stopped feeling wary of her. But I could no longer demonize her as I had until that silent, sunlit moment. (Parker Palmer, *A Hidden Wholeness* [San Francisco: Jossey-Bass, 2004] 155–6)

Think about this reading. And find other stuff on compassion. You need to supplement your spiritual practice with spiritual wisdom.

Now for the really important part. At the end of the day, take some time to review the day in the light of your spiritually grounded value of compassion. No doubt you will notice some things that could have been done differently if you had remembered your value of compassion.

Well, get on the phone or email and redo that situation. Don't let embarrassment stop you. Just do it. You may be awkward at first, but you'll get used to it.

This is repenting. Repentance is not what bad people have to do. It is what people who live out of transcendent values find necessary. Most of us don't get it right the first time. We only notice we could have done it differently "over our shoulder." But when we see a more compassionate way, we have to act on it. This is how we get better. A little.

Getting better means seeing a compassionate way while a situation is actually unfolding. Most likely the first time this happens you will have to pause to figure out what is going on. In the pause a response will come to you. Yes, a response will come to you. It will not be a carefully worked out strategy with all the pluses and minuses lined up in columns for you to evaluate. You will suddenly see it. Like it was there all along but you didn't notice it. When it comes to you like that, this is the Holy Spirit. Say, "Thank you."

And act on what you see. The courage to act on what you see will also come from the Holy Spirit. Say, "Thank you."

Although you have compassion in your heart and you saw what to do and you did it, it may not have worked out very well. That's not the Holy Spirit. That's you. Redo it. Redoing and pausing/pausing and redoing are partners. Where there is one, you'll find the other.

After a while, you'll think, "I'm getting pretty damn good at this. I am probably the most compassionate person in this whole organization (family, neighborhood, etc.)." That's your ego wanting to separate you from other people in order to feel superior. Say, "No thank you."

Instead, humbly recommit yourself to your spiritual practice on compassion, your spiritual reading on compassion, and your experiments in bringing compassion into all you do. That's fire, the steady burning that does not burn out. Of course, by now you know where this perseverance comes from, so say, "Thank you."

One last thing. This process is never over. Repenting is forever. Get used to it.

Fourth Sunday of Advent
Luke 1:39-45

❦

Evangelizing the Child in the Womb

A Spiritual Commentary

Mary set out and went with haste to a Judean town in the hill country, where she entered the house of Zechariah and greeted Elizabeth. When Elizabeth heard Mary's greeting, the child leaped in her womb. And Elizabeth was filled with the Holy Spirit and exclaimed with a loud cry, "Blessed are you among women, and blessed is the fruit of your womb. And why has this happened to me, that the mother of my Lord comes to me? For as soon as I heard the sound of your greeting, the child in my womb leaped for joy. And blessed is she who believed that there would be a fulfillment of what was spoken to her by the Lord."

Zechariah and Elizabeth both come from priestly families, and Elizabeth is pregnant with a child who will become a prophet. She represents both the priestly and prophetic traditions of Israel. So when the infant in her womb leaps for joy at Mary's greeting, and when she humbly asks, "But how does this happen to me, that the mother of my Lord should come to me," the theological priorities are clear. Mary carries the fulfillment of Hebrew history. The promise at the heart of Israel's faith, both its priestly and prophetic traditions, is Jesus.

Besides this theological consideration, there is a very personal and individual note in Elizabeth's praise of Mary. She is blessed because she has learned to trust the process of hearing the Lord's word with such attentiveness that it leads to fulfillment. Elizabeth is referring to the previous episode in Luke's Gospel. Mary has just had a mind-boggling conversation with the angel Gabriel who speaks the Word of the Lord. (See the Fourth Sunday of Advent, Year B.) In a surprise visit, he greeted her as a reality bursting with grace and destined to be involved in a divine plan. This troubled her, but she did not dismiss it. She pondered his strange address of "full of grace" and "the Lord is with you."

As she was considering his unusual salutation, Gabriel continued unabated, telling her not to be afraid and spelling out the mission in detail. It entailed conceiving and bearing a son who would inherit the throne of a king, the house of a patriarch, and lead a kingdom that would never end. The angel spared no superlative or extravagance. The mission is about God, history, and the future of the world. Needless to say, the virgin is both overwhelmed and overmatched.

Mary protested she did not have the necessary physical prerequisites. She is not qualified. "Who said anything about the physical?" Gabriel insinuates. He counters her objection with the promise of the Holy Spirit who would permeate her and would provide whatever was needed. In the last analysis, this is God's doing. He strengthens his case by mentioning Elizabeth, her kinswoman. She is already on board—the barren one is bearing a son. Then he hammers the lesson home: nothing is impossible with God. The tendency of the mind to shy away from what it perceives as impossible is directly refuted. This is the angel's trump card and it wins the hand. Mary says "yes" with what the poet Denise Levertov called "a courage that opened her utterly" (*A Door in the Hive* [New York: New Directions, 1989] 88). The angel departed, and Mary "set out and traveled to the hill country in haste."

Although angels can be imposing and, more often than not, get their point across, they can also be ephemeral. They belong to a species of special spiritual experiences. They arrive unexpectedly, leave suddenly, and the ones whom they visit find themselves pregnant. "What exactly has happened here?" is a common response. There is a need for more down-to-earth human conversation, a conversation that can process what happened and evaluate it. But this conversation has to be with someone who will respect the experience, who knows the ways of angels. Gabriel has dropped the name Elizabeth, and Mary has picked up on it. However, she is not hastening to the house of the priest in the mystical hills of Judea to check out the angel's story. Is Elizabeth really pregnant? Rather, she is looking to explore her transcendent experience with someone who knows about them. She has come to the right place.

However, the confirmation does not come through tortured conversation and labyrinthine discussion. Mary's greeting triggers the Holy Spirit in Elizabeth, and her loud outburst not only tells Mary all she needs to know but also begins Mary's mission. The storyteller does not say what the exact greeting was; but both in the narrative and Elizabeth's witness the connection is made between the greeting and the infant leaping for joy. Mary's salutation activates what is growing in Elizabeth, what is coming to birth in her. What is growing in her is God-grounded and God-directed and, as Gabriel has indicated, breaks through the way the human mind constructs laws of possibility and impossibility. Therefore, humility and lowliness are the proper responses. "Why has this happened to me, that the mother of my Lord comes to me?" These interior attitudes open the door between human impossibility and divine possibility.

What is going on here?

Mary's work with the angel has made her not only the mother of Jesus but an exemplary disciple of the Word. As one who has realized and integrated the truth of the Word, she is capable of starting the process in others. Her greeting can touch the interior where the promise of God is growing and stir it into activity. In the presence of fulfillment, the embryonic growth in Elizabeth recognizes its goal and what it must serve. The path of trusting the Word is not only the individual achievement of Mary. Her presence activates the divine gestation in others.

Teaching

Spiritual teachings often use images from physical and social reality as analogies to understand and cooperate with the more subtle movements of spiritual reality. However, these images are open-ended, and an adequate understanding of the point of comparison between the image and the spiritual reality has to consider the context.

Womb is an important image that is used to illumine spiritual reality. It is taken from female reproductive anatomy and is used in variety of contexts. In the highly poetic early centuries of Christianity, it was said that Mary conceived through the ear. In other words, it was the Word of the Lord spoken by Gabriel and heard by Mary that initiated the pregnancy. It was also said that Mary conceived in her heart. In other words, she pondered the Word of the Lord in the space where the human person is connected both to God and to the world of action. It was also said she conceived in her womb. In other words, the Son of the Most High took flesh in the human condition. These three forms of conceiving—ear, heart, womb—came together as a spiritual process of incarnation. Mary heard the word in her ears, pondered its deeper meaning in her heart, and embodied it in action, conceiving the Word in her womb and giving birth. In this context, womb means the embodiment of the spiritual.

The image of womb is also used to suggest the slow movement of growth from darkness to light or from the hidden to the revealed. The

Word of the Lord is a seed that is planted in darkness, in hiding. It grows slowly in that place, gradually becoming more visible. When it is fully matured, it pushes forth into the world. The pregnant womb bears the meaning of a slow ripening with the attendant wisdom, "When the fruit is ripe, it falls from the tree." In this context, womb is the place where the fruit ripens and Jesus is called the "fruit of Mary's womb."

The image of womb is also used to convey God's complete knowledge and guidance of each person. "O Lord, you have searched me and known me. . . . For it was you who formed my inward parts; you knit me together in my mother's womb" (Ps 139:1, 13). "Can a woman forget her nursing child, or show no compassion for the child of her womb? Even these may forget, yet I will not forget you" (Isa 49:15). In this context, womb is the origin of the human person whom God knows from the beginning and to whom God is unalterably committed.

In the story of Mary and Elizabeth, the emphasis is on Elizabeth's womb. A child is growing there who is sensitive to the greeting of Mary that arrives through the ears of Elizabeth. We are told twice, once through the storyteller's description and once through the witness of Elizabeth, that the greeting was positively received. The child leapt for joy. In this context, I suggest the "child in the womb" is a promise that accompanies each human birth, and Mary's greeting is the fulfillment of that promise.

That Jesus is the fulfillment of human history as well as Hebrew faith is suggested throughout Luke's Gospel. When the child Jesus is in the arms of the aged Simeon, Simeon sings to God that what he holds is both "a light for the revelation to the Gentiles and for glory to your people Israel" (Luke 2:32). Jesus is meant for the Gentiles as well as the Jews. Also, the Lukan genealogy, which is placed after the baptism of Jesus, moves through a long line of Jesus' Hebrew ancestors to arrive climactically at "son of Adam, son of God" (Luke 3:38). The Hebrew lineage is ultimately rooted in the single progenitor of the human family making Jesus the Son of Man. However, Adam has been directly created by God, making Jesus the Son of God. The full truth about Jesus is—Jew, human being, and divine son.

The meeting of two pregnant women symbolizes this threefold truth. The historical Jewish level is assured by their ethnic identities. The universal human level is assured by the pictures of pregnancy, the way all people are introduced into life. The divine dimension is assured by the angelic appearances to Zachary and Mary and the fact that Elizabeth's directly addresses God's activity. Therefore, Mary's greeting causes the infant to leap for joy in the womb of Elizabeth, in the womb of every woman, and among the angels in heaven.

Although we are not told what this joy-producing greeting was, I speculate that it was the standard Christian greeting, "Peace." Mary is not only the mother of the Lord but the perfect disciple who hears and keeps the word. When these disciples enter a house, they are to say, "'Peace to this house!' And if anyone is there who shares in peace, your peace will rest on that person; but if not, it will return to you" (Luke 10:5-6). Mary entered the house of Zachariah and her greeting of peace rested on one who shares in peace, for it had been predicted of John that he would guide people's "feet into the way of peace" (Luke 1:79). In the Christian community, peace connotes the restoration of relationships based on God's initiative. This is what the angels sing at the birth of Jesus. "Glory to God in the highest heaven, and on earth *peace* among those whom he favors!" (Luke 2:14). The connections between heaven and earth and among all creatures on earth are rightfully ordered.

This is the promise accompanying each child growing in the womb. Of course, this hope for a world of communion rather than alienation will not be fulfilled. The divine and the human will not be integrated, and the relationships between people will not be harmonious. But the Christian response is: it was in one man. Jesus was one like us in all things save sin. He was, as Paul Tillich said, essential God-Manhood, the New Being, under the conditions of existence (*Systematic Theology, Vol. II: Existence and the Christ* [Chicago: University of Chicago Press, 1957] 118–35). He lived in communion with God and neighbor in a world that lived in alienation from God and neighbor. He was the fulfillment of the promise of every child in the womb. And, by the way, he was a "firstborn" (Luke 2:7). There can be others. But first they must hear this good news. When Christians celebrate the birth of Jesus, they evangelize the child in every woman's womb.

Second Sunday in Ordinary Time
Second Sunday after Epiphany

John 2:1-11

٧

Supplying Wine

A Spiritual Commentary

On the third day there was a wedding in Cana of Galilee, and the mother of Jesus was there.

Jesus and his disciples had also been invited to the wedding.

When the wine gave out, the mother of Jesus said to him, "They have no wine."

And Jesus said to her, "Woman, what concern is that to you and to me? My hour has not yet come."

The story starts with a time designation—"on the third day." This does not mean the third twenty-four-hour period. Rather, it is part of a symbolic sequence. The first day is the beginning; the second day is the middle; and the third day is the end. Therefore, the third day symbolizes the fulfillment of the activities of the first and second days and the start of something new. It is a transitional day, something is ending and something is beginning. Also, "third day" carries the connotation that this transition is overseen by God. It is a manifestation in time of the divine plan.

This transition is happening at a wedding where the mother of Jesus is present. On the surface level, a wedding is an event where two, male and female, become one in order to create a third. Weddings are about human love that co-creates human life. On the depth level, a wedding, especially a wedding where the mother of Jesus is present, symbolizes the relationship between the divine and the human, how the two embrace each other to create vitality. The wedding symbolizes how God and people are united in love to co-create spiritual life.

The mother of Jesus is the spokesperson for the people side of this divine-human relationship. She is humanity aware of its lack, conscious that it cannot live to the fullest without continual communion with God. So she speaks to Jesus, the God side of the divine-human relationship, the haunting and poignant words of all human insufficiency. "They have no wine." Humans have lost their union with God and, by implication, their communion with one another. Without this spiritual union the wedding of life cannot continue.

These words of human need spoken by the mother of Jesus will be echoed by all who seek the presence of God as a remedy for human failing. The royal official will say, "come down before my little boy dies" (John 4:48). The lame man describes his helplessness as, "I have no one to put me into the pool" (John 5:7). In the face of the overwhelming numbers of people, Philip realizes the scarcity of money and bread. "Six months' wages would not buy enough bread for each of them to get a little" (John 6:7). Even though he has been healed, the blind beggar remembers, "I was blind . . ." (John 9:25). Mary and Martha send a message to Jesus, "Lord, he whom you love is ill" (John 11:3). These statements combine to create a chorus of human afflictions. They do not reflect moral evil, the terrible pain humans inflict on one another. They are the cries of finitude—illness, lameness, blindness, hunger, and death. In short, the human condition is so jeopardized that people cannot celebrate. They have no wine.

In response to the mother of Jesus' bold statement of lack, Jesus addresses her as "woman." He recognizes her as Eve, the mother of the living, who cares for her children and whose responsibility it is to seek their well-being. And when he asks her how the imperiled human condition whom she represents is connected to God whom he embodies, it is a question that sets up the revelation of his glory. Jesus' glory is to bring divine abundance into the world of human lack. The incarnate love of God is geared to prevent perishing. "For God so loved the world that he gave his only Son, so that everyone who believes in him may not perish, but may have eternal life. Indeed, God did not send the Son into the world to condemn the world, but in order that the world might be saved through him" (John 3:16-17). The answer to the question, "What concern is this to you and me?" is: everything. The very reason for Jesus' being is to supply wine for the imperiled marriage of divine and human life. The mother of Jesus knows who to come to when the wine runs out.

However, the fullest revelation of how divine love embraces human lack will take place at Jesus' "hour." Jesus acknowledges this hour has not yet come. Yet this hour holds the clue to the way the divine and the human are united, and it must be taken into account whenever human need and divine love face each other. The mere mention of this hour corrects a conventional misunderstanding of the divine and the human. God is not a king who arbitrarily decrees blessing or curse; and Jesus is not a miracle worker. Jesus' hour shows a different way.

Early in the gospel, the disciples of John follow Jesus and ask, "Where do you live?" He invites them to, "Come and see" (John 1:39). Jesus lives "close to the Father's heart" (John 1:18). So the invitation to John's disciples is to enter into Jesus' relationship with the Father and to receive God's love. But later in the gospel, when Jesus asks where they have laid Lazarus, the tables are reversed and *he* is told, "Lord, come and see" (John 11:34). Then when he sees Mary and the Jews weeping, Jesus himself weeps. Now he is one with those he loves. He himself has entered into the vulnerability of human existence.

This is the path divine love takes. It does not save from the outside, by divine fiat and/or overwhelming force. Divine love compassionately shares human suffering in order to save from the inside. Therefore, the condition for making good wine at the wedding of Cana is drinking sour wine on the cross of Golgotha (John 19:29). This is the truth of his "hour," a truth that must never be forgotten.

> **His mother said to the servants, "Do whatever he tells you."**
>
> **Now standing there were six stone water jars for the Jewish rites of purification, each holding twenty or thirty gallons.**
>
> **Jesus said to them, "Fill the jars with water."**
>
> **And they filled them up to the brim.**
>
> **He said to them, "Now draw some out, and take it to the chief steward."**
>
> **So they took it.**
>
> **When the steward tasted the water that had become wine, and did not know where it came from (though the servants who had drawn the water knew), the steward called the bridegroom and said to him, "Everyone serves the good wine first, and then the inferior wine after the guests have become drunk. But you have kept the good wine until now."**
>
> **Jesus did this, the first of his signs, in Cana of Galilee, and revealed his glory; and his disciples believed in him.**

The mother of Jesus now knows the intent of divine love and the path it will take. As the representative of imperiled humanity, she instructs the servants to do whatever Jesus tells them. Now the transitional nature of the revelation, what is ending and what is beginning, comes into play. The six stone water jars are for Jewish rites of purification. The water is used to ritually wash the body, the outside, in order to make it clean. The assumption is that the divine and human are related and kept in communion by the human effort to remain pure. Humans must ritually atone for their sins if they are to stay in touch with the divine. However, this way of humans placating God is eliding into a different way of thinking and acting. The time has come for purifying water to be transformed into exhilarating wine.

At Jesus' instruction, the jars are filled to the brim with water. The emphasis is no longer on the water washing the outside of a body but on the water filling the inside of the jars to their maximum. This is the beginning of the abundance of grace that wells up from within, a fullness that characterizes Spirit. "The water that I will give will become in them a spring of water gushing up to eternal life" (John 4:14). At Cana when the water gushes up into eternal life, it becomes wine. Wine is a symbol for Spirit, vivifying the entire human person from within. The divine and the human are related and kept in communion by the divine Spirit entering into the threatened human condition and supplying what it needs.

In a concluding remark, the storyteller calls this action of Jesus a "sign." A sign works on two levels. There is a surface/physical/literal level directly available to the five senses. Consciousness focuses on what the eyes see, the ears hear, the hands touch, the nose smells, and the tongue tastes. There is also a depth/spiritual/symbolic level not immediately available to the senses but that must be discerned through what is sensibly available. Readers are invited to follow the clues of the surface/physical/literal level into the depth/spiritual/symbolic level and experience the Christian revelation.

However, the ingrained human tendency is to stay on the surface, to become mired in the sensible. The common sense dictum, "What you see is what you get" encourages us to go no further. So the storyteller minimizes the miraculous aspects of the story so readers will not be so dazzled by the surface that they will not proceed to the depth. The actual change of the water into wine in this story is so completely downplayed that it almost appears as an afterthought. It is casually mentioned within the context of another activity—tasting. "When the steward tasted the water that had become wine . . ." There is no spotlight thrown on the transformation. The change is slipped in, for this story is more interested in revealing how the divine and the human are married to one another than in ballyhooing a miracle.

But who can read this sign correctly? Who can see it as the revelation of Jesus' glory and come to believe in him? The storyteller says the disciples were able to do so. But they had help, both positively and negatively.

Positively, they watched the servants hear and obey Jesus' instructions to the letter. In particular, the servants both filled the jars to the brim with water and drew the water made wine out from the inside of the jars. They learned how to connect what is ending with what is beginning and to make the transition. The revelation of Jesus is not something completely new. He is the fulfillment of what came before. The prologue of the gospel puts water and wine together. "The law indeed was given through Moses; grace and truth came through Jesus Christ" (John 1:17). The wine transcends the water even as it includes it. The servants know where the wine came from.

Negatively, the steward to whom the servants bring the wine does not grasp the sign. He is mired in the sensible and he cannot follow his taste buds to the spiritual. He judges by gastronomical standards, and by those standards all he knows is that he is drinking finer wine than was served at the beginning of the feast. This late arrival of the good wine confuses him. It reverses his expectations. The usual wedding strategy is to bring out the good wine, the finer vintages, first. This allows the guests to get drunk on good wine and allows the steward to give them lesser quality when they cannot tell the difference. This is the practical and proper protocol for wine and weddings, and the steward calls the bridegroom over to let him know where he has gone wrong. The steward's limited appreciation of what is happening is summed up in the simple observation that the steward "did not know where it [the wine] came from." He is caught on the surface/physical/literal level. For him, there is no sign.

But for the storyteller this is the *"first"* of his signs. "First" does not mean number one in a series of seven. It means this sign displays a pattern that will be present in all the signs. It is "first" in the sense of archetypical. The dynamics that are found in this story will be woven throughout the entire gospel—the transition from exterior religion to interior faith, the many faces of imperiled human existence, divine love compassionately entering human life to save it, and the division between those who can read the signs and come to belief and those who cannot read the signs and remain unbelieving.

Teaching

Popular Christian imagination has always loved this story of the wedding feast of Cana and has never ceased to puzzle over it. Is Jesus curt to his mother? Does Jesus save the bride and groom from the social embarrassment of not having enough wine? Is Jesus the ultimate party animal, the man who can always find a better vintage? Is the steward a wine snob? This sparse story is suggestive enough to generate long-standing questions.

Also, few gospel stories get as much Rorschach treatment as this wedding snapshot. As a grinning woman once confided, "I dreamed I danced with Jesus at the wedding feast of Cana." Whatever details the story lacks, Christian readers have cheerfully supplied them. The sheer abundance of midrash intuits there is some hidden fun in this brief tale.

In the spirit of all the poems and stories that have read and played between the lines of the wedding feast of Cana, the mother of Jesus has something to say.

> "Come now, my Son,
> do you tease these gray hairs?
> Late and laughing you arrive and find me finding you.
> An entreaty is my greeting,
> 'They have no more wine.'
> But you sweep me up
> in mock debate,
> a young man's arms
> around my seriousness,
> wresting from me a conspiratorial smile.
> 'What has that to do with you and me?'
> you say,
> winking words which invite the memory of our meals.
> And I tell you quick,
> in hushes,
> how
> I lit the fire in your eyes
> and held your head of dreams
> and poured water in your hands
> when you came burning
> from the desert sands.
> Beyond that,
> I say,
> you and I,

are strangers,
I say.
But games aside,
I say,
Jesus,
I say,
these empty glasses mock your Father's feast."
'My hour has not yet come,'
you say,
making me say it all
right here
in the midst of sober guests.
You hold me now
in roles reversed,
a son giving birth,
a mother young again.
Steward,
I say,
this man who kisses my eyes,
this Son of my love
has need of a canyon
to hold the grapes
that his fast feet
will crush to marriage wine.
Now,
the teeth of our laughter
blinds the steward
who does not know what we do,
my secret friend.
Your hour is the minute
the wine fails."

(John Shea, *The Spirit Master*
[Allen, Texas: Thomas More Press, 1996] 206–7)

Third Sunday in Ordinary Time
Third Sunday after Epiphany
Luke 1:1-4; 4:14-21 *LM* • Luke 4:14-21 *RCL*

〰

Deepening Spiritual Knowledge

A Spiritual Commentary

Since many have undertaken to set down an orderly account of the events that have been fulfilled among us, just as they were handed on to us by those who from the beginning were eyewitnesses and servants of the word, I too decided, after investigating everything carefully from the very first, to write an orderly account for you, most excellent Theophilus, so that you may know the truth concerning the things about which you have been instructed. (Luke 1:1-4, NRSV)

Luke wants to join the many who have preceded him in telling "the events that have been fulfilled among us." He does not tell the readers in general or Theophilus in particular why he has decided to write another narrative. Instead, he indirectly recommends his account because of his careful investigations that go back to the beginning. But if we read between the lines, we may sense Luke is dissatisfied with previous renditions.

This dissatisfaction may not be at the level of facts but at the level of interpretation. He is concerned that Theophilus know the truth (the literal Greek word means "deeper knowledge") concerning the things about which he has been instructed. In other words, he already knows what happened; he probably has the correct facts. But does he have the right meaning, the deeper spiritual knowledge of what happened? For Luke the right meaning of the life, death, and resurrection of Jesus of Nazareth is tied to the idea of "fulfilling events." Past divine promises have been fulfilled, and this theological perspective is the proper lens to interpret what has happened. Reading events properly, from a deeper theological point of view, is an ongoing concern of Luke's Gospel.

Then Jesus, filled with the power of the Spirit, returned to Galilee, and a report about him spread through all the surrounding

country. He began to teach in their synagogues and was praised by everyone. (Luke 4:14-15, NRSV)

After his baptism, while he was at prayer, Jesus had a profound religious experience. He experienced himself as God's beloved Son who was filled with God's Spirit. This Spirit drove him into the desert where the devil tempted him to understand and act out his Son of God identity as a personal privilege. Satan suggested that his beloved status meant he would always be physically full, socially powerful, and religiously safe. (See First Sunday of Lent.) Jesus refused this self-centered understanding of "Son of God." His powerful "No" allowed the Spirit to fill him more completely. The Spirit that was given him in the experience of prayer inhabited him more thoroughly as he purified himself of false understandings. So it is "filled with the power of the Spirit" that he returns to Galilee.

But there is still more. A full understanding of "Spirit-filled Son of God" has not been developed. What the religious experience does not mean has been clarified in the duel with the devil on the desert floor, in midair, and on the pinnacle of the Temple. What it does mean will unfold in his hometown as he consults the past promises of Scripture.

When he came to Nazareth, where he had been brought up, he went to the synagogue on the sabbath day, as was his custom. He stood up to read, and the scroll of the prophet Isaiah was given to him. He unrolled the scroll and round the place where it was written:

"The Spirit of the Lord is upon me,
because he has anointed me
to bring good news to the poor.
He has sent me to proclaim release to captives
and recovery of sight to the blind,
to let the oppressed go free,
to proclaim the year of the Lord's favor."

And he rolled up the scroll, gave it back to the attendant, and sat down. The eyes of all in the synagogue were fixed on him. Then he began to say to them, "Today this scripture has been fulfilled in your hearing." (Luke 4:16-21)

The importance of this moment is highlighted by its dramatic rendering. The book of Isaiah is handed to Jesus, but he is not doing an assigned reading. He searches to find the words that will spell out the meaning of "Son of God." He finds the Spirit-driven mission language of Isaiah. To be the Son of God is to be on a mission of liberation. Wherever human life is impoverished, imprisoned, impaired, it will become enriched, free, and enabled. All this will be done by the power of divine favor. Son of God is not a title of privilege. It is a call to transformative action.

This passage is in "the book of Isaiah *the prophet.*" As such, the assumption is that it looks to the future, announcing something that is to come. It is a word of hope to a hopeless situation. But this is not the teaching Jesus takes from it. Sitting in the position of the teacher with the entire synagogue focused on him, Jesus tells them the promise has been fulfilled. The waiting is over. When Jesus spoke the words and they heard them, they were no longer words of prediction. They were words of inauguration.

Luke has made good on his own promise. He is giving Theophilus the deeper knowledge, the theological point of view of the events that have been fulfilled among us.

Teaching

Religious experiences entail a shift of consciousness in which we realize we are grounded in a transcendent reality. In the case of Jesus, this realization is expressed in the historical symbolism of the heavens splitting, a dove descending, and a voice speaking, "You are my beloved Son in whom I am well pleased." However, it is only after the religious experience ends and consciousness shifts back to more mundane concerns that we notice the experience did not come with a complete set of instructions. In the case of Jesus, the Spirit remained with him, but it needed to lead him into other experiences to complement his prayer revelation. It led him into the temptations for further clarity about his identity and back to Nazareth to publicly read the prophesy that would clarify his mission. Temptations and homecoming were needed to deepen his knowledge of the ripped heavens, the dove, and the voice.

This is a classic pattern of how religious experiences unfold. They begin with a consciousness of our eternal grounding in God. Aware that this grounding is unconditional, we quickly interpret it as love. But when consciousness returns to the rough-and-tumble of time, we do not know how to translate what we experienced into our conflicted minds and our concrete decision-making processes. In this context, deepening spiritual knowledge entails discovering the path from transcendent identity to historical mission.

To be more concrete, a person may have a profound awareness of communion with ultimate reality. This awareness may be triggered by nature, by the death of a parent, by the birth of a child, by the love of a woman or a man, by the quest for scientific truth, by compassionate protest on behalf of the poor and oppressed, etc. In and through these events and activities, God's love breaks into consciousness and grasps a person.

But this depth awareness is fleeting. Ordinary consciousness, not of the Source, but of work, family, finances, etc., returns. How will the Spirit of this religious experience be courted and pursued? Will the person test out its meaning with other ideas? Will sacred books be consulted? If they are, chances are the experience will grow in significance. The meaning and implications of the experience will be deepened. The Spirit of the experience wants this to happen, but the person must cooperate.

Although this way of deepening spiritual knowledge is alive and well in contemporary life, there is another way, a backward way, so to speak, of deepening spiritual knowledge. The classic way begins with a transcendent experience and gradually understands what this experience means for ongoing life in time and history. The movement is from the sacred to the secular. The reverse way begins with direction and action in time and history and only gradually realizes this direction and action is grounded and inspired by transcendent reality. The direction is from the secular to the sacred. We discover we are responding to an immanent God we had not previously noticed.

Michael Novak tries to map this deepening spiritual knowledge in his effort to interpret business as a noble calling. He admits that, for the most part, business people do not see themselves in terms of responding to a divine call.

> I know from talking to and corresponding with business people that many have never been asked whether they regard what they do as a calling. They don't think about themselves that way. That has not been the language of the business schools, the economics textbooks, or the secularized public speech of our time. . . . But most of them, they say, do start mulling the idea of calling once it is raised. Some confess that they could think of what they do as a calling, even if they have not. That would not be much of a reach from what they have already been doing. It's just one of those things that, so far, few people say. (*Business as a Calling: Work and the Examined Life* [New York: The Free Press, 1996] 36)

This is a crucial start to deepening spiritual knowledge: an openness to a possibility not previously considered and willing to "start mulling the idea."

This "mulling the idea" does not immediately lead to the awareness of an eternal grounding for business striving. What it may lead to is recognizing values that transcend profits. The caricature of business as a ruthless bottom-line enterprise may be too lopsided to account for all that is going on in business men and women. People are engaging in their work because they have the gifts and talents for it and because it contributes in some way to the common good. Once they open themselves to the possibility that they are struggling with deep drives for fulfillment and contribution, further reflection is inevitable.

Novak unravels the fulfillment and contribution drives. He suggests that people's work can give them a sense of fulfillment.

> But fulfillment of what? Not exactly a standing order that we place ourselves. We didn't give ourselves the personality, talents, or longings we were born with. When we fulfill these—these gifts from beyond ourselves—it is like fulfilling something we were meant to do. It is a sense of having uncovered our personal destiny, a sense of having been able to contribute something worthwhile to the common public life, something that would not have been there without us—and, more than that, something we were good at and enjoyed. (Ibid., 18)

Perhaps as we searched out meaningful work, we were responding to a call deep within us, a call that comes with the very fact of our being alive.

This type of approach backs into the sacred grounding of our secular activities. It is gradual and modest in what it comes to know. It discovers the impulses of soul and takes its time in establishing these as real. But if we stay with these impulses, we will arrive at the insight that they are grounded. We will discover the rock in a weary land and the shelter in a time of storm. Our knowledge will be deepened to include the ever-present but ever-elusive Spirit.

Fourth Sunday in Ordinary Time
Fourth Sunday after Epiphany

Luke 4:21-30

🕯

Pleasing and Displeasing

A Spiritual Commentary

After his baptism, in an ecstatic moment of prayer, Jesus received a revelation that he was the beloved Son of God filled with divine pleasure. However, the full import of this revelation was not immediately known. At this point in the story (Luke 3:23-38), Luke helps the readers gage what is at stake by inserting a "backward" or "downward" genealogy. The genealogy starts by saying "Jesus was the son (as was thought) of Joseph." Then it recounts Jesus' Jewish ancestors all the way back into prehistory where Jesus becomes "Son of Adam." Then, in a glorious leap, the lineage ends with Jesus as the "Son of God."

This genealogy acknowledges Jesus belongs to the Jews, to the human family as a whole, and to God. But the way it is structured, with the telltale parenthesis, "Jesus was the son (as was thought) of Joseph," focuses the upcoming tension. People will stay on the first level of Jesus' Jewish identity and be unable or reluctant to acknowledge his universally human and divine identities. The people most prone to do this will be the people of his own hometown.

Then he began to say to them, "Today this scripture has been fulfilled in your hearing."

All spoke well of him and were amazed at the gracious words that came from his mouth. They said, "Is not this Joseph's son?"

Jesus has just read the prophesy from Isaiah about one who is anointed with the Spirit and destined to bring about a better world. (See Third Sunday in Ordinary Time, Cycle C.) His startling commentary on this prophesy is that it is no longer a prophesy. It has been fulfilled. The quickly drawn implication is that Jesus is the fulfillment. He has borrowed Isaiah to flesh out what the voice said to him when he was at prayer after his baptism. "You are my beloved Son. In you I am well pleased." The mission associated with his identity as the Beloved Son has been clarified.

But the exact language can lead in another direction. The prophesy is fulfilled in *their* hearing. If they have the capacity to receive Jesus and his message, the prophesy will be fulfilled. A better world will come about. But if they do not have the capacity to receive Jesus and his message, the prophesy will not be fulfilled. Their capacity to hear is essential to the fulfillment of the prophesy. Their first response is encouraging for they seem to welcome these challenging words of Jesus.

Although the hometown people in Mark reject Jesus because they know him too well and cannot take his wisdom seriously (Mark 6:1-6), these hometown folks claim him and marvel that one of their own is so eloquent and privileged. However, the reason for their pleasure is the assumption that he is Joseph's son. As Joseph's son, the benefits of which he speaks—the vision of divine favor and human liberation culled from Isaiah—will be bestowed on the village of Joseph. Those who are speaking favorably of Jesus are smacking their own lips. They will ride Jesus into a better life. Jesus senses this is the source of their praise and approval.

> **He said to them, "Doubtless you will quote me this proverb, 'Doctor, cure yourself!' And you will say, 'Do here also in your hometown the things that we have heard you did at Capernaum.'"**

It is so obvious that the son of Joseph of Nazareth should help Nazarenes that it is enshrined in a proverb. But Luke's genealogy warned (it was thought) he was the son of Joseph. His Jewish ancestry was real but not the whole picture. It was a first level that led to deeper considerations. His hidden roots were Son of Adam and the Son of God. These deeper connections may elude the people of Nazareth, but they are clear to the one who heard the voice during prayer after his baptism and purified himself of the desire for exemption and privilege in his exchange with the tempter.

> **And he said, "Truly, I tell you, no prophet is accepted in the prophet's hometown. But the truth is, there were many widows in Israel in the time of Elijah, when the heaven was shut up for three years and six months, and there was a severe famine over all the land; yet Elijah was sent to none of them except to a widow at Zarephath in Sidon. There were also many lepers in Israel in the time of the prophet Elisha, and none of them was cleansed except Naaman the Syrian."**

Jesus reminds the Nazarenes of an unpopular strand of Jewish tradition. They were not chosen by God to form a closed society and become the beneficiaries of divine blessings of abundance. They were chosen to bring the benefits of the one God to all people. The focus is not on themselves but on what they can do for others. Even Elijah and Elisha, two prophets who staunchly defended the covenant with Israel, knew this. Jesus' words suggest the Nazarenes must undergo the same consciousness shift that has transformed Jesus. To be loved means to be sent to others.

When they heard this, all in the synagogue were filled with rage. They got up, drove him out of the town, and led him to the brow of the hill on which their town was built, so that they might hurl him off the cliff. But he passed through the midst of them and went on his way.

When they thought Jesus would bring them untold blessings, they spoke favorably of him. When they understand he is asking them to bring blessings to others, they are enraged. It is a short trip from approval to condemnation. The angry actions of these hometown folks prefigure the Jerusalem elite. The chief priests and scribes will crucify Jesus outside Jerusalem, the city built on a hill. But their murderous execution will not be final. In the resurrection Jesus will walk through the midst of them. Physical force cannot kill his spiritual reality.

Teaching

In these times when meditation is engaged in for a variety of reasons, I have always appreciated Ken Wilber's insistence on its ultimate purpose:

> There are many ways to explain meditation, what it is, what it does, how it works. Meditation, it is said, is a way to evoke the relaxation response. Meditation, others say, is a way to train and strengthen awareness; a method for centering and focusing the self; a way to halt constant verbal thinking and relax the body-mind; a technique for calming the central nervous system; a way to relieve stress, bolster self esteem, reduce anxiety, and alleviate depression. . . . Whatever else it does, and it does many beneficial things, meditation is first and foremost a search for the God within. (*Grace and Grit* [Boston: Shambhala Publications, 1993] 76)

But on the way to the God within, we become acquainted with the mind and the fascinating games it plays. This is definitely one of the "beneficial things."

One of these games is the pleasure-displeasure continuum. Perhaps the better image is one taken from the world of computers. The mind runs a pleasure-displeasure program. And it runs it fast, so fast we do not notice the program itself. All we know is we are carried away by the program. A certain word or event pleases us; another word or event displeases us. We smile and frown, swinging back and forth. Better said, since pleasing and displeasing are full-throttle responses, we gush and growl. We are completely into pleasure and displeasure. This vacillation may confuse and tire us, but we accept these alternating emotional inner states as normal.

This is one way of understanding what Jesus ran into when he returned to his hometown. When Jesus says things that please the Nazarines, he is praised. What they like is the idea that the promises of the messianic age will be theirs. This supports and blesses their self-centered focus. It also validates the proverbial wisdom they have used to assure themselves of divine favor. They are God's people. The Messiah will come from them and, naturally, be for them. The doctor's cure begins at home. When they interpret Jesus' speech in this way, "gracious words" are coming from his mouth.

When Jesus says things that displease the Nazarines, he is attacked. What triggers the displeasure is Jesus' words that suggest these blessings that they thought were theirs alone would also be given to the Gentiles. Worse, they would be the ones who would bring those blessings to the Gentiles. The depth at which this message was heard is hard to imagine. It touched on the emotional energy of racial hatred and survival. The Nazarines exploded in rage and attempted murder.

Of course, it is not just the citizens of Nazareth that are run by pleasure-displeasure programs. We all are. Ask any politician who has ever tried to "curry favor" to win votes. People sit on the pleasing-displeasing teeter-totter of their ego. They go up and they go down depending on whether they feel enhanced or threatened by what is happening. Everything that protects and promotes them creates pleasure and everything else is viewed neutrally or hostilely. But this dynamic is more easily seen in others than it is in ourselves. We see other people behind bars, but we look out from our own prisons without noticing the bars.

So inner attention is a way to be free of this mechanical pleasing-displeasing behavior. We must learn to become aware of the pleasure-displeasure program *while it is running*. This awareness will allow us to modify the fierceness of our reactions and eventually to experience times when we break free of its hold. But this is a long-term goal, something that becomes possible after extended spiritual training.

A quicker but more painful exercise is to join the good no matter where it is happening. The good moves through life-seeking people to cooperate with it. Sometimes it visits us and, at other times, it visits others. But it always needs hearts and hands to increase its effectiveness. Begin by lending a hand and see what will happen to the heart. Join the good when we will get nothing out of it, when we cannot evaluate it in terms of our pleasure or displeasure. After we stop grumbling about the sacrifice, we will find ourselves filled with the goodness with which we are cooperating. A breakthrough realization will arrive: we can be joyful whenever or wherever the good is happening. Suddenly, we will feel no resentment for the widow at Zarephath in Sidon and Naaman the Syrian. We will rejoice that her hunger has been filled and his skin has been cleansed. And finally, the prophesy of *human* liberation, not just our own well-being, will be fulfilled in our hearing.

Fifth Sunday in Ordinary Time
Fifth Sunday after Epiphany
Luke 5:1-11

❧

Going Fishing

A Spiritual Commentary

Once while Jesus was standing beside the lake of Gennesaret, and the crowd was pressing in on him to hear the word of God, he saw two boats there at the shore of the lake; the fishermen had gone out of them and were washing their nets. He got into one of the boats, the one belonging to Simon, and asked him to put out a little way from the shore. Then he sat down and taught the crowds from the boat.

The crowd is eager to hear the word of God ("the crowd was pressing in on him"), and Jesus casts about for a pulpit ("he saw two boats there at the shore of the lake"). The purpose of hearing the word is to be "caught" by it, to have it illumine the mind and inspire the will to such an extent that it changes the processes of thinking and acting. Therefore, teaching from a boat is symbolically appropriate. When fish are caught, they move from the darkness beneath the sea into light. So those who hear Jesus' teaching will be pulled from darkness into light. In particular, Jesus will reach into the interior darkness and release a fullness beyond what they had previously known.

But in order for this to happen, two hearings are necessary. A first encounter acquaints the hearers with the teaching and prepares the way for further exploration. Then a second, deeper encounter brings greater realization and integration of what the teaching means. The first encounter is symbolized both by the fishermen "washing their nets" and Simon pulling his boat "out a little way from the shore." The nets are prepared, but they are not yet used. The boat has pushed off a little, but it has not yet found open water.

In the second, deeper encounter the washed nets will be let down into the sea and haul in a tremendous catch of fish, and Simon will be asked to move away from the shore and put out into deep water. The crowds who stay on shore become acquainted with the teaching, but they remain in the first encounter. Simon, James, John, and the other fishermen who follow Jesus' instructions enter the second encounter and realize the truth of the teaching in a life-transforming way.

> **When he had finished speaking, he said to Simon, "Put out into the deep water and let down your nets for a catch."**
>
> **Simon answered, "Master, we have worked all night long but have caught nothing. Yet if you say so, I will let down the nets."**
>
> **When they had done this, they caught so many fish that their nets were beginning to break. So they signaled their partners in the other boat to come and help them. And they came and filled both boats, so that they began to sink.**
>
> **But when Simon saw it, he fell down at Jesus' knees, saying, "Go away from me, Lord, for I am a sinful man!"**
>
> **For he and all who were with him were amazed at the catch of fish that they had taken: and so also were James and John, sons of Zebedee, who are partners with Simon.**
>
> **Then Jesus said to Simon, "Do not be afraid; from now on you will be catching people."**
>
> **When they brought their boats to shore, they left everything and followed him.**

When Jesus finished speaking the word, it is time for Simon and the others to experience what they have heard. It is one thing for Jesus to articulate a teaching; it is quite another thing for hearers to grasp it so it becomes their own. Jesus gives symbolically simple directions for the disciples to personally appropriate the teaching. Simon must go deep inside himself (put out into deep water) and wait to receive (let down your nets for a catch). But Simon, James, John, and the others have never had success with these directions. They have tried them and experienced only the absence of light (night) and emptiness (caught nothing).

Yet Simon has called Jesus "master." A master, by definition, has more knowledge than a disciple. So Simon will do what Jesus says, even though he does not think it will work. This is the classic position of disciples. They have to obey the master until through their own experience they discover what the master knows. Simon is exteriorly obedient, but interiorly dubious.

Following Jesus' instruction leads to abundance and fullness. If people open themselves to God, God obliges. Divine reality suffuses the disciples. The nets are filled to the breaking point and the boats are filled to the sinking point. Since this is not how they usually experience themselves, Simon and the others are amazed and overwhelmed. Simon's response reflects the proper and prescribed attitude for all who happen upon the immensity of God. The fullness and abundance of divine reality dwarfs him. He experiences his own smallness and inadequacy. He is not worthy of what he has experienced. The greatness of the Creator and the smallness of the creature go hand in hand. Simon is in a long line of quaking humans.

But Jesus names Simon's response differently and offers another possibility. Simon is not conventionally pious but wrongly fearful. The awareness of God makes him tremble and crushes him down. If he clings to the knees of Jesus, he must be on his own knees. Simon does not embrace the fullness; he wants it to go away. This is hardly what Jesus wants. So he instructs Simon not to be afraid. Instead, he is to use what he has experienced to bring others to the same experience. As Jesus has caught him, he is to catch others. Forget fear, it is time for adventure. So when they brought this fullness (their boats) to shore, when they moved out of the deep waters of abundance, they left everything they used to do and dedicated themselves to catching men and women. The word has been heard.

Teaching

It is known by everyone who cares to know that the Lord Jesus and St. Peter used to retire to the local tavern after a hard day of ministry to break bread and drink wine together.

On a certain rainy night St. Peter turned to the Lord Jesus and grinned, "We're doing real good."

"We?" asked the Lord Jesus.

Peter was silent. "Alright, you're doing real good," he finally said.

"Me?" asked the Lord Jesus.

Peter pondered a second time. "Alright, God's doing real good," he finally admitted.

But the Lord Jesus saw how reluctant St. Peter was to admit the source of all goodness. He laughed and hit the table with his fist.

It was the laugh that got to St. Peter. He pushed his face toward Jesus and blurted out, "Look! I was somebody before you came along.

You didn't make me. I know now everybody says, 'There goes the Lord Jesus and his sidekick St. Peter. Jesus cures them and Peter picks them up.' But it wasn't always that way. People knew me in my own right. I was respected and looked up to. They would say, 'There goes Peter, the greatest fisherman in all of Galilee.'"

"I heard that you were a very good fisherman, Peter," said the Lord Jesus who was always quick to praise.

"You're damn right I was. And tomorrow I am going to prove it. We are going fishing, and you will see how the other fishermen respect me and look to my lead."

"I would love to go fishing, Peter. I have never been fishing," said the Lord Jesus, who was always looking for new adventures. "But what will we do with all the fish we are going to catch?"

"Well," Peter smiled the smile of the fox. "We'll eat a few, store the rest, wait till there is a shortage, then put them on the market at top dollar and turn a big profit."

"Oh," said the Lord Jesus, who had that puzzled and pained look on his face that Peter had often observed, as if something that had never crossed his mind just made a forced entry. Peter wondered how someone as obviously intelligent as Jesus could be so slow in some matters.

The next morning at dawn the Lord Jesus and St. Peter were down at the shore readying their boat. And it was just as St. Peter had said. When the other fishermen saw Peter, they sidled over. "Going out, Peter?" they asked.

"Yeah," answered Peter, not looking up from the nets.

"Mind if we come along?"

"Why not?" shrugged Peter, pretending to be bothered by them.

When they left, he glared over at the Lord Jesus and said, "See!"

St. Peter's boat led the way. The Lord Jesus was in the prow hanging on tightly for he was deeply afraid of the water. Now St. Peter was a scientist of a fisherman. He tasted the water, scanned the sky, peered down into the lake, pointed off to the side, and gave the word in a whisper: "Over there."

"Why isn't anyone talking?" asked the Lord Jesus in a voice much too loud for the quiet work of snaring fishes.

"Shhhh!" Peter put his finger to his lips and glared at the Lord Jesus.

The boats formed a wide circle around the area Peter had pointed to. "Let down the nets," Peter's voice crept over the surface of the water.

"Why don't they just toss them in?" blurted out the Lord Jesus, who had hopes of learning about fishing.

A second SHHHH! came from St. Peter.

The fishermen let down their nets and then began to pull them in. But something was wrong. The muscles of their arms did not tighten under the weight of fish. The nets rose quickly; the arms of the men were slack. All they caught was water.

The fishermen rowed their boats over to St. Peter. They were a chorus of anger. "The greatest fisherman in all of Galilee, my grandmother's bald head! You brought us all the way out here for nothing. We've wasted the best hours of the hours of the day and we have nothing to show for it."

And they rowed toward shore shouting curses over their shoulder.

The Lord Jesus said nothing.

St. Peter tried a second time. He checked the nets, scanned the sky, tasted the sea, and peered into the depths. At long last he looked at the Lord Jesus and, pointing out into the sea, said, "Over there!"

No sooner had he said, "Over there!" than the Lord Jesus was at the oars, rowing mightily, the muscles of his back straining with each pull.

And all day long under the searing sun the Lord Jesus and St. Peter rowed from place to place on the sea of Galilee. And all day long, under the searing sun, they let down their nets. And all day long, under the searing sun, they hauled in their nets. And all day, long under the searing sun, they caught nothing.

Evening fell and an exhausted St. Peter raised the tattered sail to make for shore. The weary Lord Jesus sat in the prow, a look of anticipation on his face.

It was then, as the boat glided toward shore, that it happened. All the fish in the sea of Galilee came to the surface. They leapt on one side of the boat and they leapt on the other side of the boat. They leapt behind the boat and they leapt in front of the boat. They formed a cordon around the boat, escorting it toward shore in full fanfare.

Then in a mass suicide of fish, they began to leap into the boat. They landed in the lap of the laughing Lord Jesus. They smacked the astonished St. Peter in the face. When the boat arrived at shore, it was brimming, creaking, sinking under the weight of the fish.

All the other fishermen were waiting. They gathered around St. Peter and slapped him on the back. "Peter, you scoundrel! You knew where the fish were all the time and never let on." They hit him on the shoulder. "Peter, you rogue! You put us on. You are surely the greatest fisherman in all of Galilee."

But St. Peter was uncharacteristically silent. He only said, "Give the fish to everyone. Tonight, no home in this village will go without food." After that, he said nothing.

But later that evening, at the tavern with bread and wine between them, Peter looked across the table at the Lord Jesus and said, "Go away from me. I wanted the fish to be over them, not with them. I wanted the fish to rule them, not feed them. You go away from me. I am a sinful man."

But Jesus smiled, not the smile of the fox, but the smile that moves the sun and the stars. And he had no intention of going away. There were other fish to catch.

Sixth Sunday in Ordinary Time
Sixth Sunday after Epiphany

Luke 6:17, 20-26 *LM* • Luke 6:17-26 *RCL*

۷

Taking Hold of the Life That Is Really Life

A Spiritual Commentary

He came down with them and stood on a level place, with a great crowd of his disciples and a great multitude of people from all Judea, Jerusalem, and the coast of Tyre and Sidon. They had come to hear him and to be healed of their diseases; and those who were troubled with unclean spirits were cured. And all in the crowd were trying to touch him, for power came out from him and healed all of them.

"He came down . . ." Jesus had spent the night praying on a mountain. When day came, he called his disciples and chose twelve of them to be apostles. Then Jesus, the disciples, and the apostles descended the mountain to meet the crowds of more disciples and people from diverse regions on the plain. The charisma of Jesus was the magnet that attracted them. He teaches and cures. Everyone wants a piece of him for he radiates healing power. All in all, it is a picture of a powerful man marshaling his forces for a mission that everyone is awaiting.

Then he looked up at his disciples and said: "Blessed are you who are poor, for yours is the kingdom of God. Blessed are you who are hungry now, for you will be filled. Blessed are you who weep now, for you will laugh. Blessed are you when people hate you, and when they exclude you, revile you, defame you on account of the Son of Man. Rejoice in that day and leap for joy, for surely your reward is great in heaven; for that is what their ancestors did to the prophets."

But woe to you who are rich, for you have received your consolation. Woe to you who are laughing now, for you will mourn and weep. Woe to you when all speak well of you, for that is what their ancestors did to the false prophets."

43

Abruptly, in the midst of this power and adulation, Jesus addresses his disciples. He details a series of blessings and woes, describing the paradoxical life that lies before them. This combination of observations and predictions sobers the intoxicating atmosphere of the clinging crowds. This realistic yet hopeful vision of Jesus is driven by a formidable theological vision that is wider than what is happening and what will happen to the followers of Jesus.

When Jesus spent the night in prayer, he was attuning his mind to the mind of God and preparing himself to act in the world as one sent by God. The emerging consciousness reflected in the blessings and woes is very much in the prophetic tradition. Although Jesus is more than a prophet, he shares the unyielding prophetic sensitivity to the discrepancy between God's vision for human life and the way humans are actually living. It is this discrepancy that drives the blessings and woes.

Since the present world is out of sync with God, all its judgments are provisional. The way the world judges success and failure or happiness and despair is neither normative nor lasting. These judgments are not normative because they do not coincide with the ultimate intentions of God's will. They are not lasting because unless the social construction of reality is built on the rock of spiritual truth, it will crumble. First Timothy 6:17-19 spells it out.

> As for those who in the present age are rich, command them not to be haughty, or to set their hopes on the uncertainty of riches, but rather on God who richly provides us with everything for our enjoyment. They are to do good, to be rich in good works, generous, and ready to share, thus storing up for themselves the treasure of a good foundation for the future, so that they may take hold of the life that really is life.

The "life that really is life" is the only foundation for the future.

This general theological vision is applied to Jesus' disciples. The first blessing lays the "foundation for the future." Although Jesus will contrast weeping now with laughing later and hungry now with filled later, he does not contrast socially poor now with socially rich later. Rather, in the initial blessing he states the underlying tension that drives the dynamics of all the blessings and woes.

The disciples are socially and financially poor now but, at the same time, they are living in the kingdom of God. In other words, they have "taken hold of the life that is really life." Since this real life is greater than social life, it can coexist with hunger, mourning, weeping, and persecution. They can participate in it even while they are socially bereft. But also this life will outlast their negative social situations that are destined to self-destruct because they are not grounded in this real life. What will happen is the ones who are in touch with this real life will necessarily be filled, laughing, and joyful. Staying faithful to the eternal values of God brings an awareness of what will surely come to pass.

There is a particular emphasis on the disciples' blessedness when they endure rejection because they are followers of Jesus and are trying to embody the new humanity called the Son of Man. The present state of the world not only resists their invitation, but it goes on the offensive to actively persecute and discredit them. The natural response to this fierce rejection would be despair. But Jesus suggests they rejoice. The reason: their fidelity in these situations will be rewarded in heaven. This does not necessarily mean life after death. Heaven is a circumlocution for a more profound indwelling with God. As the rejection of the outer world grows, the communion with God grows more intensely to overcome the persecution. This is what a long line of prophets discovered as they held out for God's world while people attacked them violently as a way of defending their own narrowly conceived lives.

The woes are driven by the same theological tension. The rich have chosen a counterfeit to the "life that is really life." Therefore, their consolation is now—as long as it lasts, and it will not last long for it is not real life. Also, those who laugh now because the present state of injustice supports them will mourn. Eventually, God will have the last word and, since they have opted against God's word, they will weep. In particular, if the disciples lose the social cutting edge of Jesus' message, woe will be visited on them. This is because they will have found a way to rationalize the present injustices. They will give to people the reasons they need not to repent. A true prophet pits God's word against the present state of injustice. A false prophet adapts God's word to justify unjust social arrangements.

As always, paths can be chosen. Some paths lead to blessing and some paths lead to woe.

Teaching

I knew a woman disciple of Jesus who said "Yes" to this paradoxical life of blessings and woes. She knew the life that was really life and was forthright in unmasking its counterfeits. She was wide awake in a world gone to sleep, and she suffered considerably because she was a true prophet. When she was dying, she told me, "I've angered a lot of people, but I have been faithful." That should have been on the memorial card.

Whenever she would call, more often than not her first words were, "Jack, isn't it awful."

"What's awful?"

"We have to help them."

"Who is 'them'?" Unfortunately, I knew who "we" were.

Although the names of "it" and "them" changed, the scenario remained the same. The "it" was some oppression, some injustice, some domination of one person or group by another. The "them" were people in trouble. If there was a person anywhere on the globe in trouble, I fantasized that she woke in the morning aware of it. She lived without anesthesia. She took in the pain of the world, not out of guilt or obligation, but just because it was there and it shouldn't be. When she died, there was a big argument about just how old she was. The correct answer was ageless.

She loved to tell the story about a talk she gave to a group of women. She drew stick figures on the board that represented various styles of relationship. One pair of figures was grossly mismatched. The first one towered about the second and glared down at it. Although it was a simple drawing, it expressed the whole world that many people knew only too well. After the talk a woman who did not speak English came up and pounded on the board, hitting the lower figure with her fist and shouting, "Me! Me! Me!"

I was in a small group where she told that story. One of the members said something to the effect of: "Well and good. But what if she gets out of the relationship? Where will she go? What will she do?" My friend was pulled forward to the edge of her chair, her arms were out in front of her, her hands parallel to each other like they were gripping some large object. I suspect it was the man's head. She was about to attack, but she didn't.

Instead, she slid back in the chair, did not talk for a moment, and then spelled out what was so obvious to her. I don't remember the exact words, but I cannot forget the drift. "Wherever there is unjust suffering, you stop it. Sure, you might not know what is next. So what. You know what shouldn't be and what won't last in the long run. It doesn't make any difference whether you are on the bottom or top of the relationship. It is oppressive and it is wrong. There is a better life. Reach for it. And don't count the cost."

When you are in touch with the life that is really life, you see through all the false impersonations.

Seventh Sunday in Ordinary Time
Seventh Sunday after Epiphany
Luke 6:27-38

❦

Pausing for Freedom

A Spiritual Commentary

"But I say to you that listen. Love your enemies, do good to those who hate you, bless those who curse you, pray for those who abuse you. If anyone strikes you on the cheek, offer the other also; and from anyone who takes away your coat do not withhold even your shirt. Give to everyone who begs from you; and if anyone takes away your goods, do not ask for them again. Do to others as you would have them do to you. If you love those who love you, what credit is that to you? For even sinners love those who love them. If you do good to those who do good to you, what credit is that to you? For even sinners do the same. If you lend to those from whom you hope to receive, what credit is that to you? Even sinners lend to sinners, to receive as much again. But love your enemies, do good, and lend, expecting nothing in return. Your reward will be great, and you will be children of the Most High; for he is kind to the ungrateful and wicked. Be merciful, just as your Father is merciful."

These injunctions appear staggeringly stupid. They go beyond the commonsense law of reciprocity. Although Jesus says, "Do to others as you would have them do to you," he really means "Do to others as you would have them do to you, and continue to do this to them no matter what they do to you." Never leave the attitude and action of loving them even if they have left the attitude and action of loving you. Although everyone does not give you kind and generous treatment, everyone receives kind and generous treatment from you.

This teaching will certainly thin the crowd of Jesus' followers. It is a suggestion that goes directly against common sense. Loving enemies just gives them a chance to hit you one more time. Doing good to those who hate you is codependency at best and masochism at worst. Giving to everyone who begs means that you will soon become a beggar and find out most people don't give to those who beg. To top it off, help the robber. If he takes your coat, hand him your shirt as well.

Did Jesus skip playground 101? Has Jesus been out in the sun too long without a hat? Where is the Moses of battle and the Elijah of slaughter? Where is the God who makes "mine enemies the footstool under my feet"? The parody of this teaching has real appeal: "Do unto others before they do it unto you."

This shocking advice is not social naiveté. It is theological courage of a high order. Jesus has seen quite clearly into the never-ending nature of violence and the never-ending nature of God. The two are incompatible, and he has opted to play the game of unconditional love rather than the game of reprisal. The key sentence is the last one. The divine is a Father of unwavering love, an infinitely merciful reality. If we are in touch with this loving God who cannot be anything but love, then neither can we be anything but love. It is our inner relationship to the loving God that determines our response to whatever is happening.

In other words, circumstances do not control us. We counter circumstances. Enemies, persecutors, and haters cannot make us into themselves, infecting us with their toxicity. This has always been their power. They make returning evil in kind appear necessary. It is simply a matter of survival. We may not have begun it, but we will end it.

However, in Jesus' teaching this seduction to imitate violent power has met a firmer resolve. This is a resolve of both the mind and the will. The mind realizes God is love, and the will integrates that realization into unloving social relationships. What Jesus is saying is: "Stop the crazy, endless slaughter by stopping it in yourself. Do not participate in evil on evil's terms."

However, the teaching goes further. It claims this contrast between love and hate, prayer and curse, give and take, is the only way God is known. The argument is not that contrast is the only way God is present. God is universally present; and when people are mutually reciprocal, the inner love of God and neighbor may be motivating them. But there is no way to know it because even those people who are alienated from God's universal presence, "sinners," scratch each other's back. From an outer, observable point of view, it is impossible to tell if grace is present. In a literal and better translation, "what credit is that to you" means "what grace is there in that." Grace is the proactive energy of the person who is interiorly related to God manifesting itself regardless of circumstances. But if circumstances are even-handed and propitious, everybody appears loving. You cannot tell the sinners from the saints. Contrast is needed for revelation.

> **Do not judge, and you will not be judged; do not condemn, and you will not be condemned. Forgive, and will be forgiven; give and it will be given to you. A good measure, pressed down, shaken together, running over, will be put into your lap; for the measure you give will be the measure you get back.**

This teaching continues the emphasis that our personal actions create the world in which we live. But it focuses that insight in a self-referential way. It startles us into seeing the connection between how we act toward others and our own destiny. If our actions are chronically judgmental and condemnatory, they will redound back on us, swallowing us with their negative fury. When we are fiercely righteous, we never see that. Our inner state of condemnation seems to target others, but it is secretly bringing us to judgment. What we think is harmful to other people is really harmful to us.

The same dynamic underlies the positive action of forgiveness. Jesus' way of forgiveness may seem at first to benefit others, but ultimately it is the path of our own fulfillment. The abundant generosity we bestow on others overflows into our lives. In the mindset of condemnation, reality is mean and scarce; in the mindset of forgiveness, reality cannot be contained. The pressed down good wheat runs amuck. The harvest is plentiful. We find ourselves, perhaps surprisingly, the recipient of our own generous living. How we treat others becomes how we are treated.

These spiritual teachings are not put forward as objects of belief. We are not asked to assent to them because they are the inspired words of Scripture. Rather, they are meant to illumine experience. If we look deeply at life, we will see what they say is true. Initially, this seeing will be fleeting. We will see it and then not see it. But with steady practice we will come to know the truth and, as Flannery O'Connor once said, the truth will make us odd.

Teaching

Jesus was walking down the road with his disciples. Some people threw stones at him and cursed him. Jesus blessed them.

The disciples asked him, "Master, why do you bless those who curse you?"

Jesus replied, "I can only give what I have in my purse."

Surely this simple Sufi story about Jesus' powerful teaching on going beyond reciprocity hides something crucial. When we are attacked, there is an instinctive drive to protect ourselves and fight back. The negative pressures of the outer world do not give us much time to think. They want us on their own terms. Those terms may not be what we choose, but they are often how we deal. Those of us who are not securely conscious of our deeper loving identity are unable to immediately find our purse. But a rock seems always at hand.

This is the distinction between reaction and response. Reaction is knee-jerk, a mindless, mechanistic imitation of what is presented to us. As I chanted in fourth grade, monkey sees, monkey does. Response, however, is mindful, a bringing forth of who we really are to engage what has approached us. Obviously, response is preferable. But response takes time. It is not only that we are to think before we act. We are to find the inner space where we are unconditionally loved by God. This love is a creative rush that fills us and overflows, making our speech and action a generous measure rather than a paltry slap back, unworthy of the merciful God's child.

While wandering through a library, Stephen R. Covey stumbled upon a book with three sentences that "staggered me to the core."

> Between stimulus and response there is a space.
> In that space lies our freedom and power to choose our response.
> In those choices lie our growth and our happiness.

> (*The 8th Habit: From Effectiveness to Greatness*
> [New York: Free Press, 2004] 43)

We have a transcendent freedom that opens a space between what acts on us and how we act back. The ability to inhabit this space is the beginning of spiritual development. Of course, Jesus' teaching goes beyond this. It is not just that we are free from compulsive reaction, we are free to embody the loved and loving identity that is our core. So much contemporary spirituality glories in the freedom that flows from our spiritual identity. It relishes the liberation from reactivity. But often there is a strange silence about what this freedom is for. Transcendent freedom is the first step of transcendent loving.

However, in actual situations it is the size of the space between stimulus and response that matters and the length of time we are able to inhabit it. In other words, the space has to be our home, a generous space of light and warmth. We have to possess the key to this space;

and we have to be able to rest in it, to be comfortable in its surroundings. If we engage in consistent spiritual practices, they will help us widen this space and lengthen our dwelling time. Therefore, we will be able to go there when need arises. Need arises when the negative flow of life wants more participants for its destructive agenda. At that time we are to go to the space that is free and loving, not to retreat out of fear but to prepare for action.

Of course, nothing is automatic. This space readies us for speech and action, but it does not supply the speech and action. "Loving enemies, blessing those who curse you, praying for those who persecute you, lending to those who cannot repay" are general imperatives for proactive, graceful living. But they are not specific instructions about what to say and do. Therefore, pausing is necessary not only to create the space of freedom and love between stimulus and response. It is also necessary to figure out the response. So if you see me in silent pause amid the swirling negativity of events, do not think I am lost or aimless. I am merely trying to find my purse.

Eighth Sunday in Ordinary Time
Eighth Sunday after Epiphany

Luke 6:39-45 *LM* • Luke 6:39-49 *RCL*

❧

Thanking Teachers

A Spiritual Commentary

He also told them a parable: "Can a blind person guide a blind person? Will not both fall into a pit? A disciple is not above the teacher, but everyone who is fully qualified will be like the teacher.

There are different levels of spiritual development. If your spiritual eyes have not been opened, you must find someone whose eyes are open. If you spiritually squint, you must find someone whose eyes are open wide. If you apprentice yourself to someone as blind or blurred as you are, you may have a soul mate. But you will also have a companion in the same darkness and together you will experience a similar catastrophe. Do the blind tend to huddle with the blind for companionship, for mutual comfort in their failure to see?

Disciples begin their training by apprenticing themselves to someone who is above them. But the goal of the training is for them to become like the teacher. Therefore, a criterion for choosing a teacher is: do you see in this person the person you want to become? In a passage below, Jesus will tell his disciples the type of person they will become if they hear, understand, and put his words into action. Today's disciple is tomorrow's teacher.

Why do you see the speck in your neighbor's eye, but do not notice the log in your own eye? Or how can you say to your neighbor, "Friend, let me take out the speck in your eye," when you yourself do not see the log in your own eye? You hypocrite, first take the log out of your own eye, and then you will see clearly to take the speck out of your neighbor's eye.

Although this spiritual warning comes with the charge, "You hypocrite," the more psychologically damning word may be, "Friend." The blind man has a condescending attitude toward the one he is trying to help. Calling him "friend" is patronizing. He sees himself as an agent of another person's self-improvement. Yet he is unaware of his own impaired condition.

Why is it we can see and expound on the slightest fault of our neighbor while we are blind to our own staggering imperfections? At least part of the answer is: it is a matter of untrained consciousness. We notice what is minutely wrong with our neighbor because our attention is always focused outward on others. We have fine-tuned our observations of others. We do not miss even the tiniest of their moral flaws. However, we are not trained in self-observation. So we do not see ourselves clearly.

This is a serious lack. Spiritual traditions always think we are complicit in our perceptions and decision. We are not paragons of objectivity, passing neutral judgments on what we see. Rather, our minds have biases, tapes, and storylines that enter into everything we say and do. If we do not know what these are, we are ignorant. Without this self-knowledge, we tend to paint perfect pictures of ourselves or, even more dangerously, innocent pictures of ourselves. Then we view the imperfect world around us as if we were not part of it. We live in disdain rather than compassion. The only effective way to help our neighbor improve ever-so-slightly is to tell the story of our own massive conversion.

There is a story told about Gandhi that illustrates this point. A woman brought her granddaughter to Gandhi and commanded, "My granddaughter eats too much sugar. Tell her to stop."

Gandhi said, "Bring her back to me next week."

The grandmother and granddaughter returned next week. But Gandhi again put them off, saying the same thing, "Bring her back to me next week." This happened three times.

Finally Gandhi said to the granddaughter, "You should not eat so much sugar. It is not good for you."

The grandmother was nonplussed. "We waited four weeks for this simple remark."

"Ah!" Gandhi sighed. "It took me that long to stop eating too much sugar myself."

The only way to help our neighbor is to tell the story of our own struggle.

No good tree bears bad fruit, nor again does a bad tree bear good fruit; for each tree is known by its own fruit. Figs are not gathered

**from thorns, nor are grapes picked from a bramble bush. The
good person out of the good treasure of the heart produces good,
and the evil person out of evil treasure produces evil; for it is out
of the abundance of the heart that the mouth speaks.**

Religious traditions often issue injunctions to moral behavior. "Be
compassionate. Be just. Be truthful." When people try to be faithful
to these injunctions, they find they are not able to carry them out. The
spiritual wisdom on this failure is: behavior is intimately tied to a sense
of identity. If we do not know we are good people, we will not be able
to do good deeds. Moral change is dependent on identity change. Good
trees bear good fruit; bad trees do not. Fig trees bear figs, not thorns.

There is in each person a spiritual center whose image is the heart.
The heart is the hidden source of speech. In fact, it has within it an
abundance, a treasure, that the mouth draws on and makes available
in the outer world. Therefore, heart appears in the outer world and can
be judged through what a person says. If a person's words spin out
evil imaginings, we can be assured the heart is corrupted. If a person's
words spin out scenarios of reconciliation and peace, we can be assured
the heart is in touch with the God of peace and reconciliation. What
appears can be traced back to what is hidden.

**Why do you call me "Lord, Lord" and do not do what I tell you?
I will show you what someone is like who comes to me, hears
my words, and acts on them. That one is like a man building a
house who dug deeply and laid the foundation on rock; when
a flood arose, the river burst against that house but could not
shake it, because it had been well built. But the one who hears
and does not act is like a man who built a house on the ground
without a foundation. When the river burst against it, immediately it fell, and great was the ruin of that house.**

Genuine spiritual teachers are always wary of over-dependent disciples. It is an occupational hazard. On one hand, teachers want the
disciples to be obedient, to absorb the wisdom, and to do the practices.
In order to grow, disciples must initially trust the teacher's directions.
However, the point of initial trust is for the disciples to come to know
for themselves what the teacher knows. The teacher creates the conditions for their discovery of spiritual wisdom. But sometimes this
process does not run true to course. Instead, disciples become more
and more dependent on the teacher. They think crying "Lord, Lord"

will compensate for their failure to learn for themselves and spiritually develop.

Spiritual development entails hearing, understanding, and acting. A question that would naturally arise for disciples would be: if we hear, understand, and act on what you say, what will we become? Jesus answers this question in a startling way. They will become flood proof. Raging rivers symbolize both the vicissitudes of life and the dark, sinister forces that seek to destroy genuine human life. What Jesus offers is a foundation that can withstand those attacks. This is not esoteric heavenly promises. This is down-to-earth, practical wisdom on how not to get engulfed. Jesus the teacher wants disciples who can act and survive in a dangerous world.

Teaching

Many years ago a friend of mine made a visit to a spiritual community in Northern California. The main teacher in the community was Eknath Easwaran, a teacher of meditation who grew up in the Hindu tradition. When my friend returned, I talked to her on the phone. She said, "He's the real thing, Jack."

Finding spiritual teachers who are the real thing is no easy task. If teachers do not know themselves and what they are about very clearly, many problems can arise. Students can pursue false forms of development and even, in some cases, become victims of sexual or financial abuse. So I said to her, "How do you know that?"

"When I was leaving, I said to him, 'I really like what you have done here.' And he said back, without batting an eye, 'Everything you see here is the result of the grace of my grandmother.'" Then my friend stopped talking.

I finally asked, "How does that make him the real thing?"

"You see, I threw a fastball at his ego and he just let it go by. Instead, he told a story of grace. His consciousness is attuned to the world of grace, and he is comfortable articulating it."

When she said this, I remembered reading about his grandmother in one of his writings. He called his grandmother his first spiritual teacher. In particular, I remembered one incident he wrote about (The Bhagavad Gita for Daily Living, Vol. 3: To Love Is to Know Me [Petaluma: Nilgiri Press, 1984], pp. 9–10).

Eknarth grew up in a little village in South India. One of the first lessons he learned in geography was that the earth is round. This was a very shocking revelation and even the teacher presented it in a diffident way. "You may not believe this, and if you don't, I sympathize completely. But this is what they gave me to understand when I did my teacher's training in Madras."

When Eknarth went home and told his mother, she laughed in disbelief. When he would go off to school in the morning, she would sometime say, "Goodbye—and don't slip off." But when he told his grandmother what he had learned, she shot back, "What does it matter? You can be selfless whether the earth is round or square or triangular."

That is the remark of a true spiritual teacher. When you are discombobulated, you should return to essentials. Find the foundation that can withstand the storm and stand there. If the earth is round or if it is flat, what is important is your ability to be selfless, to put others first. As long as that is not threatened, there is no need for confusion or fright.

"Everything you see here is the result of the grace of my grandmother."

Many of us have had formal spiritual teachers and explicit training in the spiritual life. But all of us have had informal spiritual teachers. These are the people who have taught us essential truths about human living. It is good to recall them, to remember who they are and what they were able to give us. We should thank our teachers. If we live in gratitude for what we have been given, we will more freely and creatively give it away.

Ninth Sunday in Ordinary Time
Ninth Sunday after Epiphany
Luke 7:1-10

ᘓ

Obeying the Higher

A Spiritual Commentary

The ultimate mystery of Jesus Christ can be appreciated as the interplay of three identities. He is the Son of David, the Son of Man, and the Son of God. These three identities are hierarchically ordered. Jesus' ethnic identity as the Son of David roots him in Jewish biology and history. However, this important grounding level is considered the lowest because if he is only a Jew, then his mission is confined to Israel. Jesus' human identity as the Son of Man is the middle level. Honoring his ethnic identity, Jesus' mission begins with the Jews. But it moves outward to include all people. Hence the maxim: salvation is from the Jews but is meant for all. The Son of Man belongs to the human family. As Luke's genealogy insists, he is the son of Adam (Luke 3:38). Jesus' spiritual identity as the Son of God is the highest level. This is the revelation of the heavenly voice at his baptism. "You are my Son, the Beloved; with you I am well pleased" (Luke 3:22). The inner being of Jesus is in complete communion with divine love. Therefore, what Jesus makes available for the Jews and all people is an authentic revelation of God.

These three identities should not be played off against one another. Each is real and must be included in a total picture of Jesus. But each is also partial; and its full truth is only known in relationship to the other two. To call Jesus the Son of David or the Son of Man or the Son of God and say no more is woefully inadequate. The three identities nest within one another. The Son of God includes and transcends the Son of Man; and the Son of Man includes and transcends the Son of David. To know the full reality of Jesus Christ, the tendency to emphasize one identity to the exclusion of the other two must be resisted. All three must be acknowledged, and how they flow back and forth into each other must be, for lack of a better word, enjoyed. The following story reflects some of the enjoyment of this flow.

> A centurion there had a slave whom he valued highly, and who
> was ill and close to death. When he heard about Jesus, he sent
> some Jewish elders to him, asking him to come and heal his
> slave.
>
> When they came to Jesus, they appealed to him earnestly, say-
> ing, "He is worthy of having you do this for him, for he loves
> our people, and it is he who built our synagogue for us."

The centurion knows the protocol. A Gentile directly approaching
Jesus might be rebuffed. So he recruits Jews to solicit a favor from a
Jew. But recruit is too mild a word. The text says he *sent* them. This may
be a foreshadowing of the mindset of the centurion that will be more
fully displayed later in the story. He is used to "sending" people.

The Jewish leaders do not object. They know what is required
of them. They approach Jesus with the universal appeal of back-
scratching. The centurion has been good to us; we should be good to
him. He is not a "Gentile dog," but one "who loves our nation and he
built our synagogue." They make their case for this non-Jew solely on
the grounds he helps Jews. They center their reasons on themselves.
The Son of David will surely listen to this appeal from fellow Jews to
help a Gentile whose chief virtue is that he loves Jews and materially
has supported their religion.

But this information about the centurion's Jewish sympathies is part
of a larger and very interesting portrait. It seems he does not draw tight
social boundaries. His care extends beyond his family and ethnic group
to include slaves and Jews. In this translation, the centurion has a slave
"whom he valued highly." This can give the impression he does not want
to lose a good and skilled worker. In another translation (RSV), the slave
is "dear to him." If the centurion loves the Jewish people, it would be consistent with his character to love his slave. He does not narrowly define
himself in terms of his individual self, his social position, or his ethnic
group. Although he honors the theological truth that salvation comes
from the Jews by sending Jewish leaders to the Jewish Jesus, he might
also surmise "from what he has heard" that the salvation that flows from
Jesus is nonrestrictive. He may know that the Son of David nests within
the larger and more inclusive Son of Man. In fact, from his inclusive way
of behaving he might know this Son of Man truth about himself.

> And Jesus went with them, but when he was not far from the
> house, the centurion sent friends to say to him, "Lord, do not
> trouble yourself, for I am not worthy to have you come under

my roof; therefore I did not presume to come to you. But only speak the word, and let my servant be healed. For I am also a man set under authority, with soldiers under me, and I say to one, 'Go,' and he goes, and to another, 'Come,' and he comes, and to my slave 'Do this,' and the slave does it."

When Jesus heard this, he was amazed at him, and turning to the crowd that followed him, he said, "I tell you, not even in Israel have I found such faith."

When those who had been sent returned to the house, they found the slave in good health.

But the centurion discerns even more. He knows that the Son of Man nests within the larger and more inclusive Son of God. It is the Son of God identity that reconfigures the other two identities, contextualizing them and positioning them properly. This recognition of Jesus as the Son of God is played out in truly spectacular fashion. The centurion, as he is in the habit of doing, *sends* friends to tell Jesus he should not come. The reason is that he is not worthy. This unworthiness is not based on a sense of sinfulness. Rather, it is the classic consciousness of finitude, an abiding awareness of the infinite qualitative difference between the divine and the human.

As the psalm attests, "The fear of the Lord is the beginning of wisdom" (Ps 111:10). Wisdom understands God has to be taken into account as a transcendent reality, something above and beyond human power and control. The proper way for humans to relate to this reality is to humbly acknowledge its superiority. The centurion is so acutely aware of this total otherness of God that he himself cannot even approach Jesus. Instead, he sends his friends to tell Jesus not to take another step. The reason is profoundly simple: his small house cannot contain God's Son.

But the centurion's care for his servant has devised an alternative strategy. God's word created the world. Jesus, the Son of God, can speak God's word and heal his servant. The centurion is sure of this for he knows how higher and lower work. Also, he is acutely aware of being in the middle. He is under authority and, in turn, others are under his authority. He obeys what is above him, and those below him obey what is above them. He recognizes Jesus as a level higher, one commissioned from the divine order. This means that everything in the earthly realm obeys him.

It also means he is not restricted by the earthly constraints of time and space. He does not have to traverse space in order to arrive "in the nick of time," before death claims the loved servant. His word, spoken anywhere, can be effective everywhere. The lower obeys the higher, and the higher whom Jesus represents is the Lord of space and time. The Lord of space and time is not subject to the laws of being in one place at one time. For the Son of God, whose Father made all things through his word, a word is enough. But, in fact, the divine realm is even greater than the centurion surmises. Jesus does not even utter a word. Yet when the friends whom he sent return, the slave is in good health. The healing has been effective without using the space-time world as a medium.

However, Jesus' observation on the centurion's way of thinking and acting is bittersweet. In the place where salvation comes from—Israel— he has not found faith. This faith entails an awareness that Jesus mediates divine life and also that the passion of this divine life is to heal. But in the place where salvation is going this faith has been so developed that the Son of God's word, even his unspoken intentionality, can be immediately effective. However, this should not be read as a criticism of Israel and a compliment to Rome. Rather, it is a commendation of a certain consciousness. When consciousness stays focused on Jesus in his full reality—Son of David, Son of Man, and Son of God—it is able to receive the healing flow of God's love.

Teaching

The centurion does not have all the lines in this story, but he has the majority of them. He is also smack-dab in the center of the action and completely turns around the travel plans of Jesus. So what he has to say cannot be avoided. With astonishing certitude, the centurion uses his experience of the military chain of command to describe the relationship between the spiritual realm and the physical realm. Far from being offended, Jesus wholeheartedly agrees with him. He sees his way of thinking and acting as a faith development that surpasses what he has found in Israel. There is no getting around the fact that what the centurion is promoting and what Jesus is approving is a hierarchical view of life.

In a strict sense, "hierarchy" refers to the origin of all things in the sacred and, therefore, how the sacred continues to exercise influence and authority on everything it has brought into being. However, the language of hierarchy has a history of associating with psychological and social dynamics that are often evaluated as misleading and destructive. To contemporary ears, hierarchy is a suspicious word.

Hierarchy implies an ascending order of ranked values. In spiritual traditions, this is often translated into the superiority of the spiritual over the physical. This superiority is based on the perception that the spiritual lasts and the physical fades. The physical is susceptible to moths and rust. Moths and rust cannot touch the spiritual (Matt 6:19-21). From this point of view, the spiritual is more intrinsically valuable than the physical. However, this does not mean the physical should be denigrated and people should engage in ascetical practices designed to completely overcome the insistent demands of the body. But this is the wrongheaded conclusion that has often been drawn.

Spiritual seekers have been led down an anti-body path with deceptive results. They fantasize they are above the body. They fast in order to give the impression that food is not essential to who they are. Of course, they either become sick or they eat in secrecy, deceiving themselves and others. Or they believe they have banished sexual desire. Of course, they become obsessed with the sexual lives of others and are tortured by sexual fantasies they vigorously try to cover up. Valuing the top member of the hierarchy has led them to devalue the whole hierarchical structure, especially its physical foundation.

Also, hierarchy as a ranked order of value has been translated into social relationships. This is where the centurion's military metaphor is particularly susceptible of abuse. The people on the top give orders to the ones below, and the ones below are meant to mindlessly obey and not talk back. Of course, the orders that are given to the lower ones are commands that serve the interests of the higher ones. The result is the oppression of the least, a social condition that the revelation of Jesus is meant to unmask and reverse.

What is prominent in the chain of command image is the absence of dialogue between the higher and the lower. This has become a hallmark of rigidly hierarchical organizations. Although all sorts of organizational mechanisms from town halls to polling procedures to consulting focus groups have been created to facilitate the higher listening to the lower, the essential hierarchical structure remains in place.

This pervasive hierarchical mood has led many to conclude that genuine dialogue cannot go on in strictly organized higher-lower settings. The goal of dialogue is to create shared meaning. It comes about when people treat one another as colleagues. However, hierarchy prohibits this sense of openness and equality. So in place of dialogue, orders are given and orders are either carried out or disobeyed. The social world that hierarchy creates and that we are forced to live in is a world of authority matched by either obedience or rebellion.

Therefore, when the word "hierarchy" is mentioned, people's minds often gravitate to negative psychological and social consequences. Ken Wilber has tried to reframe hierarchical thinking so that its dysfunctional tendencies are curbed. For him hierarchy is "a ranking of orders of events according to their *holistic capacity*" (*Sex, Ecology, Spirituality: The Spirit of Evolution* [Boston: Shambhala Publications, 1995] 17). Each level of the hierarchy is both a whole and a part in relation to a larger whole. For our purposes, Jesus, the Son of David, is both a whole and a part in the larger whole of Jesus as the Son of Man; and Jesus as the Son of Man is both a whole and a part in the larger whole of Jesus as the Son of God. Therefore, the lower levels are not dismissed or violated when they are enveloped in larger wholes. Hierarchy recognizes different levels of value and initiates a holistic process of inclusion and transcendence.

Therefore, honoring every level is important in holistic thinking and acting. But so is recognizing different gradations of value and that lower levels are meant to be open to and influenced by higher levels. But what type of influence does the higher divine level exert and what type of obedience is required by the lower human level? The military example of the centurion leaves the impression that there does not have to be any conscious cooperation from the lower levels. The higher issues commands and the lower obeys without question or under-standing. The integrity of the lower is sacrificed to the higher.

But what if the higher divine level was self-giving love? What if its fundamental intention was to heal the isolation of the lower levels by communing with them? What if this communion with the spiritual fulfilled the full potential of the lower levels? Then, although the lower would be obeying the higher, the higher would be serving the lower. Under certain circumstances, the higher would even take off the clothes of superiority and reveal the towel of a slave (John 13:3-5). Service is its essence. And in the revelation of this Love all the false consciousness around hierarchy must itself become obedient. The fantasies of domina-tion would be seen for what they are—fearful expressions of isolation. What would emerge would be a world of nested dimensions mutually indwelling in one another. It is no accident that the higher divine level of the Son of God is revealed in the healing of a beloved slave.

First Sunday of Lent

Luke 4:1-13

❦

Rejecting Strategies

A Spiritual Commentary

Jesus, full of the Holy Spirit, returned from the Jordan and was led by the Spirit in the wilderness, where for forty days he was tempted by the devil.

There are two major biblical traditions about the devil. One tradition portrays him as a divinely assigned tester. He works in league with God to uncover what is in people's heart. For example, in the book of Job, God and Satan have a heavenly conversation about Job. Is he really a righteous servant of the Lord or, as Satan suggests, is his righteousness only because God has put a fence around him, kept him safe from the vicissitudes of life? (Job 1:10). God agrees to put Job to the test to find out. This testing tradition is the deep background for the sacred event (forty days) of the Spirit leading Jesus into the wilderness in order to be tempted. The temptations will expose Jesus' heart.

The second tradition portrays the devil not as an agent of God's purposes but as the enemy of God's purposes. "Like a roaring lion your adversary the devil prowls around, looking for someone to devour" (1 Pet 5:8). This is the evil one, the one who enters into Judas (John 13:1), a murderer and liar from the beginning (John 8:44). Overtly and covertly, this evil one is bent on undercutting God's salvific activity. He must be resisted; no suggestion of his can be entertained. This tradition of an evil one who seduces people into activities that go against God's will is also present in the temptations of Jesus.

The two traditions come together as the symbolic narrative reveals the steadfast heart of Jesus as he rejects Satan's strategies. These suggested strategies immediately follow Jesus' baptism where in prayer he heard the voice of the ripped heavens address him, "You are my beloved Son, in whom I am well pleased." Therefore, most properly, these temptations focus on Jesus' identity. They are wrong ways of thinking about what it means to be the Son of God. "If you are the Son of God . . ." (See the First Sunday of Lent, Cycle A.) But they can also be approached as messianic temptations. They are wrong ways of thinking about God's mission and how to carry it out. This is how we will interpret them—as faulty mission strategies that Jesus sees through and rejects.

Also, these temptations are placed at the beginning of Jesus' ministry and his rejection of them is definitive. But actually they will haunt his kingdom activity from the beginning to the end. There will always be the temptation to see himself as a miracle worker who caters to people's insistent physical demands, as someone who is ultimately trying to become king or, at least, increase his political and religious power, and as someone who has yet to demonstrate that God approves of his words and deeds. These false interpretations are how other people saw him, and how they wanted him to perform. Jesus sees it differently.

> **He ate nothing at all during those days, and when they were over, he was famished.**
>
> **The devil said to him, "If you are the Son of God, command this stone to become a loaf of bread."**
>
> **Jesus answered him, "It is written, 'One does not live by bread alone.'"**

This temptation to turn a stone into bread is a "good temptation." A "good temptation" cannot be blatantly wrongheaded. It must have a semblance of truth about it. It must be attractive enough to be seriously considered. Who can deny that God is concerned about human hunger? God fed the Israelites with manna and quail in the desert after they escaped from Egypt (Exod 16–17). This showed God's love for his children. If Jesus is the son of this loving liberator and provider, he will perform a similar miracle to feed himself and, by implication, those to whom he is sent. The desert cannot grow food, but the Son of God, who has access to the miraculous power of God, can provide food in the desert. This is certainly how the mission should be carried out—targeting physical needs that all people acknowledge and meeting them.

As seductive as this strategy is, it did not work well in the past. The full story of Exodus shows how this approach provided temporary relief but ultimately produced effects that were not desirable. God provided manna and quail for the Israelites in the desert, but then they wanted water. In fact, they demanded water as a sign of ". . . [if the] LORD [is] among us or not?" (Exod 17:7). Reliance on God did not make them grateful to the Provider and caring of one another. Instead, they became arrogant, insisting God serve their physical needs. The people stayed on the physical level of existence and never moved beyond it, dragging God down to the level of slave. The problem with miracles is that people passively wait for God to do all the "heavy lifting."

But God is a reality that speaks to the human heart in order to transform it. This is referred to as "not living by bread alone." Although Jesus will be concerned with feeding the hungry, his strategy will not be the miraculous provision of food. God's kingdom will be preached, taught, and lived as a call to conversion. People are more than recurrent physical needs. The spiritual relationship to God, to one another, and to the earth is primary. The fact that Jesus refrains from food for forty days suggests he personally knows that "one does not live by bread alone." Satan's strategy misses the point of human transformation, and so it is rejected.

> **Then the devil took him up higher and showed him all the kingdoms of the world in a single instant. He said to him, "I will give you all this power and the glory of these kingdoms. The power has been given to me and I give it to whomever I wish. Prostrate yourself in homage before me, and it shall all be yours."**
>
> **In reply, Jesus said to him, "Scripture has it, 'You shall do homage to the Lord your God; him alone shall you adore.'"**

The devil, who is devoted to showy material, takes Jesus up higher. The first temptation has been successfully resisted and more sophisticated seductions are necessary. He shows Jesus all the kingdoms of the world in a single instant. In other words, he reveals to Jesus the essence of these kingdoms, the inner dynamics that make them work. Their power and glory belong to the devil because they work by the devil's power. This power is captured in his names. Satan, "Satanas," means the accuser. Devil, "diabolus," means the one who tears things apart, the divider. The kingdoms of the world work by the strategies of accusation and division.

If Jesus wants political and social power, he must play the games of accusation and division. The Son of God should certainly be concerned about bettering the social conditions that structure human life. If he wants to be in a position to influence society, he must be in a position of power. In order to get to a position of power, he must play the games that will get him there. The way of Satan is the path of advance. All Jesus has to do is commit himself to the strategies of accusing other people and dividing them from one another.

But Jesus is already committed to another strategy. He adores the Lord whose way is forgiveness and reconciliation. Once again, Jesus will bring about the kingdom not by the reigning tactics of temporal power but by the personal call to conversion. Forgive one another and be reconciled is the way forward. This path is not found in the kingdoms of the world. They are not to be imitated. They are to be transformed.

> **Then the devil led him to Jerusalem, set him on the parapet of the temple, and said to him, "If you are the Son of God, throw yourself down from here, for Scripture has it, 'He will bid his angels watch over you'; and again, 'With their hands they will support you, that you may never stumble on a stone.'"**
>
> **In reply, Jesus said to him, "It also says, 'You shall not put the Lord your God to the test.'"**
>
> **When the devil had finished all the tempting, he left him, to await another opportunity.**

The context of this last temptation is the difficulty of knowing if God authenticates the preaching and teaching of any individual. The authentication cannot come from the preaching or teaching itself. It must come from an accompanying sign. So if people could not determine if a person spoke for God or spoke for their own interests, they could be "put to the test." They could deliberately put themselves in harm's way or be forcefully put in harm's way. If they survived, then obviously God was behind their actions and everyone would fall in line. If they did not survive, God was not behind their actions and everyone could go home and await someone else. Either way it was a sign.

So the devil's suggestion is that Jesus engage this criterion of discernment up front. If he leaps from the pinnacle of the Temple, from God's highest point, and floats down, it would be a demonstration that God is with him. Most people who would leap from the Temple would crash on the floor of the Temple, proving the God of the Temple was not with them. But Jesus' angelically supported descent would be spectacular proof of divine approbation. It would be Jesus' way of presenting his credentials. There would be no opposition to his preaching and teaching. This sign would convince all.

This last temptation will reappear in full force at the Crucifixion. The execution of Jesus is "another opportunity" the devil awaits. At that time, if Jesus would save himself, come down from the cross, it would prove that God was with him. Or, as the bystanders in the Gospel of Mark hope, Elijah might come to rescue him and provide divine authentication beyond refutation (Mark 15:36). The book of Wisdom lays out this discernment theology very clearly, and lays it out in the devious ways the authorities used it.

> "Let us lie in wait for the righteous man, because he is inconvenient to us and opposes our actions; he reproaches us for sins against the law, and accuses us of sins against our training. He professes to have knowledge of God, and calls himself a child of the Lord. He became to us a reproof of our thoughts; the very sight of him is a burden to us, because his manner of life is unlike that of others, and his ways are strange. We are considered by him as something base, and he avoids our ways as unclean. He calls the last end of the righteous happy, and boasts that God is his father. Let us see if his words are true, and let us test what will happen at the end of his life; for if the righteous man is God's child, he will help him, and will deliver him from the hand of his adversaries. Let us test him with insult and torture, so that we may find out how gentle he is, and make trial of his forbearance. Let us condemn him to a shameful death, for, according to what he says, he will be protected."
>
> Thus they reasoned, but they were led astray, for their wickedness blinded them, and they did not know the secret purposes of God. (Wisdom 2:12-22)

This method of telling the God-appointed from the self-appointed is really a blind and wicked way of getting rid of people who insist on conversion.

But from Jesus' point of view, the problem with this strategy is not its wicked use but its underlying assumption. Jesus is a Jew of the first commandment. His loyalty and commitment are to the One God. Human creatures, the sons and daughters of the One God, are called to act like God in love, peace, and justice. Genuine religious and moral action is the essential sign people are living in God's covenantal love. This is the only test, the test to which God invites his children. Can we imitate the love of God?

However, creatures have a tendency to forget this fundamental truth and the priorities that flow from it. They confuse the Creator-creature relationship and take up the wildly wrong position of testing God, of demanding a sign to assuage their misgivings. What they are really doing is demanding God be like them, to share their fear, ignorance, and lust for certitude. They are deifying their own doubt and soliciting God to solve it. But the Son of God sees through this. Jesus' refusal comes from the clarity of a Jew of the first commandment and the profound reverence that flows from that realization.

Teaching

The CEO has brought a young man to the board meeting. The hospitals in this large Catholic system are hurting financially. The young man has designed a way to organizationally downsize to cut costs. He lays out his plan. Board members ask questions about the effectiveness of this plan to turn around the hospitals. However, even the questions show the board is on its way to adopting this proposal.

A religious sister on the board raises her hand and asks. "How are you going to do this?"

The young man is silent. He has not thought much about this and, to the extent he has, it would be pink slips through the office mail. Suddenly, the focus is not on the survival of the hospitals but on the survival of the people who will be let go. A long and labored conversation ensues on how to do this very difficult but very necessary thing. What are the values that will guide it? How will compassion and respect inform the strategy?

This scenario reflects the way the gospel is brought forward into contemporary Christian life. We distill values from gospel narratives and try to allow them to influence the way we do things. Are gospel values evident in the strategies we employ in education, health care, family life, community life, etc.? For many, just to ask this question is a new, and often not comfortable, step. Also, it is often not clear how the values are really gospel values. The values are often expressed in general language—love, compassion, justice, respect, etc. Supposedly, these words summarize the key dynamics of gospel texts. But the text is often forgotten, leaving the word to float in a vacuum and attract random meanings.

I often think that if we paid closer attention to actual gospel texts, we might find more specification to the values and make them better instruments to guide contemporary strategies. Of course, people quickly reply that the gospels are ancient documents and not immediately applicable to current situations. They can only have influence when they are mediated through the general values that were present in the past and are present today. That may be true, or some version of that may be true. Still, a closer look at the texts may sharpen the values we blithely state in general terms. In the case of the temptations of Jesus, we might find examples of strategies that should be rejected. These ancient temptations may have contemporary individual and corporate embodiments.

In the first temptation Satan suggests that people can be appeased if their physical needs are met. Everyone knows that "bread and circuses" is the proven form of people control. People can be attracted and kept on board by glutting them. Promise them they will be full and safe, and they will let you get away with anything. Admit it. This is what they want. Give it to them. Strategies of this sort are basically manipulations of physical needs. They do not take into account the spiritual and moral dimensions of people. But this general type of strategy is not a stranger to both personal relationships and political campaigns.

In the second temptation Satan suggests that accusing others and dividing people from one another is the proper way to power and glory. Do not look at yourself or your organization as the problem. Find outside causes and accuse them of fomenting the problem. "Outside agitators" takes the heat off inside scoundrels. Look out the window at the enemy, but never let the window become a mirror and look at yourself. Also, do your best to keep people fighting with one another. Thus you can do your own plundering without attracting attention. Strategies of this sort are basically clever ploys to keep you looking good and everyone else looking bad. The tempter is the primordial spin doctor.

In the third temptation the devil suggests that accompanying credentials are more important than the way a person actually thinks and acts. Judge and promote people by their wealth, or their style, or their cleverness. Show is always to be preferred to substance. Keep saying he is a "nice guy" or she is a "go-along" woman. Since when should a principled person be a recommendation for anything? Strategies of this sort avoid essentials and spend their time manipulating the surfaces.

The devil did his best to seduce Jesus into using strategies that looked like they might further his ambitions. But Jesus saw them for what they were—betrayals of his identity—and he refused them. It remains to be seen if we can do the same.

Second Sunday of Lent
Luke 9:28-36

🌿

Risking Listening

A Spiritual Commentary

Jesus took with him Peter and John and James, and went up on the mountain to pray.

This opening line suggests all four "go up" to pray. But as the episode unfolds, only Jesus will pray. The storyteller paints two pictures of Jesus at prayer. The first highlights his transparency to God. The second focuses on Jesus' conversation with past prophets about how God's will is going to be manifested in his life. In other words, both Jesus' identity (the Son of God who is transparent to the Father's light) and his mission (the Messiah who saves the people) enter into his prayer.

The locale of this prayer activity is a mountain. If God dwells in the sky, a mountain is an ideal place to pray because it is closer to God. Later in the episode a cloud will descend and a voice will speak from it. The symbolic import is: prayer is both the process of the ascending human and the descending divine. It is a combination of human effort and divine grace. People climb the mountain; God descends from the sky.

And while he was praying, the appearance of his face changed, and his clothes became dazzling white.

This is the first picture of Jesus' prayer: his transparency to God. His prayer takes place in the interior of his being. Jesus is connected to God in the deepest part of himself. When he goes into this closet to pray (Matt 6:6), he consciously contacts his Father who sees in secret and this Father rewards him. The reward of the Father is to give God's Spirit into Jesus. This giving of Spirit permeates Jesus entirely. It radiates in his face and turns his clothes dazzlingly white. In other words, it moves through body and garments.

Mark's rendition of the Transfiguration says his clothes were "dazzling white, such as no one on earth could bleach them" (Mark 9:3). This image is meant to point to the divine source of the whiteness, just in case the earthbound reader might think it was just a case of exceptional good laundry. However, clothes symbolize more than just garments, outerwear. They mean the whole outer world, the arena of engagement and action. What begins in the interior of Jesus flows out into the world. This reinforces the path of how spirit becomes flesh. It flows from the inner to the outer.

> **Suddenly they saw two men, Moses and Elijah, talking to him. They appeared in glory and were speaking of his departure, which he was about to accomplish at Jerusalem.**

This is the second picture of prayer and it is no surprise to find Moses and Elijah occupying the mountain with Jesus. They often sought out the mountain during their prophetic careers. Their mountaintop experiences were basically times when they consulted God about what was happening in the valleys and on the plains. In other words, God sent them, and so they had to consult God as events unfolded and next steps were envisioned. On the mountain they received both illumination and courage for the tasks of earth.

This is why they are talking about Jesus' exodus, his divinely conceived mission. They are not absorbed in Jesus' transfiguration, but concerned about his liberating action in Jerusalem. They are on the mountain, but they are considering the affairs of earth. Prayer on the mountain is the preparation for action on the earth.

This is also why all three are appearing in glory. Glory is not the isolated individual in touch with God. Glory is how people enact God's plans for the earth. Jesus the Messiah is the premier example of this glory. This glory will be a fulfillment because it is part of a plan, a plan that reaches back to Adam and includes the prophetic struggles of Moses and Elijah. Of course, this fulfillment will be in Jerusalem, the Holy City, and the city to which Jesus journeys throughout the gospel.

> **Now Peter and his companions were weighed down with sleep; but since they had stayed awake, they saw his glory and the two men who stood with him.**

The storyteller presents the disciples in somewhat of a twilight zone. They are weighted down with sleep and yet they are managing to stay awake. This combination of waking and sleeping symbolizes they "get" it and they "don't get it." They are in an in-between space. They are like the man in Mark's Gospel whom Jesus had to touch twice in order to heal his blindness (Mark 8:22-26). After the first touch, he saw people but they looked like trees. After the second touch, he saw people clearly. The disciples are in a one-touch state. They see, but they see blurred. This is a familiar space in spiritual perception. Something is seen, but there is also the realization that something more is to come. This in-between space opens the door for mistakes, and one is about to be made.

> **Just as they were leaving him, Peter said to Jesus, "Master, it is good for us to be here: let us make three dwellings, one for you, one for Moses, and one for Elijah"—not knowing what he said.**

Moses and Elijah are not making a mistake. They know their place and they are about to leave. But Peter detains them with the suggestion of three tents. In the Hebrew Scriptures a tent could symbolize a dwelling place for the divine. Peter wants to make three tents as if Moses, Elijah, and Jesus are on the same level. It is true that Jesus is in the prophetic tradition. But if John the Baptist looms larger than a prophet, even more so is Jesus (Luke 7:26). We are about to hear a more appropriate way of situating Jesus. Making three tents is a mistake, a mistake that is about to be corrected.

> **While he was saying this, a cloud came and overshadowed them, and they were terrified as they entered the cloud. Then from the cloud came a voice that said, "This is my Son, my Chosen; listen to him!" When the voice had spoken, Jesus was found alone.**

Peter's wrongheaded suggestion is interrupted in a spectacular way. A cloud descends, overshadows the disciples, and they are enveloped into it. In this cloud of divine presence a voice reprises what the heavenly voice told Jesus at this baptism. "You are my Son, the Beloved; with you I am well pleased" (Luke 3:22). Only now the voice is not addressing Jesus directly. It is talking to the disciples, and it is not mincing words. Jesus is the Son of God, God's chosen One. The task of discipleship is not to build three tents or even one tent. Jesus is not to be housed and worshiped. He is to be heard. The strong imperative, "Listen to him!" shatters the cloud and reveals Jesus alone—without Moses or Elijah. Get it, Peter?

> **And they kept silent, and in those days told no one any of the things they had seen.**

They *should* keep silent. They have just been corrected by a divine voice from a cloud. When they talk, they are partially right and partially wrong, asleep and awake, seeing and not seeing, hearing and not hearing. What they know is provisional. But, most importantly, when they are not talking, they are in the first stages of listening. Superficial silence—not talking—is the beginning of listening. Profound silence—an empty, receptive mind—is the goal of listening.

The story suggests the content of their listening. They are to ponder the "things they have seen." Seeing is one thing, but understanding is another. Insight is hindsight. It will take time to penetrate and appropriate what they have seen. Learning to listen to the events of Jesus' life is one way his followers pray. They meditate on the events of his life until the truth of those events deepens, and they understand what they must do. This is one way the voice from the cloud is obeyed. "Listen to him!"

Teaching

In ancient China, on the top of Mount Ping stood a temple where the enlightened one, Hwan, lived. One of his disciples was Lao-li. Lao-li had studied and meditated for many years, but he had yet to reach enlightenment. Finally, he decided he had to accept his destiny, gracefully resign himself to his lot, and retreat down the mountain, giving up his hope of enlightenment.

When he went to tell Hwan of his decision, the enlightened one was meditating. Before Lao-li could say anything, Hwan spoke. "Tomorrow I will join you on your journey down the mountain."

The next morning, before their descent, the master looked out into the vastness surrounding the mountain peak. "Tell me, Lao-li, what do you see?"

"Master, I see the sun beginning to wake just below the horizon, hills, and mountains that stretch on for miles, and far below a lake and an old town."

The master smiled, and they took their first steps down the mountain. When they arrived at the foot of the mountain, the master asked Lao-li again, "What do you see?"

"Master, I see roosters as they run around barns, cows asleep in the meadow, children romping by a stream."

The master remained silent and they walked together to the gates of the town. There the master gestured to Lao-li and they sat down under an old tree. "What did you learn today, Lao-li?" the master asked. "Perhaps this is the last wisdom I will impart to you." Lao-li was silent.

After a long while, the master continued, "The road to enlighten-ment is like a journey down the mountain. It comes only to those who realize that what one sees at the top of the mountain is not what one sees at the bottom. Without this wisdom, we close our minds to all that we cannot view from our position and limit our capacity to grow and improve. But with this wisdom, Lao-li, there comes an awakening. We recognize that alone one sees only so much—which, in truth, is not much at all. This is the wisdom that opens our minds to improvement, knocks down prejudices, and teaches us to respect what at first we can-not view. Never forget this last lesson, Lao-li: what you cannot see can be seen from a different part of the mountain."

When the master stopped speaking, Lao-li looked out to the hori-zon, and as the sun set before him, it seemed to rise in his heart. Lao-li turned to the master, but the great one was gone.

From a Christian point of view, Jesus is the "different part of the mountain." He sees things which, from our position on the mountain, are not able to be seen. That is why the voice from the cloud assures the disciples of Jesus' special stature and urges them to listen to him. Whenever we follow someone more illumined than ourselves, we must be open to what they say. This does not mean we become gullible or acritical or mindlessly obedient. But it does mean we temporarily sus-pend our own assumptions to work with words that may be, on a first hearing, strange to us. Jesus has greater wisdom and courage than his followers. They must realize this and risk the act of listening. They must not immediately argue with everything they cannot comfortably accom-modate to their present worldview. As we learn to listen to the Word of God through gospel stories, we must cultivate a similar openness.

In moments of honesty, we will all admit to dismissing many of Jesus' words. The sayings about hating our very selves, or not calling someone a fool, or taking no heed for tomorrow, or letting the dead bury the dead, or lending to those who cannot repay, or resisting not evil, so powerfully assault common sense that we do not entertain them. But perhaps they are invitations to a deeper level of wisdom. But we will never know unless we are willing to engage in an act of deep listening, an act that entails the letting go of some mental defenses as well as the letting in of these strange words.

The gospels contain a strange spiritual wisdom. It conflicts with conventional understandings and preferred ways of behaving. In order to hear it and to cultivate it until we understand it and are able to in-tegrate it into our lives, we may have to let go of some of our favorite certainties. But if listening to Jesus leads to greater life and love, then the "letting go" will be done in joy. ". . . then, in his joy, he goes and sells all he has and buys that field" (Matt 13:44).

This is the ultimate reasoning for listening to him. He has the words of eternal life (John 6:68). But in order to receive them, we must let go of the words of death. Therefore, we listen to these words until life overcomes death. The Transfiguration takes place on the road to Jerusalem and the road to Easter.

Third Sunday of Lent
Luke 13:1-9

❦

Bearing Fruit

A Spiritual Commentary

Some of those present told Jesus about the Galileans whose blood Pilate had mingled with their sacrifices.

Jesus asked them, "Do you think that because these Galileans suffered in this way they were worse sinners than all other Galileans? No, I tell you, but unless you repent, you will all perish as they did. Or those eighteen who were killed when the tower of Siloam fell on them—do you think that they were worse offenders than all the others living in Jerusalem? No, I tell you, but unless you repent, you will all perish just as they did."

The "some who were present" seems an innocent enough designation, but their anonymous status makes them part of the crowd. When Jesus responds to the crowds, he is addressing his words to a wide audience who embodies a conventional point of view. The target group is not the disciples, or the Scribes and Pharisees, or the Sadducees, or a particular individual, such as the centurion, the Canaanite woman, etc. This is not wisdom tailored to a specific group or individual. It is a brush stroke on the broad canvas of common humanity.

These "some present" are concerned with how to bring order to the vicissitudes of life. A horrendous incident is alluded to in the text. It seems some Galileans were visiting Jerusalem and offering sacrifices in the Temple. These sacrifices involved the killing of animals. Pilate sent in troops and murdered the Galileans, mingling their blood with the blood of the sacrificed animals. If the sacrificed animals were part of a ritual for the atonement of sins, the Galileans were murdered as they were repenting. This makes the crowd think that perhaps the magnitude of their sins had something to do with their tragic fate.

Jesus, the reader of hearts, surmises their thoughts, discerns the path of their misguided thinking.

> "These Galileans must have been the worst of sinners for this to happen. God would not accept their sacrifice, but through the agency of Pilate

sacrificed them instead. Is not this always the case? Whenever random moral evil occurs, there are proximate players like Pilate and the Galileans. But there is also an ultimate actor hidden in the background. Is not the hand of the punishing God in this?"

Thinking along these lines is common. It seems almost hard-wired into the human mind.

Before Jesus resists this way of thinking, he extends it. He gives it its due before he shows how it is misleading. "What about physical evil" he seems to say, "the accidental events that tragically affect people's lives? You have heard how, without warning, a tower fell in Jerusalem and eighteen were killed. Was the hand of God in this, the hand of a God who sees sinners and punishes them?" The thought is seductive. All the events of life are within a divine plan. Therefore, incidents of moral and physical evil are somehow connected to the divine will. The most probable explanation is punishment for sin.

Jesus gives an adamant "No" to this theological way of thinking. However, the text does not explain this "No." He does not engage in theological debates that later Christian thinkers will relish. Where are his rebutting arguments? There is no insistence on a divine love that seeks repentance rather than punishment. There is no laborious explanation of God's permissive will that allows evil to happen. There is no appeal to a higher wisdom and a hidden plan that humans cannot appreciate. There is just a strong denial that the people were killed because they were egregious sinners. It is almost like he is issuing a command, "Stop that way of thinking right now!"

Then there is a surprising confrontation. Jesus says that unless they repent, they will all likewise perish. This is another example of how dealing with Jesus can turn dangerous. They are asking about the fate of others, and suddenly they are faced with their own fate. And this fate is not dependent on the caprice of Pilate or the poor mortaring of bricklayers. Their fate is in their own hands. They have to repent (or, more accurately, "change their mind") or they will perish. The conversation changes from questions of abstract theology to demands for personal decisions.

But what exactly is entailed in this change of mind and how can it keep them from perishing? The crowd looks outside themselves and wonders about the tragic fate of others. Even more, they connect this fate with the will of God. This habit of looking outside at already accomplished events to uncover the workings of God needs to be turned around. People must look inside to be in touch with the will of God and then make that will happen in the events of their lives. They are the ones who bring God's will onto the earth. Speculating about tragedies is a misplaced emphasis, matching earthly events to divine will leaves us puzzled and enervated. It takes consciousness away from the more important work, bringing the divine will to earthly events. This is the change of mind that is needed, as the attached parable makes clear.

> **Then Jesus told this parable.**
>
> **"A man had a fig tree planted in his vineyard, and he came looking for fruit on it and found none. So he said to the gardener, 'See here! For three years I have come looking for fruit on this fig tree, and still I find none. Cut it down! Why should it be wasting the soil?'**
>
> **The gardener replied, 'Sir, let it alone for one more year, until I dig around it and put manure on it. If it bears fruit next year, well and good; but if not, you can cut it down.'"**

In this context the parable reveals the toughness of the mind of Christ. We are fig trees called upon to bear fruit. This is the purpose of human life. Each person is on a mission to do the will of God on earth. In the parable the fig tree is presently unfruitful. In its unfruitful state, it is described as wasting the soil. The intent of this image connects with other gospels images. Wasted soil is similar to a squandered inheritance, a light under a basket, and salt that has lost its savor. In other words, the tree is not doing what it should do. It is meant to bear fruit and it is not performing. The gardener begs for time and treatment. It is assumed the owner accedes to his request. But the hard message remains: produce or perish.

There is a saying: if you are struck in the leg with a poison arrow, it is not the time to inquire what type of feathers are on the shaft. There is definitely a perishing that happens from the uncontrollable events of life. Those events strike terror in us, and we wonder why one is taken and one is left. If we are preoccupied by these situations of the outer world, our minds hypothesize explanations and we shrink from life and its unknown intrusions. However, this type of conjecture is "inquiring about the feathers."

In Jesus' mind there is a more urgent situation. It is not theoretical but immediate and practical. We are in jeopardy now. The poison arrow is in the leg. We must act immediately. A tree meant to be fruitful is in danger of being cut down. This possibility of perishing without producing frustrates our whole life project and compels us to change. The conditions of change are favorable. There is soil, manure, a gardener to hoe, and time. But the time is not endless. We must change now or we will perish, not by a sudden tragic event but by our own failure to respond. Leave to the fabrications of the mind the question of whether terrible events are God's will. The will of God that is beyond debate is that we change and produce fruit, that we bring heaven to earth.

The regrettable conclusion of this episode, especially for those of us who play the mind games of theology, is: Jesus was not a theologian.

Teaching

What happens when one way of thinking is too much with us? What happens when a single question occupies our consciousness? What happens when we say of some thought, "I can't get it out of my mind" or "It gives me no rest"?

Many people think that when the mind can be single-minded, it is on the path of discovery. Highly focused attention is the precursor to breakthroughs in thinking and solutions to problems. However, there can be a downside to this ability to concentrate. The mind that is preoccupied with one thought excludes many others. There is only so much "room" in the mind. When all the space is taken by one way of thinking, there is no place for another thought. Therefore, if a new thought is to be allowed to influence a person, it must replace the current thought that monopolizes the mind or, at least, make that thought "move over" so that the space of the mind can be shared.

This seems to be the background for one of the teachings of this text. The crowds are filled with the question of tragic events and divine will. They ponder outer events, evaluating them as blessings or curses, rewards for righteousness or punishments for sins. They worry about why bad things happen to good people or why good things happen to bad people. This is an important train of thought, and it has an honored place in Christian theology. The problem is not with these questions surrounding divine will and tragic events, but how these questions crowd out other questions: in particular, how these questions of divine will preclude the most significant question about divine will.

The divine will is not in outer events, but in the soul where the person is connected to God. The path of contacting and enacting the divine will is to go within and then to go without. When we go without, we carry the divine will with us. God's will is done in and through us.

That is the thrust of Jesus' prayer. We are the sons and daughters of "our Father in heaven." When we open to this Father in heaven, we are to hallow his name, bring his kingdom, and do his will "on earth as it is in heaven." The assumption of the prayer is that God's will is not done on earth. Therefore, to look at the events of the earth to find God's will is to look in the wrong direction. It is in the heavenly space of prayer that we touch this will and it is in the struggles of the earth that we enact it.

This is what it means to bear fruit, to bear God's being and love into the world. If, at the moment, we are not doing this, the gardener will go to work. Our tree is planted in good soil. In other words, we are grounded in God, in the reality of "the hidden ground of love" (the title of a Thomas Merton book.) But we are not attending to that grounding or opening to its nurture. The art of the gardener (the Second Adam who has not lost the intimacy of the Garden of Paradise) will revitalize our contact with the ground of God. He begs for time and with hoeing and fertilizing creates the conditions of fruitfulness.

But, in the last analysis, what drives Christ to pull attention away from speculative matters and redirect it to this fundamental intercourse between divine and human wills? There is little indication in the episode. However, I fanaticize he is moved by a great sadness brought on by the sight of wasted soil and fruitless trees. I recently read of a very successful business leader who had died. His wife was asked if he was a happy man. She replied that he had trouble with happiness because he was almost "physically revolted by the idea of unrealized potential left on the table." There is something of that intensity in Jesus' plea for repentance.

Fourth Sunday of Lent

Luke 15:1-3, 11-32

🔥

Failing to Rejoice

A Spiritual Commentary

Now all the tax collectors and sinners were coming near to listen to him. And the Pharisees and the scribes were grumbling and saying, "This fellow welcomes sinners and eats with them."

The groups that will listen to the story of the Prodigal Father are clearly designated. The tax collectors and sinners are those outside the law; the Pharisees and scribes are those inside the law. These two antithetical groups have gathered around Jesus. The Pharisees and scribes have a criticism, and they are characterized as grumbling. Grumbling signifies a lack of understanding, a mindless objection, a thought that is agitating them deeply because it is confusing them greatly. As their minds construe it, the problem is: Jesus is welcoming and accepting people whose behavior puts them outside the law. In doing this, he is approving them and sanctioning their actions.

Of course, this is not how Jesus sees it. It is doubtful whether Jesus ever ate with a "sinner" or argued with a "Pharisee or scribe." Instead, he shared food with lost sons and daughters and had conversations with other lost sons and daughters. Jesus is clear about what he does. He seeks out the lost. In the story that follows, a father welcomes two lost sons. The younger lost son parallels the sinners and tax collectors; the older lost son parallels the Pharisees and scribes. Although these two groups see themselves as opposite of one another, Jesus sees them as sharing a common malady—the failure to rejoice. The ultimate intention of the story is to replace this common malady with a common cure—celebration.

So he told them this parable: "There was a man who had two sons. The younger of them said to his father, 'Father, give me the share of the property that will belong to me.' So he divided his property between them."

This "man who has two sons" is not a typical patriarch. The younger son insults him by asking for his share of the inheritance. Inheritances are only received when the patriarch dies. To ask for it before his death is to implicitly desire that the father die. But instead of responding with offended honor and beating or banishing the son, the father gives everything he has, keeping nothing for himself. He gives his property to both his sons, dividing it equally.

This magnanimous self-giving goes completely against cultural type. Patriarchs are not known to bankrupt themselves. This odd behavior, which will continue throughout the story, provides a clue to the interpretation of the story. Although on one level it is a story about family relationships, it is not meant to be a social commentary. The father represents the self-giving spiritual reality of God and the two sons symbolize two predicaments in which people find themselves. The younger son will be lost in sin and the older son will be lost in self-righteousness. But both are lost and have the mindsets to prove it. It is these mindsets that the father will have to work with and correct.

> **"A few days later the younger son gathered all he had and traveled to a distant country, and there he squandered his property in dissolute living. When he had spent everything, a severe famine took place throughout that country and he began to be in need.**
>
> **So he went and hired himself out to one of the citizens of that country, who sent him to his fields to feed the pigs. He would gladly have filled himself with the pods that the pigs were eating; and no one gave him anything."**

This is a picture of ever-greater descent. It is meant to show complete degradation. The son goes into a far country, abandoning his day-in day-out connection to home and father. Then he squanders the inheritance, his only remaining contact with his father. Immediately he experiences famine and need, becomes a hireling who not only tends swine but becomes a pig himself, desiring their food. His situation, "no one gave him anything" is starkly contrasted with his situation in the home of his father who freely gave him whatever he had.

Although this story is directed at specific historical groups of first-century Jewish people and uses symbols designed to emotionally impact them (e.g., pigs), it depicts the universal situation of people before God. If people take the gift of God but do not stay in touch with the Giver, they begin a process of dehumanization. Since they are no longer in touch with the Source of life, what little life they manage to take with them is quickly dissipated. Quite literally, it dissolves, having no

Source to refresh it. Therefore, this dissolute living leads to emptiness. In place of fullness there is famine. Symbolically, people live the life of a slave in a far country rather than the life of a son in the home of their father. They are reduced to the physical level of life and defined by its unmet hungers. But empty stomachs concoct plans.

> **"But when he came to himself he said, 'How many of my father's hired hands have bread enough and to spare, but here I am dying of hunger. I will get up and go to my father, and I will say to him, "Father, I have sinned against heaven and before you; I am no longer worthy to be called your son; treat me like one of your hired hands."'"**

He is presently a hired hand and not eating. Perhaps he can be a hired hand and eat. The house he knows is the house of his father. There the hired hands eat well. So he prepares and practices a script to get back into the house of food. It is a script that acknowledges his sin, his straying from the Source of life. In fact, the confession of sin is so thorough that he becomes the sin. He imagines the full consequences of his sin are a permanent loss of sonship. He resigns himself to being treated like a hired hand. His sin has become his identity. He is no longer son; he is sinner.

> **"So he set off and went to his father. But while he was still far off, his father saw him and was filled with compassion; he ran and put his arms around him and kissed him."**

> **"Then the son said to him, 'Father, I have sinned against heaven and before you. I am no longer worthy to be called your son.'"**

The lost son makes the first move. He turns and moves toward the father. But that is all he needs to do. He does not have to walk the whole way home, the humiliation of his sin and the fierceness of his need driving each step. "While he was still far off, his father saw him . . ." The reason his father sees him is that he has been keeping vigil, waiting and watching. At the sight of his son, the father's heartfelt compassion covers the distance between them before his body covers the ground between them. This compassion moves him so completely that he runs, embraces, and kisses. It is hard to overestimate the emotional force of these three sequential actions. They combine to create a picture of overwhelming love and reconciliation.

Humans have to turn back to God, but they do not have to crawl back. Divine love meets them more than halfway. Grace is a proactive energy that seeks whoever is willing to be found. But when the identification with sin is strong, the welcome of grace can be resisted. The lost son has privately practiced his script. Its sentiments are lodged deep within him. Now he publicly performs it. Even in the embrace of his father, he clings to the power of his sin to make him unworthy. We have a standoff—a sullen sinner and a wildly joyous father. Joy is always more inventive than dejection.

> **"But the father said to his slaves, 'Quickly! Bring out a robe—the best one—and put it on him; put a ring on his finger and sandals on his feet. And get the fatted calf and kill it, and let us eat and celebrate; for this son of mine was dead and is alive again; he was lost and is found!'**
>
> **And they began to celebrate."**

In a wonderfully ironic move the father does not engage his son who would be a hired hand. Instead, he talks to the slaves about how to treat his son. He is to be visibly reinstated as a son with robe, ring, and shoes. Then the fatted calf is to be killed and the entire community is to celebrate. All this has to be done quickly. It has to reverse the negative thinking in his son's head that already has had too much time to develop. The reason for this wholehearted welcome is symbolically stated: my son was dead and has come back to life; he was lost and now he is found. This is all the father cares about. Celebration is the only appropriate response.

> **"Now his elder son was in the field; and when he came and approached the house, he heard music and dancing. He called one of the slaves and asked what was going on.**
>
> **He replied, 'Your brother has come, and your father has killed the fatted calf, because he has got him back safe and sound.'**
>
> **Then he became angry and refused to go in.**
>
> **His father came out and began to plead with him."**

As the younger son represented the tax collectors and sinners but was also a universal type, so the older son represents the scribes and the Pharisees but is also a universal type. There is no better way to introduce the elder son than he "was in the field." The older son is a worker. He does not come to the house of his father from famine in a far country but from laboring in the fields. And he is not accustomed or even attracted to the sound of music and dancing. He does not immediately go in. He is suspicious, and when he finds out what is going on, he is angry. His refusal to go in and join the celebration is an insult. It is an insult on a par with asking for the inheritance while the father is still alive. But the father who ran toward one lost son now comes out after the other lost son. This father does not let insult turn him away.

> **"But he answered his father, 'Listen! For all these years I have been working like a slave for you, and I have never disobeyed your command; yet you have never given me even a young goat so that I might celebrate with my friends. But when this son of yours came back, who has devoured your property with prostitutes, you killed the fatted calf for him!'"**

This complaint, spoken in anger, reveals the heart of the older son. Although he has stayed home, he has not stayed home as a son. He sees himself as a slave and his father as one who issues commands. He has obeyed these commands but not with the full heart of a son. He works with the calculating mind of a slave, wanting to be paid for his labor. But he sees himself as underpaid and his father as so stingy that he keeps him from celebrating with his friends. Therefore, he lives with a smoldering resentment that has now come to the surface and demands the attention of his father. "Listen!" This is the speech of a self-pitying man who thinks he has been treated unfairly, while his profligate younger brother has been treated indulgently. The question is: "Does he have it right, or is this a skewed and self-righteous account?"

> **"Then the father said to him, 'Son, you are always with me, and all that is mine is yours. But we had to celebrate and rejoice, because this brother of yours was dead and has come to life; he was lost and has been found.'"**

The father does not share the older son's rendition of their relationship. From the father's point of view, the important thing is that they have always been together and the father has held nothing back from him. At the start of the story, the father divided and shared all he had with *both* sons. But the older son has not focused on the presence and self-giving of the Father. Instead, he has fabricated a demanding father who withholds love from the one who deserves it while giving love to the one who does not deserve it. Although there has been no inequality or favoritism, this is the inner world the older brother inhabits.

The real problem is the older son has turned the free gift of the father into a burden for which there is never adequate compensation. His own lack of joy makes him a lost son. Like his brother, but with different motivation, he has chosen the identity of a hired hand, with all the resentments and angers that enforced employment brings. If the older son had lived in the house and fields of his father as a free and vibrant worker in the vineyard, he would now be dancing in celebration at the return of his brother. He would know that unless we turn it into drudgery, the presence of the father always makes us joyous. Celebration is just the natural overflow of divine love. Given the nature of God who finds the lost and brings the dead back to life, it is something necessary. "We *had to* celebrate and rejoice . . ."

Teaching

As often as I have read and meditated on this story of the Prodigal Son or, as some contemporaries have renamed it, the Prodigal Father, it still has the power to move me emotionally. I am not alone. When I have told this story to others, even those who have heard it many times, I look out to see glistening eyes. Some spiritual traditions interpret tears as the consciousness of the border between the sacred and the profane, between time and eternity. I think this story has that kind of power. It brings certain listeners to the space where God and the soul are in conversation.

But the story has some very difficult things to say about how God and soul converse. Better said, how God and the soul do not converse, how they stay separate from one another. A first target of the story is the mindset of the younger son. He obsesses on his mistake, allowing it to hold him tighter and tighter. Although the father shows no signs of holding on to it, the son is not able to let it go. He would have trouble following the advice of Isaac Meir of Ger.

> Whoever talks about and reflects upon an evil thing he has done is thinking of the vileness he has perpetrated, and what one thinks, therein is one caught—with one's whole soul one is caught utterly in what one thinks, and so he is still caught in vileness. And he will surely not be able to turn, for his spirit will coarsen and his heart rot, and beside this, a sad mood may come upon him. What would you? Stir filth this way of that, and it is still filth. To have sinned or not to have sinned—what does it profit us in heaven? In the time I am brooding on this, I could be stringing pearls for the joy of heaven. That is why it is written: "Depart

from evil and do good"—turn wholly from evil, do not brood in its way and do good. You have done wrong? Then balance it by doing right." (Quoted in *A Jewish Reader: In Time and Eternity*, ed. N. N. Glatzer, 2nd ed. [New York: Schocken Books, 1961] 111)

This makes fine psychological sense; and it would seem to be required if forgiveness is ever going to be integrated into a person's life.

But it is also difficult to do. Letting go of sin is different than repressing the memory of wrongdoing. When wrongdoing is repressed, it sits and waits until the censor of the mind relaxes. Then it reappears in consciousness and undercuts the capacity for joy. When we let go of past sins, we can remember them without identifying with them. Then they can be triggers of gratitude and compassion. They do not interfere with joy. They actually promote it. But this inner dexterity takes a long time to learn.

The second target of the story is the mindset of the older brother. As a representative of the scribes and the Pharisees, his way of thinking particularly afflicts those who see themselves as righteous. The book of Deuteronomy chastises the Jews "because you did not serve the Lord your God joyfully and with gladness of heart for the abundance of everything" (Deut 28:47). When our consciousness cannot stay focused on the abundance of God and creation and, therefore, serve the Lord in joy and gladness, other motivations emerge. The first and foremost is reward. We work for our own profit. We may convince ourselves that this is a pure motivation because we are working for a *spiritual* reward. But spiritual reward is still spiritual reward; treasure in heaven is still treasure in heaven.

Working for external rewards and not out of inner abundance eventually brings us into the emotional state of resentment. Resentment is built on comparison and a perceived inequality. The older brother evaluates himself in relation to his younger brother and, not surprisingly, comes off favorably. He has obeyed his father's commands and his brother has squandered the father's living with whores. These are the hard facts that cannot be denied.

However, these calculations are not part of the Father's equation. The running Father is the symbol of divine grace; and grace is grace is grace is grace. It just gives to whoever is able to receive it. When the reward-driven mind encounters this indiscriminate grace, it regards it as unjust because it is not playing the game of merit. It erupts in a red-hot blast of resentment. There may be many fine points to this story that people do not understand. But everyone gets it when the older brother explodes. We instinctively understand him because his mindset is deeply embedded in each of us.

The revelation of God as grace should make us rejoice. But before we can celebrate, we must deal with the mindsets that the appearance of grace uncovers. We are attached to our past sins, and so cannot quite believe we are sons and daughters of love. This keeps us from joy. We also are alienated from the simple presence of abundance, and so we work for reward and find ourselves resentful and envious. This keeps us from joy. Only when we break the stranglehold of these two blocking mindsets will we hear the music in the house and know that we are home.

Fifth Sunday of Lent
(Lectionary for Mass)

John 8:1-11

◖

Holding in Sin or Forgiving for Life

A Spiritual Commentary

Then each of them went home, while Jesus went to the Mount of Olives. Early in the morning he came again to the temple.

Everyone went home. Jesus' home is in the Temple. However, he must follow a prescribed path to get there, a path that includes an overnight stay on the Mount of Olives. The reason for this strange itinerary is Jesus is the bearer of the exiled divine glory. According to legend, the divine glory once resided in the Temple. But the sins of the people were so offensive that the divine glory departed from Israel. It "leapt" from the Temple to the Mount of Olives, and from the Mount of Olives into the heavens.

Now the divine glory in the person of Jesus is returning by the same path, only reversing the direction. Jesus is the One Who Comes Down from Heaven or the One Who Comes Down from Above (John 3:13, 31). He proceeds to the intermediary Mount of Olives, and then returns to his home to the Temple. In this way the divine glory "comes again" into the Temple.

It is early in the morning. So it is a new day. We can expect a new relationship between divine glory and human sinfulness. In the past, sin drove divine glory away. Who knows what will happen when they meet again?

All the people came to him and he sat down and began to teach them.

"All the people" could not gather in the Temple area. So it is not helpful to picture a mob trying to get close to Jesus. But what is about to transpire is meant for all the people. The intended audience is not just disciples or an isolated seeker or the adversarial Pharisees or the hardened rulers. Every life is involved in the processes that are about to unfold. The human condition is about to be revealed. All people are implicated. Therefore, "all the people came to him."

Jesus is seated, the position of a teacher. He has begun his teaching. However, the storyteller does not allow us to hear the teaching. We are not directly treated to the wisdom of Christ. As so often happens in gospel stories, there will be an interruption. We will not hear Jesus talk; we will watch him engage people. Jesus is not portrayed as a speculative thinker. He is someone who puts together thought and action, who encounters people in an effort to change them.

> **The scribes and the Pharisees brought a woman who had been caught in adultery; and making her stand before all of them. . .**

"Caught–brought–made to stand there"—these are verbs of power, control, and dominance. In two short sentences the scribes and Pharisees are characterized clearly. What they are about is finding people in sin and holding them there. In particular, the picture of the woman "made to stand before all of them" conveys this holding action. They are staring at her. The stare is the special tool of the self-righteous. The stare fixates the person, turns them into an object, tries to hold them in the mistake they have been caught in. The unflinching eyes of the stare attempts to stay the flow of time and the newness it always brings.

> **"Teacher," [they said] "This woman was caught in the very act of committing adultery. Now in the law Moses commanded us to stone such women. What do you say?" They said this to test him, so that they might have some charge to bring against him.**

If they are nothing else, the scribes and Pharisees are predictable. They have caught the woman, and they are holding her in her sin. But they have no sin to hold Jesus in. So they devise a trap to catch Jesus in sin. Then they will hold him in the sin they have trapped him into. The scribes and Pharisees hold people in sin for a living. They are single-minded in this pursuit. Jesus is their target.

But their deceitful question has unwittingly given Jesus the raw material of his response. In the imagination of Jesus, the mystic-prophet, Moses/stones/the-very-act-of-adultery stirs up the founding events of Israel. Jesus is about to reenact them—with his own peculiar spin.

Jesus bent down and wrote with his finger on the ground.

When they kept on questioning him, he straightened up and said to them, "Let anyone among you who is without sin be the first to throw a stone at her."

And once again he bent down and wrote on the ground.

Almost everyone at one time or another has given in to curiosity and asked, "What did he write?" However, it is not important what he wrote. What is important is he wrote with his finger, he wrote on the earth, and he wrote twice. It is also important he bent down, straightened up, and bent down again. These actions bring us back to the Law of Moses and provide the answer to the question of the scribes and Pharisees, "Now what do you say?"

In the book of Exodus, God writes the Ten Commandments and gives the two stone tablets to Moses. We are assured of divine authorship because we are told they were written with "the finger of God" (Exod 31:18). Human authors use quills and parchment. God uses his finger that is capable of carving into the hardness of rock. Jesus also writes with his finger, showing his closeness to God and that he writes for God.

When Moses descends from his mountain encounter with God, he carries the stone tablets to the people. As he draws close, he hears noise coming from the camp. Joshua thinks it is the noise of warfare. Moses, forewarned by God, correctly identifies it as the noise of revelry. He catches the people dancing around the golden calf. He throws down the tablets and breaks them. Then with the help of the sons of Levi he slaughters 3,000 of the revelers. The price of breaking the covenant is death. "In the law Moses told us to stone such women."

As the Hebrew tradition evolved, this first breaking of the covenant and every subsequent breach was envisioned as adultery. Yahweh and his people were married, but Israel whored after strange gods. Yahweh even asked the prophet Hosea to symbolize this infidelity. "Go, love a woman who has a lover and is an adulteress, just as the Lord loves the people of Israel, though they turn to other gods" (Hos 3:1). Given the overall evaluation of the Pharisees in the Gospel of John, this woman caught in adultery is an image of Israel who has strayed from the true God. In particular, it is the religious elite of Israel who have broken the covenant because they do not know the true teachings of Moses, teachings that Jesus is about to show them.

The story in Exodus does not end with the death of the idolaters/ adulterers. Moses returns to the mountain, pleads for the people, and in a long conversation with God suddenly asks to see God's glory. God accedes to Moses' wish but with a strange condition. "And while my glory passes by I will put you in a cleft of the rock, and I will cover you with my hand until I have passed by; then I will take away my hand, and you shall see my back; but my face shall not be seen" (Exod 33:22-23). The glory of God is too great to take face to face. Then the Lord tells Moses to cut two more tablets. "I will write on the tablets the words that were on the former tablets which *you* broke." The emphasis is on the fact it was Moses who did the breaking.

So God writes a second time. But between the first and the second writing the glory of God passes by Moses. When it does, it has something to say.

> "The LORD, the LORD,
> a God merciful and gracious,
> slow to anger,
> and abounding in steadfast
>   love and faithfulness,
> keeping steadfast love for the
>   thousandth generation,
> forgiving iniquity and
>   transgression and sin,
> yet by no means clearing the guilty,
> but visiting the iniquity of the parents
> upon the children
> and the children's children,
> to the third and fourth generation." (Exod 34:6-8)

The divine glory, too great to look on directly, is steadfast love and endless forgiveness. Yet this does not keep iniquity from being passed on from generation to generation. The way of the earth is the forgiveness of God meeting the entrenched iniquity of people, the releasing God pleading with the holding people.

"Now what do *you* say?" is the question the Pharisees put to Jesus.

Here then is what Jesus has to say. It is an incomplete understanding of the Mosaic Law to stone people who have broken covenantal laws. The God who wrote the Law is not punishing and vindictive. The true interpretation of the Mosaic Law is that God always writes twice. And between the first and second writing is the reason why two writings are always needed. There are no sinless ones. Israel herself is only alive because God has forgiven her many adulteries. No one can cast the first stone for everyone lives by the grace of the forgiving God. Holding people in their sins while holding yourself innocent is delusional. The question is not the condemnation of adultery but the continuing blindness of people to the universal necessity of forgiveness.

There is an alternative to the holding stare of the scribes and Pharisees. Jesus exemplifies it. He bends down, stands up with words that hold up a mirror to the scribes and Pharisees, and then he bends down again. He does not stare. He does not hold them. He shows them their hidden sinful selves and returns to the earth. This self-knowledge is what is needed for them to change. The divine glory does not have to return to the sky. It has found another way to deal with the sinfulness of the earth.

So, Jesus writes with his finger—the sign of God's authorship. He writes twice—the sign of God's forgiveness. He writes on the earth—the sign of a universal condition. He refuses to stare at them—the sign that sins are not held.

Are the Pharisees able to read these symbolic signs? Are they able to hear this complex blend of criticism and invitation?

When they heard it, they went away, one by one, beginning with the elders.

"When they heard this" does not mean that Jesus spoke loud enough. It means they "got it." It penetrated into their minds and hearts. This offer of a different self-understanding—not righteous and vengeful but sinful and forgiven, not judge of this woman but the brother to her straying, not faithful to the Mosaic Law but ignorant of the true meaning of the Mosaic Law—became a clear invitation.

They refused it. They walked away. No reasons are given. In a way none are needed. Is there anyone on earth who has not seen themselves in a way that contradicted their cherished and scrubbed-up image and not looked away? We know how hard it is to look, especially when to look means to join with people we have previously despised.

However, to refuse the invitation to community is to live in isolation. They walk away "one by one," alone and unconnected. The oldest begin this procession of refusal. The longer people live in self-righteousness and condemnation, the more difficult it is to see the truth and life-giving potential of an alternative.

And Jesus was left alone with the woman standing before him. Jesus straightened up and said to her, "Woman, where are they? Has no one condemned you?"

Earlier "they made her stand there." Now there is just the simple fact of mutual presence—no force, no "caught–brought–made to stand." Jesus stands up to look at her without staring, to show her to herself. In a gentle and nonholding way, Jesus showed the scribes and Pharisees a distorted self they did not know and yet needed to know in order to turn and have life. The scribes and Pharisees had to see distortion before they could embrace life. This woman needs to see life before she can leave distortion. So Jesus shows her a deeper self that has always been present but now needs to be seen and believed. He calls her "Woman." This is not a simple designation that she is female. In the Gospel of John the Mother of Jesus is called "Woman" twice, once at the wedding feast of Cana and once at the cross. "Woman" is a title of honor, pointing to a deep life-giving power.

Augustine said about this scene, "Only two are left—mercy and misery!" However, was Jesus ever satisfied with only two? Did he not want all people—"All the people came to him"? "Where did they go?" is not a rhetorical or ironic question. Neither is it cynically gloating over a victory in a theological jousting match. It is a poignant question that I fantasize comes out of a hidden grief. Its impact is to cause us to scrutinize again the mystery of turning away from the offer of salvation.

The woman cannot answer the question of where the ones who refused the offer went. Did they walk away into the night like Judas? Perhaps not. Although they might not have been able to drop the stones, they could not throw them either. Perhaps they are in that troubled space between identities, the space where a life of hardness and judgment brings us all, and a space where Jesus' next question to the woman presses us for an answer. "Has no one condemned you?"

"No one, Lord," she said.

For a story that traditionally has been titled "The Woman Caught in Adultery," it is significant she has only one line. But it is an important line. There is no condemnation in the outer world. The circle of accusers has dispersed. It has often been remarked that there is a personal, deeper resonance to "no one." She does not condemn herself. For at least a brief moment the human judgmental world is nowhere to be found. What will life be without it?

"Neither do I condemn you. Go your way, and from now on do not sin again."

She calls Jesus, "Lord." So she knows he represents the Divine Source. His refusal to condemn means there is no condemnation in God. We are now invited into a world of change without condemnation. All judgment in this world is in the service of hope. Everything is geared toward the unfolding of new life. We must all, "Go!" Is there not an echo of God's ancient desire spoken through the mouth of Moses to whatever enslaves us, "Let my people go!" With what we now know from this carefully crafted story, are we able to heed its final command? Can we walk without sin?

The Divine Glory has returned. Sin will not drive it back into the heavens. It has written the "truth of twice" upon the earth and a new temple of forgiveness has been built in the precincts of the old. The divine glory is back home.

Teaching

A friend of mine is fond of paraphrasing a line from the movie *Steel Magnolias*, "If you can't say anything good about anybody, you just come over here and sit right next to me." Holding people in their mistakes is a popular pastime. Few can resist it. Even fewer understand the "handcuffing of people" that is really going on.

Holding people in sin is not the "special gift" of the scribes and Pharisees. It is an all-too-common human procedure. In fact, it is so common it is taken for granted. We do not consciously choose to do it, we just mindlessly engage in it. It is both pervasive and unconscious. We just assume the obituary of a lawyer who died at eighty-two will prominently feature the scandal he was involved in when he was thirty-five. We unreflectively remark that she is doing quite well for an ex-addict, thereby using addiction as the permanent reference point for her life. Jail sentences are never over. We look at the fifty year old and see the twenty-two year old behind bars. Sin sticks. Ask anyone who has been caught, brought and made to stand there.

Perhaps that is why the resurrected Christ in John's Gospel brings the "glue of sin" to the attention of his disciples. He is trying to bring into their awareness an active and alienating habit. The resurrected Christ breathes on them and says, "Receive the Holy Spirit. If you forgive the sins of any, they are forgiven them; if you retain the sins of any, they are retained" (John 20:22-23). This is the condition that characterizes our communal life. We can hold each other in our mistakes or let each other go. We can be a prison to one another or the source of release. Both are possibilities. But it seems we easily gravitate toward "holding in sin" and have to work at letting go. Perhaps this is part of what John means when he says, "People *loved* darkness" (John 3:19).

I have caught myself many times holding other people in their sin. But the strength and compulsiveness of this habit came home to me a number of years ago. I found a man who had tried to commit suicide—pills and booze. I called an ambulance. They pumped his stomach and got him to the hospital on time. The suicide attempt was unsuccessful.

However, every time I saw him after that, I saw him through the memory image of his attempted suicide. I could not shake it. I knew I was holding him in his sin, paralyzing him in his worst moment. Yet I could not let go. I wish I had a nice moral for this tale, but I do not. Although not many people knew of his attempted suicide, he moved away. I do not know where he is or what he is doing.

How does this "holding in sin" work?

It is quite simple and yet not easily grasped. I know something you have done. It was a wrongful action. It can be placed somewhere on the continuum beginning with indiscretion and ending with outright evil. But no matter where it fits on the continuum of wrongdoing, it has lodged squarely in my mind. It has become a permanent mental perspective. Whenever I see you, I see you through the lens of this mistake. I am holding you in your sin because the sin is the filter through which I approach and relate to you. To me you are always the guy with a DUI or the teenager who had an abortion or the cheat who did eighteen months for tax evasion, etc. I cannot let go of your sin and, therefore, I hold you in it.

People whose mistakes are well known and are "held in sin" by large numbers of people often leave for other communities or countries. People cannot or will not let go of their sin so they seek the company of people who do not know their sin. These new people are not more virtuous than the people they are fleeing. It is only that they do not know the sin. You cannot hold what you do not know. We hide our sins because we know that if they are not hidden, they will be held. Skeletons are kept in the closet because we know other people will hang them on the porch. Then the only access to our house will be through the dead bones of our mistakes.

The opposite of "holding in sin" is "forgiving for life." This is not the usual understanding of forgiveness that focuses on a past transgression and its consequences. This understanding sees every human being poised on the edge of a future, a future that promises to be more aligned with the deepest truth about him or her. Often they are moving out of an alienated past that leaves residues both in them and in others. These "leavings" will have to be dealt with.

However, the focus is on the next free step into the future. Other people are called to help them toward this new future, to "forgive" them. The "for" before the verb "give" is an intensive. It signifies a complete and total giving into the future that is emerging. The person is not identified with the past but with the free future they are struggling toward. In this vision the most profound word of forgiveness is the word Jesus speaks to the woman, "Go!"

Fifth Sunday of Lent
(Revised Common Lectionary)

John 12:1-8

〰

Walking Us Home

A Spiritual Commentary

**Six days before the Passover Jesus came to Bethany, the home
of Lazarus, whom he had raised from the dead.**

**There they gave a dinner for him. Martha served, and Lazarus
was one of those at the table with him. Mary took a pound of
costly perfume made of pure nard, anointed Jesus' feet, and
wiped them with her hair. The house was filled with the fragrance of the perfume.**

This anointing story is closely connected to the story of the resuscitation of Lazarus (John 11:1-45). (See "Causing and Consoling Grief," The
Fifth Sunday of Lent, Vol. 1, Cycle A.) On the one hand, the Lazarus story
begins by looking forward to the anointing. "Now a certain man was ill,
Lazarus of Bethany, the village of Mary and her sister Martha. Mary was
the one who anointed the Lord with perfume and wiped his feet with her
hair" (11:1-2). On the other hand, the anointing story begins by looking
backward to the resuscitation of Lazarus. Jesus is in the home of Lazarus,
"whom he had raised from the dead." The two incidents are meant to be
considered together. They mutually interpret one another.

The background of both stories is the ultimate identity of Jesus as
the eternal Word who connects God and creation (John 1:1-4). This
connection is established by communicating God's love and life into
precarious human existence. Although this divine-human communion
is spiritual and invisible, it manifests itself through certain physical-
social events. These manifestations are signs, revelations that express
and communicate the spiritual dynamics that make them possible.
The resuscitation of Lazarus is such a sign. It is a manifestation of the
Divine Love that animates Jesus' mission to the world.

Therefore, Jesus and Lazarus are bound together as spiritual reality and visible manifestation. The people who swirl around Jesus

know this. When they hear that Jesus is at the house of Lazarus, "they came out not only because of Jesus but also to see Lazarus whom he had raised from the dead" (John 12:9). Jesus' enemies also know the ultimate truth of Jesus and his mission is embodied in the resuscitated Lazarus. They not only plot to kill Jesus but "the chief priests planned to put Lazarus to death as well, since it was on account of him that many of the Jews were deserting and believing in Jesus" (12:9-10). Jesus and Lazarus are partners in the revelation.

Therefore, the dinner honoring Jesus ("They gave a dinner for him.") at the home of Lazarus and with Lazarus in attendance celebrates both God's glory and the glory of the Son of God. "This illness does not lead to death; rather it is for God's glory, so that the Son of God may be glorified through it" (11:4). God's glory is manifested when people are freed from the confining power of death. This is what happened to Lazarus. "The dead man came out, his hands and feet bound with strips of cloth, and his face wrapped in a cloth. Jesus said to them, 'Unbind him, and let him go.'" (11:44). The glory of the Son of God is how Jesus brings about this freedom from death, how he mediates divine love and life to perishing human existence. Although this glory of the Son of God is compressed into the actions of the Lazarus story, it is the sole focus of Mary's anointing. The anointing continues the perceptive insights of Mary that began in the Lazarus story.

Mary is best understood as the deeper dimension of her sister, Martha. In the Lazarus story Martha has a conventional faith. She believed that God would hear any prayer of Jesus and that the dead would rise at the end of time (11:20-27). But when Jesus said to her that he was the resurrection and the life and those who believed in him, even though they die, will live, and everyone who lives and believes in him will never die, he invited her deeper. Then he ended his self-disclosure with a pointed question, "Do you believe *this*?" She could not answer. Instead, she strung together the titles of Messiah, Son of God, and the one coming into the world. Martha stays on a confessional level, an important level but one that falls short of the mystical illumination that Jesus offers. Her limit is clearly stated. When Jesus orders the stone that covers the entrance to the grave to be taken away, she responds, "Lord, already there is a stench for he has been dead four days" (11:39). Her consciousness is permeated by the odor of physical death. She does not know any other fragrance, so she will not anoint Jesus.

But Martha does intuit that Jesus' teaching is reaching for another level. So she goes to her sister, and privately tells her, "The Teacher is here and is calling for you" (11:28). Mary immediately goes to Jesus and kneels at his feet. Kneeling at the feet of Jesus is the position of the disciple who receives the teaching. Mary the student went out to meet Jesus the teacher. She is a beloved disciple who is able to comprehend the deeper spiritual identity of Jesus. What she says to Jesus continues the word play that began with Martha. Mary is the dialogue partner Jesus seeks.

When Jesus said, "I am the resurrection and the life. Those who believe in me, even though they die, will live, and everyone who lives and believes in me will never die" (11:25-26), he was contrasting physical and spiritual life. Those who believe in Jesus, even when they die physically, will live spiritually because they will be in communion with God's love through the eternal Word. Therefore, these same people will never spiritually die. When Mary says, "Lord, if you had been here, my brother would not have died" (11:32), she is effectively saying, "Lord, if you had been here in this place of physical death where Lazarus is now, then my brother would not have died spiritually because your presence to physical death would have sustained him into spiritual life." When Jesus' question, "Do you believe this?" is addressed to Mary, it turns out to mean Jesus has to go where Lazarus is in order to bring him through death to life. Mary not only understands Jesus' identity and mission, she tells him what it entails in order that her brother, whom both she and Jesus love, will experience life.

But Jesus shudders at the prospect. Twice he is "greatly disturbed" (11:33, 38). But his trepidation is overcome by the realization of how much he loves Lazarus. When he sees Mary and the people from Jerusalem weeping, Jesus asks, "Where have you laid him?" They tell him, "Lord, come and see" (11:34). It is an invitation to enter into the world of the tomb, to join Lazarus in the land of the dead. In response to this invitation, Jesus also begins to weep.

This weeping is given two interpretations, one correct and one incorrect. When some saw him weeping, they read it as a sign of weakness. "Could not he who opened the eyes of the blind man kept this man from dying?" (11:37). This comment presupposes that Jesus keeps people from dying, and he does it by some disengaged superior power that is completely at his command. He had this power with the man born blind, but now it seems to have deserted him. When others saw him weeping, they read it as a sign of love. "See how he loved him!" (11:36). This comment suggests something completely different. Jesus does not stop people from dying. Rather through his love he shares in their suffering and in the suffering of the ones who loved them. As the beginning of the story indicated, it is Jesus' love for Lazarus and Martha and Mary that drives him (11:1-3). What only gradually comes to light is that this love, if it is to effectively communicate the life that is stronger than death, entails Jesus' own death and entombment. The glory of the Son of God is that out of love he enters into the full human condition in order to save the full human condition.

Mary discerns this empowering love as the real meaning of the death and burial of Jesus. She expresses and communicates her perception through the anointing. The death and burial of Jesus is a perfume that thrills and fills the entire house of those who serve and eat with him. When the eternal Word dies and is buried, he sustains all who believe and live in him through physical death and burial into endless spiritual life. Mary, as a faithful disciple, learned this truth about love and death at the feet of Jesus. She knelt at his feet when he was on the outskirts of Bethany. Now she returns to his feet in the home of Lazarus to revel in the full revelation, a revelation in which she participates. When she wipes the feet of Jesus with her hair, it is not to clean them of excess perfume. It is to share in the abundance of nard. It is to scent her hair with the love that flows from him. "While the king was on his couch, my nard gave forth its fragrance. My beloved is to me a bag of myrrh that lies between my breasts" (Song 1:12-13).

> **But Judas Iscariot, one of his disciples (the one who was about to betray him), said, "Why was this perfume not sold for three hundred denarii and the money given to the poor?" (He said this not because he cared about the poor, but because he was a thief; he kept the common purse and used to steal what was put into it.)**
>
> **Jesus said, "Leave her alone. She bought it so that she might keep it for the day of my burial. You always have the poor with you, but you do not always have me."**

There is another disciple besides Mary in the house. This disciple does not know what Mary knows and has not received Jesus. The revelation from the Song of Songs is alien to him.

> Seat me as a seal upon your heart,
>   as a seal upon your arm;
> for love is strong as death,
>   passion fierce as the grave.

> Its flashes are flashes of fire,
>   a raging flame.
> Many waters cannot quench love,
>   neither can love drown it.
> If one offered for love
>   all the wealth of his house,
>   it would be utterly scorned. (Song 8:6-7)

Love is as strong as death and is a passion as fierce as the grave. It cannot be quenched and it cannot be bought. Love is above all else.

But Judas knows none of this. He reduces the perfume to denarii. He does not discern the spiritual; he knows only what he can count. This lack of spiritual sensitivity means he cannot receive Jesus, who teaches people how to be born "not of blood or of the will of the flesh or the will of man, but of God" (John 1:13). But Judas's betrayal goes beyond mere obtuseness. On the outside, Judas presents himself as one who wants to alleviate the plight of the poor. But on the inside he is plotting how to enrich himself. He portrays himself as a philanthropist, one who gives money to others, but he really is a thief, one who takes money for himself. This portrait is in complete contrast to Jesus. Jesus is unified, his interior love flowing into the outside world and entering into the mortal human situation. Judas is split, the words of his mouth do not match the thoughts of his heart (see Luke 22:48); and the thoughts of his heart are only about how to secure himself. Judas is the opposite of the Good Shepherd who came to give life and give it abundantly. He is the thief who "comes only to steal and kill and destroy" (John 10:10).

Jesus answers Judas' question, "Why was this perfume not sold for three hundred denarii and the money given to the poor?" by interpreting the symbolic anointing by Mary and confronting Judas's blatant hypocrisy. In the Gospel of John, Jesus is prescient. He foresees future events and discerns how they are foreshadowed in present happenings. Mary should keep doing what she is doing for it is only "six days before the Passover." Soon the reality of what she symbolizes will happen.

> Nicodemus, who had at first come to Jesus by night, also came, bringing a mixture of myrrh and aloes, weighing about a hundred pounds. They took the body of Jesus and wrapped it with the spices in linen cloths, according to the burial custom of the Jews. Now there was a garden in the place where he was crucified, and in the garden there was a new tomb, in which no one had ever been laid. And so, because it was the Jewish day of Preparation, and the tomb was nearby, they laid Jesus there. (John 19:39-42)

The burial of Jesus signals the full participation of the Eternal Word in the human condition. He does not move from death to ascension and resurrection. As the Nicene Creed insists, "He suffered, died, and *was buried.*" The burial reveals his loving commitment to be with his friends wherever they are, even in the tomb.

But this symbolic account of Jesus' burial is evocative. The excessive spices cover the odor of death with a larger and more powerful perfume. The scent that fills the home of Lazarus also fills the tomb. In fact, this is a tomb unlike all other tombs. This tomb does not house death. No one has been laid in it. Also, it is in a garden, the garden of paradise where people lived forever before sin and death inaugurated history east of Eden. These allusions suggest that the divine love in Jesus accompanies humans all the way into the tomb in order to break open the confinement of the tomb and bring them out of it. This is the full truth of Mary's anointing. That is why the perfume is meant to be kept for his burial.

Once the meaning of Mary's anointing is illumined, Jesus confronts the hypocritical split between the inside and the outside of Judas. His remark, "You always have the poor with you, but you do not always have me," is not a general philosophical observation that contrasts the eternal historical conditions of rich and poor with the limited time left before Jesus' death. Rather it is an "in your face" comment to Judas. It wants Judas to own his hypocrisy and acknowledge what is really going on. Jesus sees through the verbal mask of social concern and dismisses this as a ruse. "You always have the poor with you" means attending to the disadvantaged can be considered at any time. But this is not what is going on in the present moment. Concern for the poor is dodging the real issue.

What is happening in the present moment is the symbolic anointing of Jesus for his death and burial. Judas is a key player in the death of Jesus. "You do not always have me" is meant to snap Judas's mind back to where it should be—on his role in actively handing Jesus over to those who will kill him. Hypocrisy is not allowed in the presence of the Unified One. Also, the emphasis is on Judas' action of pushing Jesus out of his life and not on Jesus simply and suddenly disappearing. At the Last Supper Jesus will give himself to Judas in the form of the "dipped piece of bread." But when Judas receives the bread, Satan—not Jesus—enters him (John 13:26-27). "*You* do not always have me" means you have not learned to receive me. This is the issue. Although the character of Judas is portrayed as destined to betray Jesus

(John 17:12), he is also free to examine his attitudes and actions and to change. This stinging rejoinder is the hammer Jesus uses to break down Judas's defenses and open him up to the possibilities of life.

Teaching

I have a print of an Albrecht Durer woodcut of Christ's descent into hell. In the background is a tomb with the large, stone slab that covers the entrance pushed to the side. In the foreground Christ has opened the gates of a prison dungeon and desperate people are climbing out. Christ has risen; but instead of ascending to the right hand of the Father in glory, he has gone down into hell to liberate ones who many consider terminally lost. Whenever I say the Apostles' Creed and come to the phrase, "He descended into hell," I imagine this print.

This picture has profound significance. In mythological narrative, it represents the final step of divine love penetrating the universe. The story begins with God the Father and his Son living in the sky and looking at the earth. They see humans living without conscious contact with God, alienated from the Spirit of life and love. The Father decides to send the Son to remedy this situation; or, in an alternate version, the Son volunteers for the assignment. But either way, "God so loved the world that he gave his only Son, so that everyone who believes in him may not perish but may have eternal life" (John 3:16).

If you are hearing this story for the first time and have internalized a conventional understanding of God, you might expect a "ride to the rescue." God has unlimited power, can do whatever he wants, and the Son has been sent to restore creation without any harm to himself. But as the story unfolds, the adventure of the Son develops in an unexpected way. Rather than "riding to the rescue," he joins the alienated humans in those experiences where they are most afflicted by physical and moral evil. However, he does not join them as alienated. He is one of them in all things except their separation from the Divine Source. He stays in communion with the Father even as he undergoes what humans consider the premier sign that God has abandoned them—suffering and death. This allows all humans, who learn to dwell in Jesus, to stay in communion with God through the loss of physical and social life. This communion brings them to new life. The resurrected Christ is the "first-born of the dead" (Rev 1:5). Others will follow. The story ends in risen triumph.

But the story is not over. The Son does not return home. He continues his descent—from his home in the sky to the surface of the earth, from the surface of the earth to the tomb beneath the earth, from the tomb beneath the earth to the depth of the underworld. The unthinkable has occurred. God's love for his people has pursued them into the territory of hell and unlocked the gates that have confined them. Now there is no place unvisited by divine love. The psalm is gloriously true.

> Where can I go from your spirit?
>> Or where can I flee from your presence?
> If I ascend to heaven, you are there;
>> If I make my bed in Sheol, you are there.
> If I take the wings of the morning
>> and settle at the farthest limits of the sea,
> even there your hand shall lead me,
>> and your right hand shall hold me fast.
> If I say, "Surely, the darkness shall cover me,
>> and the light around me become night,"
> even the darkness is not dark to you;
>> for night is as bright as day,
> for darkness is as light to you. (Psalm 139:7-12)

This mythological story can be translated into more rational theological concepts. God is present to all creation. Even though people are not conscious of this presence, God is never missing. It is just that human consciousness is only dimly aware of its communion with the Divine Source. The human spiritual journey is to break through the consciousness and actions of sinful alienation and open to God who sustains people in the depths of their being. As Teresa of Avila heard God say, "Soul, you must seek yourself in Me, and in yourself seek Me" ("Seeking God" in *The Collected Works of Teresa of Avila*, Vol. 3, translated by Kieran Kavanaugh and Otilio Rodriguez [ICS Publications] 385). God is a never-abandoning presence.

This theological unfolding can go on and on, and I love to read the many people who do the unfolding. They quiet my mind's clamor for coherence. But when I want to *feel* Divine Love, I close my eyes and put myself back in the mythological narrative. I see Jesus weeping and moving unwaveringly through his tears, each step bringing him closer to where his beloved Lazarus is confined. Then this image dissolves, and Mary's hair is slick with the abundance of fragrance from the feet of Jesus, and the perfume has purified the air of every smell that does not intoxicate. Then this image dissolves, and Jesus is breaking out of the tomb in a most unconventional way. He is pushing through the floor of the tomb to find the lost children of the underworld, refusing to return to the Father until he brings everyone with him.

I smile, and I know that Paul is praying for me. "I pray that you may have the power to comprehend, with all the saints, what is the breadth and length and height and depth, and to know the love of Christ that surpasses knowledge, so that you may be filled with all the fullness of God" (Eph 3:18). Then for a moment I grasp the truth that "perfect love [Divine Love] casts out fear" (1 John 4:18). It is then I sense that Someone is trying to walk us all home, striding both in front of us and resolutely at our side.

Second Sunday of Easter

John 20:19-31

❦

Resurrecting with Questions

A Spiritual Commentary

On the evening of that first day of the week, when the doors were locked, where the disciples were, for fear of the Jews, Jesus came, stood in their midst and said to them, "Peace be with you." (LM)

It is still the first day of the week because the processes of the new creation are still unfolding. Earlier on this first day of the week the disciples, in the persons of the Beloved Disciple and Mary of Magdala, realize that Jesus is with God (John 20:1-18). Now on the evening of that same new day of creation, the disciples discover that he is simultaneously in their midst. Jesus is both with God (ascension) and with them (resurrection). This simultaneous presence emphasizes that he is a bridge, connecting the disciples with God and God with the disciples. He is the mediator between the divine and the human. That was what he was in his incarnate life, and that is what he is in his resurrected life. "And there was evening and there was morning, the first day" (Gen 1:5).

However, there is a major difference between the pre-Easter and post-Easter presence of Jesus. The post-Easter Jesus does not enter through doors, as people with physical bodies must do. The doors are locked, yet "he was in their midst," as a literal rendering of the Greek says. This strongly suggests that the disciples have a spiritual realization of the presence of Jesus. He does not appear as an outer form as he previously did, but he manifests himself as a presence emerging from within and allaying their inner panic. His presence is known by the fact he brings peace in the midst of fear.

This peace is the fulfillment of his promise. "Peace I leave with you; my peace I give to you. I do not give to you as the world gives. Do not let your hearts be troubled, and do not let them be afraid" (John 14:27). Jesus leaves them peace, and this giving of peace is contrasted with how the world gives. The text does not go further with this contrast.

107

But the overall sense is the world gives and takes away. The security of one moment is replaced by the anxiety of the next moment. The world cannot sustain an abiding peaceful presence. Yet that is precisely how Jesus sees himself, an abiding presence that transcends the vagaries of the world. Jesus does not stop the chaos of the world. Rather, he is present within it, calming and untroubling the heart, bringing peace.

When he had said this, he showed them his hands and his side. The disciples rejoiced when they saw the Lord. (LM)

The showing of his hands and feet accompany and make real his word of peace. The disciples are able to read these signs of his wounded and opened body, and so they see the Lord. "Seeing the Lord" does not mean a physical sighting of the resuscitated body of Jesus. Rather, it is a code phrase for knowing the revelation of Christ at such a depth that life is changed. This knowing happens when the disciples see the opened wounds.

But what is it they know? How do they read the signs in the hands and side?

Jesus is interiorly united to the Father. But this interior unity is not a private possession. It is meant to flow forth, bringing divine life to all who are disposed to receive it. This flowing forth is how Jesus glorifies the Father. The Crucifixion is the supreme hour of this glorification. It is the time and place when divine life and love are most powerfully visible and available, present and transcendent in and through physical death. The throes of death reveal the greater flow of life.

The symbolic carrier of this spiritual truth is the lancing of the side of Jesus from which flows blood and water. Although this image triggers many interpretations, the gushing of blood and water is universally connected to the process of birth. And that this gushing comes from Jesus' side recalls the birth of Eve from the side of Adam. Therefore, the opening in Jesus' side is how his interior union with God becomes available as a life-giving birth for others. The openings in his hands perform the same symbolic function. They are channels that make available his interior life with God. This is what constitutes "seeing the Lord," receiving divine life through the symbols that mediate his "love that lays down its life for his friends." This is the truth of his death, and its realization leads them to rejoice.

They are living out the situation Jesus described earlier.

"A little while, and you will no longer see me, and again a little while and you will see me," and "Because I am going to the Father. . . ." Very truly I tell you, you will weep and mourn, but the world will rejoice; you will have pain, but your pain will turn into joy. When a woman is in labor, she has pain, because her hour has come. But when her child is born, she no longer remembers the anguish, because of the joy of having brought a human being into the world. So you have pain now; but I will see you again, and your hearts will rejoice, and no one will take your joy from you." (John 16:17, 20-24)

The sorrow they had at the loss of Jesus' physical presence is now replaced by a joy that cannot be taken away. The reason this joy cannot be taken away is that it is grounded in a spiritual presence that is not subject to loss the way physical presence is. In this sense, this new situation is superior to the old situation. It is a never-ending presence. Therefore, this "joy no one will take from you" complements a "peace the world cannot give."

Jesus said to them again, "Peace be with you. As the Father has sent me, so I send you."

And when he had said this, he breathed on them and said to them, "Receive the Holy Spirit. Whose sins you forgive are forgiven them, and whose sins you retain are retained." (LM)

Jesus offers them peace a second time. The beloved disciple had to look twice into the tomb before he came to belief. Mary Magdalene had to turn twice before she recognized the gardener as the teacher. Now the disciples hear the word of peace twice. It brings them into the fullness of revelation. The first time Jesus' word of peace expelled fear because it was the reception of perfect love, the love of God for God's children. "There is no fear in love, but perfect love casts out fear" (1 John 4:18).

Now that the disciples are grounded in the peace that perfect love brings, Jesus confers peace a second time. This time peace is the power of mission. The disciples have received the divine life that is stronger than death mediated through the open wounds of Christ. However, divine life cannot be possessed. It can only be received and given away. Therefore, they are immediately sent, commissioned by Jesus in the same way the Father commissioned him. They have to give the life they have received to others. The chain is established—from the Father to Jesus to the disciples and, by implication, whomever the disciples will commission.

The key to this mission is the capacity to receive the Holy Spirit. Just as in the Genesis story God breathed into the clay of the earth and the human person became a living soul, so now the risen Lord breathes into his disciples and they become a new creation, a creature living by the breath of God. Living by the Spirit, they join the work of the Spirit. The work of the Spirit is to make things one.

The path to this oneness is through the forgiveness of sins. Sin is what separates God from the world and people from one another. Jesus has taken away the sin of the world, replaced the fundamental separation between God and the world with communion. The communion with God is the condition for the possibility of people forgiving one another and coming into unity. However, people must realize and engage this responsibility. If they hold onto the sins that separate, then separation will continue. If they let go of (forgive) those sins, unity will develop. The Holy Spirit enlivens people to co-create the human condition. This is the power of the Resurrection, the freedom to overcome separation and bring unity.

> **Thomas, called Didymus, one of the Twelve, was not with them when Jesus came.**
>
> **So the other disciples said to him, "We have seen the Lord."**
>
> **But he said to them, "Unless I see the mark of the nails in his hands, and put my finger into the nailmarks, and put my hand in his side, I will not believe." (LM)**

The story line shifts. Thomas, who is called the Twin, was not present when the other disciples "saw the Lord." The other disciples bear witness to what they have seen, but it is not enough for Thomas. Taking the word of another does not suffice. He has his own criteria for believing, and it is not community attestation. He wants to probe the flesh. In particular, he wants to probe the marks of Jesus' death. Presumably, this physical confirmation will convince him it is really Jesus. The one who was crucified and the one whom he once knew in the flesh will be confirmed as alive. This is sense knowledge, the type of knowledge most people rely on as an indication of reality.

This demand for physical verification is misplaced. Jesus is not a resuscitated corpse and resurrection is not a return to earthly life. However, there is irony in what he wants. The only way he will see the Lord is if he enters into the wounds. But these wounds are not available for his intrusive probing. These wounds are ones that Jesus shows to people so they may receive God's life and realize his true identity. The criteria for knowing the ultimate truth about Jesus are the same after his death as before his death. The person must go beyond the physical level and open himself or herself to the communication of divine life and recognize Jesus as God's incarnate presence. This is spiritual knowledge; the type of knowledge most people think is too subtle and evasive.

> **Now a week later his disciples were again inside and Thomas was with them. Jesus came, although the doors were locked, and stood in their midst and said, "Peace be with you." (LM)**

The coming of Christ into their midst is a regular happening. Every first day of the week Jesus is with them. When they gather, he gathers with them. Once again, he is not there physically because the doors were locked. He is in the midst of the disciples, emerging from within, as the communication of peace and the presence of joy. This time Thomas is present. More importantly, Thomas is with the other disciples. He is part of the community, and it is as part of the community that he will experience the risen Lord.

> **Then he said to Thomas, "Put your finger here and seek my hands, and bring your hand and put it into my side, and do not be unbelieving but believe."**
>
> **Thomas answered and said to him, "My Lord and my God!" (LM)**

Jesus invites Thomas into his wounds, into the correct understanding of his death and through that understanding into the reception of divine life. Although Jesus uses words similar to what Thomas said was essential for him to believe, he is not complying with Thomas's demands. The meaning is quite different. Jesus is encouraging Thomas to reach for the divine life that flows through him. It plays upon a line from the Adam and Eve story of Genesis. "See, the man . . . might reach out his hand and take also from the tree of life, and eat, and live forever . . ." (Gen 3:22). Jesus is asking Thomas to reach out and live forever. Thomas must have obeyed Jesus' command, for his cry, "My Lord and My God," signals both the reception of divine life and the recognition that Jesus and the Father are one. It might also signify that Thomas now knows he is not the twin of Jesus, not on the same level as the Son.

But there is a large omission in the story. What Thomas does not do is physically probe the wounds. He does not get his flesh and blood verification, but he does come to belief. The message, a consistent message, a consistent message in the Gospel of John, is that believing is not a matter of physical observation but of realizing spiritual truth. In fact, it is in the community of believers enlivened by the presence of the risen Christ that Thomas comes to know Jesus at a level that eluded him when he knew Jesus in the flesh.

In John's Gospel the character of Thomas has an ongoing difficulty in grasping the true meaning of Jesus' death. In the Lazarus story, when Jesus decides to go back to Judea where he will be in danger from the authorities, Thomas enthusiastically speaks to and for the other disciples, "Let us go and die with him." It is a statement of bravado, perhaps even loyalty. But it is without understanding. They are not to die with Jesus; their task is to learn to receive the divine life that will come to them through Jesus' death. Jesus is not a reckless revolutionary courting death, and they are not kamikaze disciples.

Thomas's ignorance of the meaning of Jesus' death continues during the Last Supper conversations. Jesus is reflecting on his transition from this world to the Father. He insists that his upcoming separation from his disciples is only to prepare a place for them. Then he will come and take them to himself so, "where I am, there you may also be." In other words, Jesus predicts a brief separation followed by a permanent, life-giving communion.

Then he tells them, "You know the way to the place I am going." Although Jesus says they know, Thomas speaks for the group and says they do not know. "Lord, we do not know where you are going. How can we know the way?" Jesus responds, "I am the way, the truth, and the life. No one comes to the Father except through me. If you know me, you will know my Father also. From now on you do know him and have seen him." We are not told whether Jesus' response to Thomas brought him from not knowing to knowing. But the whole context suggests that it didn't. Although Thomas has seen Jesus in the flesh and talked to him, he does not know him in his theological identity as being both the path to God and the very presence of God. In particular, he does not know that the way to this simultaneous knowing of Jesus and the Father is through grasping the spiritual truth of Jesus' death.

Therefore, Thomas's interactions with the incarnate Jesus, the Jesus available for physical probing, did not facilitate the deepest truth about him, namely, his oneness with the Father and communication of divine life through his death. Thomas learns this truth through

Jesus' spiritual presence within the gathered community. There is an important implication of this path of belief. The fact that Thomas knew Jesus in the flesh is not an extraordinary privilege to understanding the revelation of Christ. Common sense would seem to suggest those who saw Jesus in the flesh have a great advantage over those who did not. But Thomas's experience suggests the spiritual presence of Christ within the community is the way to come to a correct understanding of the pre-Easter Jesus. Thomas moves from darkness to light only on the evening of the first day of the week.

Jesus said to him, "Have you come to believe because you have seen me? Blessed are those who have not seen me and have believed." (LM)

How would the literary character of Thomas answer Jesus' question, "Have you come to believe because you have seen me?" "Seeing the Lord (me)" in the sense of probing his wounded flesh was how Thomas thought he would come to belief. That was his condition for believing, and that condition kept his consciousness on the level of the flesh. However, he never did that and yet he came to belief. So physically seeing Jesus is not how belief comes about. The answer to the question is no. Thomas did not come to faith through physical sight.

Thomas came to belief by spiritually grasping the meaning of Jesus' death and, through that understanding, he received the divine life that is stronger than death. He expressed and communicated this experience by exclaiming Jesus as *his* Lord and *his* God, the one who "took him to himself" and in the process took him into God. This experience is available within the community of disciples who gather each week and who find that Jesus is among them offering them the life that flows through his open wounds. It is not necessary to see him physically in the flesh. In fact, even those like Thomas who saw him in the flesh in his pre-Easter days only understood him and believed when they contacted his spiritual presence within the believing community. This experience of the risen Lord is not relegated to the past. It is present and available when the disciples gather next week. The time and date of the gathering is: "the evening on the first day of the week."

Now Jesus did many other signs in the presence of his disciples that are not written in this book. But these are written that you may come to believe that Jesus is the Christ, the Son of God, and through this belief you may have life in his name. (LM)

The life of Jesus is a life of signs—words and deeds that were capable of pulling people into the mystery of Spirit. His disciples were present for these signs, only some of which have been written down. Therefore, the disciples know much more than is written in this book. The living Christ of the community supersedes any written material.

However, this writing is important. It is not only that these signs have been committed to written form and therefore can outlast the death of the disciples. It is also the way these signs were written. They were written in a way that reflects the signs in the actual historical dynamics of Jesus' life. In particular, the writing reflects the complex interplay between the physical and spiritual dimensions of life.

Therefore, this writing is itself a sign. It is meant to draw the reader into full belief that Jesus is God's Son and Messiah. This belief will open the reader to the flow of divine life that comes from Jesus. Readers, even though they have not met Jesus in the flesh, will experience the imparting of divine life through this written text within the community of disciples.

Resurrecting with Questions

Rainer Maria Rilke, the German poet, is often quoted as encouraging us not to excessively prize answers but to live questions. Behind this advice is a sense that we, as human beings, have not completely explored who we are and who we might become. One way this adventure in self-discovery could be pursued is by paying close attention to the questions that emerge in human consciousness. Sometimes these are questions about the adequacies of old ways of thinking and behaving. Sometimes these are questions that are tied to inklings in the present, or flashes of insight, or intuitions that challenge the dominance of rational logic.

Whenever I ponder St. John's Gospel in general and the resurrection stories in particular, a number of questions enter my mind. I usually dismiss them because they threaten the comfortable boundaries of my confined consciousness. I sense that even asking them in a sustained way will take work, and living them will demand stepping off the edge of security-consciousness into a night of trust. Ordinary people may hold unexamined opinions about these questions or entertain them after a third beer. But they are seldom seriously pursued. However, once you accept that humans are only aware of a small fraction of what they are experiencing, the door is opened into a world where people can be present even though the doors are locked.

I wonder: what kind of a barrier is death? While people are alive, we often talk of a spiritual presence to one another. At least part of what that means is we sense a reality deeper than body and mind that is crucial to the identity of a person. We presume this deeper reality is mediated through body and mind. Therefore, when body and mind have fallen away, this deeper reality is inaccessible. Body and mind constitute "remains"; spirit goes into another world, the spirit world. The deceased is with God and at rest, i.e., inactive. However, in St. John's Gospel ascension and resurrection are distinguished. Ascension means Jesus is with God; resurrection means he is still present to the ones he loved. His love relationships are intact. The disciples do not have to go on without him. They have to go on with him in a new way.

Is Jesus a special case? Or is the disciples' experience of the death, ascension, and resurrection of Jesus a revelation of the spiritual structure of reality, a spiritual structure in which all participate? Do all who have given and received love in this incarnate life continue to do so after the death of the body? Is love really stronger than death?

Perhaps our advice to those grieving the loss of a loved one is too influenced by the powerful, yet limited, capacity of physical sight. We expect those left behind to grieve their loss and then get on with life, accepting the absence of the one they once loved. Is it crazy to think they should assume a spiritual presence that cannot enter fully into most human consciousnesses and then get on with their life? If so, how should we think about this in such a way that consciousness may eventually open to it?

When we are impressed with the power of death to sever ties, we often seek signs that something of the person has survived. The person may not be with us in the way they once were, but we want some indication that they are somewhere and they are at peace. It seems we will accept the loss if we know the person is happy in another reality. Separation is presupposed. But we would like a word from beyond that everything is all right. When it comes our time to die, this loved one is often imagined as someone who has gone ahead and prepared a place and will be waiting for us. We have all heard stories of people who are close to death seeing visions of deceased loved ones. It is assumed they are a welcoming committee, guiding the about-to-die person to the other side. Death means reconnecting with those we have loved and lost.

This rendition is often the way Christian faith in life after death is characterized. However, it is not the spiritual consciousness of resurrection in John's Gospel. John's Good News is not impressed with the separation power of death. Jesus may be going to God, but that does not mean he is leaving his loved ones on earth. Just the opposite. His death will bring about a condition in which the disciples will be able to see his abiding love clearly. "I will not leave you orphaned; I am coming to you. In a little while the world will no longer see me, but you will see me; because I live, you also will live. On that day you will know that I am in my Father, and you in me, and I in you" (John 14:18-20). The world that sees with physical eyes will no longer see Jesus after his death. But the disciples, the ones whom he loves, will see him because they will perceive him with spiritual eyes. This will happen "on that day," the day when he physically dies.

Why will the death day of Jesus be also his resurrection day, and the day the disciples will grasp the communion between God, Jesus, and themselves? The human person is a composite being. In classical language, we are body and soul, material and spiritual. When we appreciate ourselves as physical, we know what it means to say we are *with* someone or *beside* someone or *above* someone or *below* someone. Physical realities are separate from one another. When they come together, they do so only to break apart again. This sense of separation is so pervasive that even the moments of togetherness are haunted by thoughts of future separation. Most of us are very aware of this combination of together and separate. When we love someone very deeply, we instinctively fear they will die and leave us. The stronger the sense of togetherness, the stronger the fear of separation.

However, we can also appreciate ourselves as spiritual beings. When we do this, we know what it means to say we are *in* someone. Spiritual beings inter-dwell. They can be in one another without displacing anything of the other within which they dwell. Inter-dwelling is the essential spiritual condition—"I am in the Father, you in me, and I in you." In spiritual consciousness togetherness hold sway with such force that separation is inconceivable. When the physical falls away, this spiritual communion remains and takes "center stage." This is why Jesus says "on that day," the day of his physical death, they will realize the truth of spiritual indwelling. When the physical is present, it monopolizes consciousness. When it is absent, the emptiness can be experienced not only as loss but also as possibility. There is a new form of presence. It is not waiting for us beyond death. Even though the doors are locked, he and she is "in our midst." On the spiritual level, we are never orphaned.

Can this be true?

How do we live this question of the resurrection?

Third Sunday of Easter

John 21:1-14 *LM* • **John 21:1-19** *RCL*

❧

Leading from Soul

A Spiritual Commentary

After these things, Jesus showed himself again to the disciples by the Sea of Tiberius; and he showed himself in this way.

The last time Jesus was by the Sea of Tiberius was during his earthly life. He fed the disciples and a large crowd with "five barley loaves and two fish" (John 6:1-14). This action was a sign, and his disciples and the people had trouble interpreting its meaning. They did not understand that Jesus was giving himself to them through the bread and fish. He was showing himself as the sustaining source of spiritual life (John 6:25-65).

Now he is by the Sea of Tiberius a second time, and, once again, he will feed his disciples with bread and fish. His resurrected presence will perform the same act as his earthly presence. He will show himself as the spiritual source that sustains life. This time the revelation will be more fully received.

> **Gathered there together were Simon Peter, Thomas called the Twin, Nathanael of Cana in Galilee, the sons of Zebedee, and two others of his disciples. Simon Peter said to them, "I am going fishing." They said to him, "We will go with you." They went out and got into the boat, but that night they caught nothing.**

In this episode, the symbolic activity of fishing focuses attention in two ways. First, it brings to mind and heart the missionary activity of the early church. Jesus called fishermen to leave their boats and nets for a different type of fishing. He promised they would become fishers of people. Therefore, "catching fish" means attracting and retaining people into the community and mission of the followers of Jesus.

Secondly, fishing is a metaphor for how hidden depths become visible. The spiritual is a present yet unseen reality. What is immediately available to the senses and the mind is physical and social appearances. However, there are times when these appearances are suffused and transfigured by their spiritual ground. These manifestations are like the moment when nets, bursting with fish, break the surface of the water. The fish were always there, present but unseen. Now they are revealed. Therefore, "catching fish" translates into bringing unconscious spiritual depths into the light of awareness.

Both these areas—spiritual depth and missionary activity—swirl around the central character of Peter. His seemingly innocent remark, "I am going fishing," reveals a lack of spiritual understanding, a failure to comprehend all that is involved in continuing the mission of Jesus. This serious deficiency, which first appeared in the foot-washing scene, was brutally exposed in Peter's denials and is again present in this futile fishing expedition (John 13:1-38; 18:15-27). The fact that seven others say, "We will go with you," shows the problem is not Peter's alone. They all share a darkened consciousness, symbolized by fishing at night. This darkened consciousness fails at missionary activity precisely because it is darkened, uninformed by the light. The reason they caught nothing is because Peter said, "I am going fishing," and others joined in without objection or modification, "We will go with you."

What exactly is the problem with what Peter and the disciples have said?

The problem has a history. In the foot-washing episode, Jesus attempted to wash Simon Peter's feet. This act symbolized the flow of divine grace through Jesus into his disciples (John 13:1-38). But Simon Peter refused, seeing Jesus' service as inappropriate. According to the consciousness of Simon Peter, the master should not wash the feet of the disciple. The proper order is for the disciple to wash the feet of the master. However, the social shock of this reversal, of a master washing his disciples' feet, contained a profound spiritual truth, a truth that had to be understood and received if Peter was to share Jesus' life. Although Peter does not understand it, he is willing to go along and suffer an entire bath if that is the requirement of being with Jesus ("not only my feet, but my head and hands as well"). Peter is in the poignant position of loving Jesus and wanting to be with him but, at the same time, not understanding him.

A subsequent scene deepens this misunderstanding. Jesus tells his disciples and Peter, "Where I am going, you cannot follow me now." Naturally, the one who does not understand about the foot-washing does not understand about his present inability to follow Jesus. The ability to follow Jesus is built on the capacity to receive and understand the foot-washing. If you are not washed, you cannot follow. But

Peter is adamant, following the logic of his lack of understanding to its disastrous conclusion. He asks belligerently, "Lord, why can I not follow you now?" In Simon Peter's wrongly directed mind, he suspects he knows the answer. Jesus does not think he has the courage. If that is the case, Simon Peter will reassure him. He blurts out, "I will lay down my life for you."

But it is not Peter's place to lay down his life for Jesus. It is the mission of Jesus, the Son, to lay down his life for Peter. It is through Jesus' dying that life is given to others because Jesus is the Son of the Father, the one who brings eternal life into the perishing of temporal becoming. But Peter has not learned that this divine life, permanently connected to human life through the death of Jesus, always has to be discerned and acknowledged as the source of "all things" (John 1:3). The project for Peter is to link the ego-based mind and will to the deeper soul in communion with Jesus and the Father. This is the source of human strength. So the first and forever posture of the disciple is to be receptive. When the ego does not acknowledge this and goes off on its own, it courts disaster. That is what the spiritually realistic Jesus tells Peter. "Will you lay down your life for me? You will deny me three times before the cock crows." The inflated ego can boast, but it cannot execute.

When Peter says, "I" am going out to fish," the tell-tale and wrong-headed word is "I." His consciousness is circumscribed by his own ego. He has screened out the source of all things and placed all his hope in his own unaided efforts. When the others joined him in his ego-centered mission, they bought into his flattened consciousness. They are destined for a night without success.

However, there is hope for Peter's lack of understanding and inability to follow. When he refused to have his feet washed, Jesus quickly pointed out to him that he was without understanding (John 13:7). But he also predicted he would understand "afterward." Also, when Jesus told Peter he could not follow him "now," he quickly added he would follow him "afterward" (John 13:36). This "afterward" refers to the three denials that would be the prelude to the "cock crowing," the advent of morning. Morning is the symbol of enlightenment, the time when Peter will simultaneously see the weakness of the ego ungrounded in God and, therefore, the need to receive the foot-washing in order to stay in living communion with divine love. Connected to the Father through the Son, he will have the ability to follow. Now the night of emptiness is over; morning is breaking. "Afterward" has arrived.

> Just after daybreak, Jesus stood on the beach; but the disciples did not know that it was Jesus.
>
> Jesus said to them, "Children, you have no fish, have you?"
>
> They answered him, "No."
>
> He said to them, "Cast the net to the right side of the boat, and you will find some."
>
> So they cast it, and now they were not able to haul it in because there were so many fish.
>
> That disciple whom Jesus loved said to Peter, "It is the Lord!"
>
> When Simon Peter heard it was the Lord, he put on some clothes, for he was naked, and jumped into the sea.
>
> But the other disciples came in the boat, dragging the net full of fish, for they were not far from the land, only about a hundred yards off.

Jesus waits on the other side of night. But the disciples have been fishing using only the willfulness of their egos. Since they have been trying to attract and retain people without acknowledging Jesus' presence as the ultimate attraction, they do not recognize him. But Jesus recognizes them. He calls them, "Children." This is a poignant reminder of what he came to teach them about the relationship to God that they will never outgrow. "But to all who received him, who believed in his name, he gave power to become children of God, who were born, not of blood or of the will of the flesh or of the will of a man, but of God" (John 1:12-13). It is because they have forgotten this relationship that the risen Jesus knows they have failed. He does not ask them if they have caught fish. He tells them what he knows to be the case and makes them acknowledge the futility of what they are attempting to do. "Children, you have no fish, have you?" They answered him, "No."

When they follow Jesus' instruction, they gather so many fish they are not able to "haul" in the net. The Greek word that is translated "haul" is more appropriately rendered in this context as "draw." It resonates with two earlier remarks in the gospel. "And I, when I am lifted up from the earth, will *draw* all people to myself" (John 12:32) and "No one can come to me unless *drawn* by the Father who sent me" (John 6:44). People come to the revelation of Jesus (fish are caught) not because of the superior skills of the disciples but because the Son and the Father are drawing them. The ultimate attraction is the drawing power of the revelation of the Father in the death of the Son. This drawing power always exceeds human abilities. "They were not able to haul it [net] in because there were so many fish."

If you have eyes to see it, abundance is a sure sign of the presence of the Lord. The Beloved Disciple has those eyes. He or she is the one who continually lives in the consciousness of being loved by God in Christ. This loved center allows him or her to read the signs of the sociophysical world. To him or her the bursting nets are revelatory of the presence of the Lord. The risen Christ and the Father are drawing people to themselves. The role of the Beloved Disciples is to remind the established leaders of this spiritual presence they so easily overlook. So the Beloved Disciple communicates this perception to Peter. "It is the Lord."

However, Peter's recognition of the presence of the Lord is tainted by his past threefold denial. He reacts—covering his nakedness by putting on clothes and hiding by casting himself into the sea. These are the two moves—covering and hiding—of the sinful Adam in the Genesis story. "But the Lord God called out to the man, and said to him, 'Where are you?' [The man] said, "I heard the sound of you in the garden, and I was afraid, because I was naked; and I hid myself"" (Gen 3:9-10). When sinners are in the presence of divine abundance, their past history of alienation from God so floods their consciousness that they become ashamed. Luke's rendition had it right. At the sight of the abundance of fish, Peter cries out, "Go away from me, Lord, for I am a sinful man" (Luke 5:8).

The sinner's self-judgment may be extremely harsh. The phrase "to cast oneself into the sea" may go beyond the mere act of hiding. It has connotations of seeking destruction. It says, "All is lost and there is no hope." Peter's impulsive and dramatic gesture is contrasted with the pedestrian response of the disciples who do not yet know the Lord's presence. The space-time continuum dominates their consciousness. They move toward shore dragging the full net. For them the distance is short, measured in yards. For Peter it is the distance between divine fullness and human emptiness, a space that is beyond measurement and is only traversed by grace. "From his fullness we have all received, grace upon grace" (John 1:16).

When they had gone ashore, they saw a charcoal fire there, with fish on it, and bread.

Peter's threefold denial of Jesus took place as he warmed himself against the cold night by a charcoal fire in the courtyard of the high priest. At that time Peter denied Jesus with the words, literally trans-lated, "I am not." This phrasing is the polar opposite of Jesus' identity, literally translated, "I am." Also, one of the people who quiz Peter about his affiliation with Jesus is a relative of Malchus, the slave of the high priest whose ear Peter had cut off in the garden. Jesus interpreted Peter's violent action as an attempt to prevent his life-giving death. "Am I not to drink the cup that the Father has given me?" (John 18:11). So Peter's denial of Jesus is more than the cowardly act of a fearful man. Peter truly does not know Jesus. He is ignorant of his ultimate identity as "I am," and he does not know the purpose of his death is to bring life into a violent and alienated world. The denials are the full flowering of his refusal to have his feet washed, of his lack of understanding.

Now, the charcoal fire is not warmth against the cold night. It cooks a morning meal at the break of a new day. It flares forth on the shore of the sea where Jesus gives instructions on how to catch fish. The fire warms bread and fish, the symbols of Jesus' identity as divine love and life for the world. Peter may think his denials have excluded him from God's love and so nothing remains but covering, hiding, and dying. But the storyteller sees his denials as necessary "turnings." They brought Peter face to face with what he had previously not been able to comprehend. His self-sufficiency, symbolized by his refusal to have his feet washed and his boast about being able to die, was in fact insuf-ficient. But it does not bring him irrevocably to the bottom of the sea. The food of his new life is being cooked on the fire of his old failures. Morning only arrives after night.

Jesus said to them, "Bring some of the fish that you have just caught." So Simon Peter went aboard and hauled the net ashore, full of large fish, a hundred fifty-three of them; and though there were so many, the net was not torn.

Jesus asks the disciples to bring to the meal he has prepared some of the new people whom they have gathered. The symbol of fish works two ways. Along with bread, it is the physical food that symbolizes divine life. But fish are also symbols that point to the people who eat the meal and receive the love of God. These people ultimately come to the meal because the revelation of the Son and the Father draws them. However, the disciples are intermediaries. They have a role to play. As Jesus instructed them to cast the net to the right side, he now instructs them to bring the fish. As long as they follow orders, the proper priori-ties are observed.

Peter, as the leader, follows the instructions. But it is difficult to envision the scene. Scholars debate various options. It seems Peter is still in the water with the net full of fish. From this position he "went on shore" rather than "went aboard." He "draws" the net with him. This "drawing" indicates he knows where the ultimate power of attraction lies. Also, Peter is not only the fisherman. He is one of the fish that the love of God—revealed in the death of the Son—has caught. This revelation draws people from every species on earth, of which there was thought to be one hundred and fifty-three. Yet this multiplicity would not break the unity of all together. The net would hold.

Jesus said to them, "Come and have breakfast."

Now none of the disciples dared to ask him, "Who are you?" because they knew it was the Lord.

Jesus came and took the bread and gave it to them, and did the same with the fish.

This was now the third time that Jesus appeared to the disciples after he was raised from the dead.

The risen Jesus is known by the same activity as the earthly Jesus. He invites his disciples to a meal that symbolizes a new day (breakfast) and feeds them. Although he says, "Come and have breakfast," it is ultimately he who comes to them and feeds them. "Jesus came and took bread and gave it to them, and did the same with the fish." Jesus is both invitation and meal, the one who initiates and sustains the divine-human dynamics. The disciples must engage in the exceedingly important task of eating. They must receive and ingest the love of God that accompanies the bread and fish. When this is happening, there is no need to inquire into "who" is really present. Whenever the community meal brings the disciples into the consciousness of loving God and one another, they know who is feeding them. It is the Lord.

This is the third time Jesus appeared to his disciples. Three is part of a symbolic sequence. The first time is the beginning; the second time is the middle; and the third time is the end. Therefore, the third time symbolizes the end of one way and the beginning of another way. It is a transitional time, participating in the past and the future. From now on Jesus will appear among his disciples in the way he has just appeared. Under the memory of his instructions, "Come," they will gather for a community meal. They will open their mouths to eat the bread and fish that will satiate their physical hunger. At the same time, they will open their minds to feed on the love of God that will fill their famished souls. And when the love of God abundantly enters into them, they will know who is present.

> **When they had finished breakfast, Jesus said to Simon Peter, "Simon son of John, do you love me more than these?"**
>
> **He said to him, "Yes, Lord; you know that I love you."**
>
> **Jesus said to him, "Feed my lambs."**
>
> **A second time he said to him, "Simon son of John, do you love me?"**
>
> **He said to him, "Yes, Lord; you know that I love you."**
>
> **Jesus said to him, "Tend my sheep."**
>
> **He said to him the third time, "Simon son of John, do you love me?"**
>
> **Peter felt hurt because he said to him the third time, "Do you love me?"**
>
> **And he said to him, "Lord, you know everything; you know that I love you."**
>
> **Jesus said to him, "Feed my sheep. Very truly, I tell you, when you were younger, you used to fasten your own belt and go wherever you wished. But when you grow old, you will stretch out your hands, and someone else will fasten a belt around you and take you where you do not wish to go."**
>
> **(He said this to indicate the kind of death by which he would glorify God.) After this he said to him, "Follow me."**

The simple phrase, "When they had finished breakfast," does more than stitch this scene to what has gone on before. When Jesus finished the foot-washing, he asked them, "Do you *understand* what I have *done* for you?" Then he explained the implications of the foot-washing—what the teacher and Lord does to the disciples, the disciples do to one another—and ended with, "If you *understand* these things, blessed are you if you *do* them." In this way Jesus unpacked the symbol of the foot-washing. Symbols are unpacked by developing the understanding they are meant to evoke and the actions they are meant to initiate. Therefore, questions about knowing and doing naturally flow from experiencing the symbol.

The meal is also a symbol; and I assume Peter participated. He ate the breakfast that was cooked and served by Jesus. There was no parody of the foot-washing scene.

> Peter says, "Lord, do *you* cook and serve *my* food?"
> Jesus responds, "You do not understand what I am doing."
> Simon Peter said, "You will never cook and serve my food."
> Jesus says, "If I do not cook and serve your food, you can have no part with me."
> Peter says, "Then not only one piece of bread and fish, but seconds and thirds."

Although Peter would not let Jesus wash him, he did let Jesus feed him. So the conversation that follows unpacks Peter's experience of being fed by Jesus. It is a dense conversation that plays out against the relationship of Jesus and Peter that has been developed throughout the gospel. But in stark outline, it is about what Peter now knows and what therefore he must do. It contrasts and reverses Peter's earlier way of knowing and doing.

Peter's responses to Jesus' insistent question, "Do you love me?" reveal a converted consciousness. Peter does not protest his love for Jesus, even when Jesus gives him the opportunity to seize comparative glory, "Do you love me more than these?" In fact, Peter does not talk for himself. Instead, he links his response to Jesus' knowing. "You know I love you." This is Peter's way of allowing his feet to be washed and receiving the laid-down life of the Good Shepherd. He is aligning his way of thinking and acting with Jesus'. What Peter knows and does is informed and transformed by what Jesus knows and does.

This conformation of Peter's way of thinking and doing to Jesus' is dramatically highlighted in the third exchange. He answers the question, "Do you love me?" with an acknowledgment that Jesus knows "all things." Even though his ego was hurt and he might be tempted to assert himself over against Jesus, he continues his reliance on Jesus' knowing. But he deepens that reliance with a full-blown understanding of Jesus as the Word through whom *all things* are made. Jesus connects God and creation, and it is precisely in the flow of that communion that Peter has learned to live. As soon as this acknowledgment is complete, Peter has the capacity to feed Jesus' sheep, to give his life for his friends as Jesus gave his life for his friends. Thinking with the consciousness of Jesus unfolds into living the life of Jesus.

And, of course, living the life of Jesus is what the enigmatic saying about a young man's freedom and an old man's coercion is all about.

Although there may be some suggestion of Peter's earlier willfulness giving way to destiny, the storyteller provides the interpretive key. Since Peter has now aligned himself with Jesus, his death will glorify God. It will be in the pattern of Jesus' death in that it will give life to the community. Peter's following will be faithful and complete "to the end" (John 13:1). Jesus concludes with a simple remark that captures the point of the entire conversation. "Follow me." This is the eternal injunction that is given to all Christian leaders. Fidelity and effectiveness go hand in hand. They will only catch fish if they move from the charcoal fire at night to the charcoal fire at dawn and allow Jesus to feed them. In other words, they will only be effective if they convert their own way of thinking and doing to the thinking and doing of Christ.

Teaching

In 1 Timothy 3:1-7 there is a list of qualifications for episcopal leadership. On the positive side the bishop has to be above reproach, temperate, hospitable, an apt teacher, respectable, well thought of by outsiders, etc. On the negative side, he should not be a drunkard, violent, quarrelsome, a lover of money, puffed up with conceit, etc. Next to these specific and measurable requirements, the Johannine criterion of "Do you love me?" seems, well . . . er, soft.

In contemporary leadership literature, there is often a distinction made between skills and values. Skills refer to demonstrable abilities that are needed to lead people in a given area. These skills can be measured and evaluated in specific ways. For example, a given leader may have to practice law, or read a balance sheet, or manage structural change, or evaluate market analyses, etc. Values are usually self-confessed commitments to which leaders hold themselves accountable. These individual values are often aligned with the values of the organization. Although values are not as easy to measure as skills, they can be translated into behaviors and evaluated. The right combination of leaders' values and skills goes a long way in predicting their effectiveness.

However, in this leadership text from the Gospel of John, Jesus does not focus on Peter's skills and values. Instead, he is hammering away at what might be called Peter's spiritual identity. Although most people are unaware of it, the human makeup has a spiritual center. Two gospel names for it are the salt of the earth and the light of the world. But if the salt "loses its flavor" or the light is "put under a bushel basket," this human potential is not developed (Matt 5:13-16). Jesus' strenuous efforts with Peter are attempts to bring Peter into this deeper identity. If Peter can achieve this deeper identity, he will order his values correctly and integrate them thoroughly into his leadership activities. Also, this spiritual identity will generate the passion to learn and perfect the necessary skills. So, in theory at least, spiritual identity perfects and elevates values and skills. In Catholic theology, *gratia elevat naturam* (grace elevates nature).

However, even with this promise of enhanced leadership abilities, contemporary sensibilities find this talk, well . . . er, soft. Spiritual traditions prefer the word subtle. They readily admit the awareness of our spiritual center is a refined form of consciousness and any sense of identification with it needs sustained practice. Certainly, the mystical and symbolic language of John's Gospel is an inspired map to the territory. But it is also an acquired taste, one for which most people do not have the time or temperament. But there is some contemporary language that tries to say much the same thing, and this language is insistent that leadership needs to become sensitive to the dynamics that the Gospel of John so highly values.

Our contemporary psychological mindset quickly spots Peter as someone who is identified with his own ego. He refuses help from Jesus the foot-washer and boasts of having the courage to face death on his own. As Jesus instructs and upbraids Peter, it may look like he is trying to kill this gargantuan ego. In fact, he is trying to resituate it, to plug Peter's ego into his soul. Ken Wilber has some insightful words on this process.

> There is a certain type of truth to transcending the ego: it doesn't mean destroy the ego, it means plug it into something bigger. . . . Transcending the ego thus actually means to transcend but include the ego in a deeper and higher embrace. . . . Put bluntly, the ego is not an obstruction to Spirit, but a radiant manifestation of Spirit. (*One Taste* [Boston: Shambhala Publications, 1999] November 17)

When the ego is plugged into the soul, it becomes a vehicle that has the ability to change the physical and social realms. Jesus loves Peter because he sees in him this enormous ego capable of shaking the foundations of the socially constructed world. His project is to get Peter to love him, for Peter to put his ego into the soul consciousness of Christ. When this happens, the isolated ego's tendencies of promotion and protection turn to acts of creative service.

When consciousness is in the soul, we are aware of an underlying unity to the diverse people and events we encounter. People who lead from the soul are not over and above others. They are always part of what is happening. Margaret Wheatley sees this as a new style of leadership:

> Many writers have offered new images of effective leaders. Each of them is trying to co-create imagery for the new relationships that are required, the new sensitivities needed to honor and elicit worker contributions. Here is a very partial list of new metaphors to describe leaders: gardeners, midwives, stewards, servants, missionaries, facilitators, conveners. Although each takes a slightly different approach, they all name a new posture for leaders, a stance that relies on new relationships with their networks of employers, stakeholders, and communities. No one can hope to lead any organization by standing outside or ignoring the web of relationship through which all work is accomplished. Leaders are being called to step forward as helpmates, supported by our willingness to have them lead us. Is this a fad? Or is it the web of life insisting that leaders join in with appropriate humility? (Margaret Wheatley, *Leadership and the New Science: Discovering Order in a Chaotic World* [San Francisco: Berrett-Koehler Publishers, 1999] 165)

In the gospel, this awareness of the web of life as the matrix out of which leadership emerges is called, "all things." This is the consciousness of Jesus and this is what Peter finally acknowledges and, with that acknowledgment, participates in that consciousness. He is "loving Christ" in a way that allows him to lead the Christian community. "Feed my sheep."

Whether leading from soul is expressed in the mystical-symbolic language of John's Gospel or reduced and adapted into the spiritual-psychological language of contemporary culture, it remains a tantalizing proposal. My guess is that any attempts to live it out will meet with powerful external and internal resistance. There will be more cries of "You will never wash my feet" and "I do not know the man" than "You know all things. You know that I love you."

Fourth Sunday of Easter

John 10:27-30 *LM* • John 10:22-30

❦

Speaking in Your Own Voice

A Spiritual Commentary

At that time, the festival of the Dedication took place in Jerusalem. It was winter, and Jesus was walking in the temple, in the portico of Solomon.

So the Jews gathered around him and said to him, "How long will you keep us in suspense? If you are the Messiah, tell us plainly."

In first-century Jewish culture one of the expectations of the coming Messiah was that he would rebuild or restore the Temple. King David had planned the Temple and his son, King Solomon, had built it. But over the years the Temple had to be physically rebuilt and spiritually restored. The festival of the Dedication recalled a physical and spiritual restoration of the Temple. Two centuries earlier the Syrians had occupied the Temple and held a sacrifice to Zeus on a pagan altar built over the altar of holocausts. This was known as the "desolating sacrilege" and triggered a successful revolt led by Judas Maccabee. The Temple area was rebuilt and rededicated to God.

So the setting is appropriate. On a feast that celebrates the physical and spiritual restoration of the Temple, a new spiritual restoration is under way. This restoration is a complete rebuilding, a new foundation that replaces the original work of Solomon. Therefore, it is winter for the building itself and for the type of worship it conducts, the end of its centrality and activity. But that does not mean that God's presence has abandoned the earth. The new Temple is walking in the old Temple—in the portico of Solomon, on a feast of spiritual renewal, in the dying days of the edifice. The replacement has arrived.

However, this is not the first time Jesus has visited the Temple. Earlier in John's Gospel he arrived with a whip of cords, overthrew the tables of the moneychangers, and set the animals free (John 2:13-22). His complaint was: "Stop making my Father's house a marketplace." At that time "the Jews" asked him for a sign to legitimate his disruption of Temple sacrifice. Jesus told them, "Destroy this temple and in three days I will raise it up." They thought he was talking about the physical edifice of the Temple. But the narrator informed the readers that Jesus was referring to his body. Jesus was not only spiritually restoring the Temple; he was spiritually replacing it.

So now the Jews take this opportunity to encircle Jesus and renew the earlier conversation that had so baffled them. They know the Messiah has the right to rebuild and/or restore the Temple. But the Messiah will be accompanied by signs that establish his position. Jesus' earlier enigmatic references to the destruction and recreation of the Temple did not grapple with their issues. In fact, it was confusing, leaving them still puzzled about what Jesus was claiming. They want literal speech, not symbolic double talk. "If you are the Messiah, tell us plainly."

But not everyone has as much trouble with Jesus' speaking style as the keepers of the Temple. Jesus does not talk plainly with the Samaritan woman, but she manages to grasp the meaning. In last exchange of this profoundly intimate conversation, he uses language in a strange way to thoroughly redefine messianic expectations.

> "The woman said to him, 'I know that Messiah is coming' (who is called Christ).
> When he comes, he will proclaim all things to us."
> Jesus said to her, 'I am he, the one who is speaking to you.'"
>
> (John 4:25-26)

The woman knows the promise of the Messiah includes a proclamation of all things. But whatever she might mean by that, Jesus' response is a quantum leap that goes well beyond her present level of understanding. His speech tries to move her attention from a future expectation to the present moment, focusing on himself and his speaking to her. But more than a shift from the future to the present is going on. By calling himself "I am" and emphasizing the action of speaking, Jesus is redefining "all things" and encouraging the woman to share his consciousness.

The background for these enigmatic, even clumsy, words of Jesus, "I am, the one speaking to you," is the opening lines of the gospel.

> "In the beginning was the Word, and the Word was with God, and the Word was God. . . . All things came into being through him, and without him not one thing came into being. What has come into being in him was life, and the life was the light of all people. The light shines in the darkness, and the darkness did not overcome it." (John 1:1-5)

The Word lives between God and Creation and holds the two together. He does this by mediating the eternal life of the Divine Source into Creation. Therefore, another name for him, in fact the proper name that conveys this dynamic function, is "I am." He is neither past nor future; he is the eternal now. "In the beginning was the Word" is not a statement about the past. It is a symbolic way of saying, "Always."

When the Word/"I am" speaks to people, he tries to illumine their minds ("the life was the light of all people") so that they might see and participate in the eternal life that he is; the life connects God with all Creation. Therefore, Jesus' answer to the Samaritan woman redefines Messiah as the Word/"I am" who mediates divine life into "all things" and is always present. His words are skillful means to have her experience the consciousness that is already in him. The eternal Word is speaking divine life into the ears of a finite person. This is who the Messiah is and he has arrived.

However, not all can "hear his voice." The authorities who pester Jesus to speak plainly think he is the problem. He will not play the game by their rules. He insists on saying something that does not directly answer their questions. They see themselves as interested people caught in the midst of a muddle, rational men insisting on clarity. Jesus sees them differently.

> **Jesus answered, "I have told you, and you do not believe. The works that I do in my Father's name testify to me; but you do not believe, because you do not belong to my sheep. My sheep hear my voice. I know them and they follow me. I give them eternal life, and they will never perish. No one will snatch them out of my hand. What my Father has given me is greater than all else, and no one can snatch it out of the Father's hand. The Father and I are one."**

Jesus thinks *they* are the problem. He has spoken and acted in a way that reveals God's life is coming into the world. This makes him the Messiah/Word/"I am." But they do not believe; they are not able to hear his word and/or read his actions as revelatory. Since they do not resonate with Jesus, they do not belong to his sheep.

Those who belong to Jesus' sheep have been saved by their interaction with Jesus and undergone a profound shift of consciousness. In symbolic code, they have heard Jesus' voice. To hear Jesus' voice means more than attending to the words he speaks. It entails discerning who the speaker is. Jesus' speech is filled with invitations to make this leap into his identity. A characteristic way Jesus talks is "Amen, Amen, I say to you." This way of speech emphasizes who is talking and encourages the listeners to discern the being of the speaker. When they grasp his unique relationship with God and they acknowledge him through a variety of titles—Messiah, Son of God, Son of Man, etc., they have heard his voice.

In hearing his voice, they have shared his consciousness. This sharing entailed knowing themselves as Jesus knew them. Believing in Jesus' name they began to believe in their own. "But to all who received him, who believed in his name, he gave power to become children of God, who were born, not of blood or of the will of the flesh or of the will of man, but of God" (John 1:12-13). Knowing who Jesus is contains the reciprocal knowledge of knowing you are a child of God, and your identity and Jesus' identity are eternally intertwined. Naturally these sheep follow Jesus and grow more fully into who they are. "Beloved, we are God's children now; what we will be has not yet been revealed. What we do know is this: when he is revealed, we will be like him, for we will see him as he is" (1 John 3:2). The simultaneous revelation of who Jesus is and who they are will continue in ways they do not yet understand.

The sheep who hear Jesus' voice also receive eternal life from him. This means that death cannot completely destroy them and that "wolves," those that want to do them harm, cannot snatch them out of Jesus' hand (John 10:12). The ultimate reason for this is that the Father (God) has given Jesus an eternal life that is stronger than all else. To be held by Jesus' hand is to be held by the hand of the Father.

Therefore, the experience of Jesus' sheep leads to one conclusion, a conclusion the religious authorities cannot endorse. If people discern God's very presence in Jesus and simultaneously know they are children of God who are meant to follow Jesus into ever greater revelations and are sustained and safe because of the eternal life he pours into them, then his voice will be heard again as he witnesses to the reality of who he is, "The Father and I are one!" Although this is not the idea of Messiah the authorities want to hear, it is plain speech.

Teaching

When the religious authorities push Jesus to speak plainly, what they mean is to adopt their theological categories and use the conventional words they understand. This becomes clear in the episode immediately following Jesus' statement about his unity with the Father. The response of the religious authorities is to pick up rocks to stone him. Jesus asks, "I have shown you many good works from the Father. For which of these are you going to stone me?" (John 10:32). The authorities answer that it is not for good works that they are going to stone him, but because Jesus is making himself equal to God. All the authorities can hear in what Jesus has said is what they have antennae for. Official ears perk up at anything that smacks of idolatry, a blurring of the boundaries between Creator and creature. Everything else Jesus has said has been lost on them.

However, when Jesus speaks plainly, he tries to detail his experience in words that are so expressive they have the possibility of communicating the experience to others. He has his own voice. Although he may borrow shepherd language from past Scripture, in particular Psalm 23, the language is recast in the light of his experience. He is speaking plainly, telling what it is like to bring true messianic hope to those who can receive it.

Those of us who grew up in Christian traditions learned to talk about Jesus in inherited language. It may have been the language of Jesus as a personal Savior, or the language of Jesus as true God and true Man, or the language of Jesus as Giver of the Spirit, or any other designations Christian denominations have developed. Although this language had been hammered out over the centuries and was necessary for community life and worship, it was basically somebody else's language. Often when we tried to use it, it was obvious we were borrowing another's voice.

I think it is important to have official christological language. But I also think believers should find their own voice about what they receive when they hear and meditate on the Christian myth and ritual. In classic theological language, faith seeks understanding. What we have received as faith, we have to appropriate as understanding. This understanding certainly includes insights, inspiration, confession, praise, and thanksgiving. But it also acknowledges lack of comprehension, lack of interest, and lack of relevance. A real faith that struggles with real understanding needs a real voice.

As we make our own the gospels, we necessarily begin to speak about what we are experiencing. At first, our voice may be stumbling and tentative. We may worry we are not orthodox enough. But, at this stage, our inner journey should not be rushed too fast into a premature doctrinal conformity. Orthodoxy can always be consulted. Or we may compare ourselves to others who seem fluent in spiritual talk about Jesus. But, at this stage, our inner journey should have its own pace. Competitive comparisons are out of place. Finding our own voice does not mean we do not learn from others. It is merely a warning that parroting ideas we do not understand will not help our faith development. We must trust our own path and the provisional yet real voice that is emerging.

This gospel text has one suggestion for us as we find a voice around our relationship with Jesus. When Jesus shifts into his own voice, he often combines descriptive language with images. His relationship to his followers is like a shepherd to his sheep. Then he plays out the image to express and communicate the nuances of what he is experiencing. We should try the same. When we hear the words of the gospel and manage to receive some of their meaning, what is it like? It is like rain on parched land, or a letter that has finally arrived, or like finding something that we did not know we had lost, or . . .

When it comes to speaking in our own voice, there is a Jewish spiritual teaching story that repays meditation.

When Rabbi Zusya grew old and knew that his time on earth was nearing a close, his students gathered around him. One of them asked him if he was afraid of dying.

"I am afraid of what God will ask me," the Rabbi said.

"What will he ask you?"

"He will not ask me, 'Zusya, why were you not like Moses?' He will ask me, 'Zusya, why were you not Zusya?'"

Fifth Sunday of Easter

John 13:31-33a, 34-35 *LM* • John 13:31-35

※

Remembering Love

A Spiritual Commentary

When Judas had gone out, Jesus said, "Now the Son of Man has been glorified, and God has been glorified in him. If God has been glorified in him, God will also glorify him in himself and will glorify him at once. Little children, I am with you only a little longer. You will look for me; and as I said to the Jews so now I say to you, 'Where I am going, you cannot come.' I give you a new commandment, that you love one another. Just as I have loved you, you also should love one another. By this everyone will know that you are my disciples, if you have love for one another."

Judas went out into the night and set in motion the proximate events that would culminate in the death of Jesus. Although there was not an explicit conversation between Judas and Jesus, Jesus knew what was happening. But he did not try to stop Judas. Instead, he hurried him on his way. "Do quickly what you are going to do" (John 13:27). Jesus understands his dying as central to the eternal purpose of God. Jesus is completely dedicated to that purpose and eager for its enactment. So when Judas leaves, Jesus' knows that his hour is near and his speech is almost an exclamation, verging on the ecstatic.

First and foremost, Jesus' death is a process of glory, a revelation of divine love saving human life. This revelation includes the truth about Jesus as the Son of Man, one who is lifted up for all to see and who draws all people to himself (John 3:14). It also includes the truth about God as a self-giving flow of life and love to his children in their most perilous experience, death. These twin revelations about the Son of Man and God redound upon each other. God is so eager to be known by his true name that God will quickly bring the Son of Man into his glory of drawing all to himself and through himself to God. The dynamic unity of the Father and the Son is expressed in this mutual and reciprocal glorification.

Secondly, the death of Jesus is a leave-taking. The bond between Jesus and his disciples is so close he can call them affectionately "little children." Little children are dependent on their parents and want to be with them at all times. But this will not be possible. This is more than a commonsense observation that death separates a person from the living and it is Jesus' time to die and not theirs. Rather, Jesus is going to the Father and they cannot come until Jesus has pioneered the way. This applies not only to them but to the "Jews." As the letter to the Colossians says, "he is . . . the firstborn of the dead. . . . For in him all the fullness of God was pleased to dwell . . ." (Col 1:18-19).

Thirdly, Jesus' death is the supreme expression of love for his disciples. "I lay down my life for the sheep" (John 10:15). This laying down of life out of love creates a new commandment. The old commandment was most likely the double commandment to love. "You shall love the Lord your God with all your heart, with all your soul, and with all your strength, and with all your mind; and your neighbor as yourself" (Luke 10:27; Mark 12:30-31; Matt 22:37-39). In this commandment the emphasis is on the human ability to love God and neighbor. But one of the towering insights of Johannine theology is that God first loved us. "We love because he first loved us" (1 John 4:19). However, this "first loving" of God is through the human person of Jesus. The first step in the new commandment is to recognize and remember the Son of Man who joins us in our deepest fears and sustains us through our greatest loss.

This new beginning—God loving us through the Word Made Flesh—is a significant psychological shift. James Mackey calls it a "universal human idiosyncrasy."

> I simply will not feel my own life, my own self, as grace or gift of God, unless someone values me. . . . I may see, at first blush, this stands the whole logic of the reign of God on its head. . . . The logic should surely read: first feel all life and existence as grace, and then feel inspired to be gracious to others. Not, first feel the grace of some human presence, feel forgiven, accepted, served, then begin to feel all life and existence as grace, and then feel inspired to be gracious to others. But it is really a universal human idiosyncrasy that is operative here, not a matter of logic. . . . [Most of us] can only sense ourselves and our world valued and cherished by God when we feel valued and cherished by others. (*Jesus: The Man and the Myth* [Mahwah, NJ: Paulist, 1979] 170)

The way people come to know and love the divine is through the human. This is the insight that grounds the new commandment.

Therefore, the disciples must always remember the laying down of Jesus' life as simultaneously his act of loving them and his revelation of God's gracious love. If they persevere in this memory, they will enact the same type of love for one another, a love that is grounded in and revelatory of divine love. This way of remembering and enacting will become a new form of Jesus' presence among his disciples. So when people see this love the disciples have for one another, they will know the source and energy of that love comes from Jesus. Love will be the tip-off that they are disciples of Jesus.

Teaching

Anne, my wife, has peppered our apartment with photographs of ourselves and all the people who are close to us. As I walk to the kitchen, I can see myself at about six months old sitting on my father's lap and playing with his police hat. If my eyes stray while watching TV, I can see Anne and Gina, her daughter, looking very much like each other. If I cannot sleep at night, I can stare at the wedding picture of my parents. We also have a rogue's gallery, a gauntlet of pictures hanging on parallel walls that will not let me pass through without stealing my attention. Although I may be alone in the apartment at times, one turn of my head reveals the captured past presence of significant others.

Of course, as I speed by, these intimate memories seem like billboards on the expressway. Even worse, I take the photos for granted. Everybody has photos; the frame business is booming. Do I pause to ponder the sofa? But then, for reasons that have always escaped me, one photo catches my eye and I find myself pondering it—smiling, or misty-eyed, or even outright laughing. If this happens, a hunger quickly follows and I move from picture to picture as if I have never seen them before. When I finish, I am stunned by the cumulative effect they have on me. I find myself filled with the love I have received.

And, not to put too fine an edge on it, I am a nicer person. I wouldn't go all the way into saying I am a more "loving" person. But I am, in the immediate aftermath, friendlier, more patient, less self-absorbed, more at peace with the everyday tensions that rack me. I recommend picture-gazing as a spiritual practice.

There is also a cross in our apartment. I see it everyday and most often it receives the "speed by" treatment. But every so often I pause and remember. Of course, it is a different type of remembering. It is not remembering my grandfather as he broke a cookie in half for both of us to eat, or my wedding day, or the double graduation of Chrissie and Robert. But I have a history with the cross.

I grew up in a Catholic neighborhood where the overriding theological story was a popularized version of St. John's vision. The Son of
God entered human life and died on the cross out of love for us. So we
should not be afraid of death and we should learn to love another. For
many years this rehearsed theology came to mind every time I looked
at the cross. And in my neighborhood and school there were a lot of
crosses to look at. But what is most important is that it sunk in. It is a
memory that had and still has an effect. I try, as the title of the movie
says, to *Pay it Forward*, to love others as I have been loved by Jesus.

Although the Jesus story can be simply told, my experience with it
is more complex. The cross only has this influence with me because
I belonged to a community and tradition that carried the memory of
Jesus through time and space so I could receive it. But they did more
than carry the memory. They tried to live the reality. When they went
wrong, they confessed and began again. I heard and read the story at
the same time as I watched and participated in the way of life the story
encouraged. The community bridged the centuries from the time the
text was written to the time it entered into my life.

John's Gospel is very much concerned with bridging time. It does
not eagerly hope for the parousia, the second coming of Christ. It
settles down into the passage of time and wonders how to maintain the
presence of Jesus on earth after he has returned to the Father. Christian
tradition has followed this lead of the gospel and emphasized the presence of Christ in Word and Sacrament. But, most fundamentally, Christ
continued through his new body, the church, the people who are im-
bued with his Spirit and remember his love as the ground and energy
of their own love. To contact Christ we do not have to psychologically
throw ourselves back into the time the scriptural text enshrines. We
have to belong to the present community of disciples who remember
and enact his love.

The fact is we need both the scriptural text and the community to
remember the love of Jesus and to love another as he has loved us. This
community is certainly the church community. But it also is wider. It
is all the people in my pictures. If I only had the Jesus story and the
church community, remembering Jesus' love would be real but, I suspect, it would be thin. If I only had the pictures, I would relish individual moments and people but I would not know the depth and extent of
their love. Remembering the love of Jesus so we can love one another
as he has loved us takes a home where photos of family and friends
stand side by side with the cross.

Sixth Sunday of Easter

John 14:23-29

ⓦ

Leaving Peace

A Spiritual Commentary

Jesus answered him, "Those who love me will keep my word, and my Father will love them, and we will come to them and make our home with them. Whoever does not love me does not keep my words; and the word that you hear is not mine, but is from the Father who sent me.

These words of Jesus are triggered by a question from Judas (not Iscariot), one of his disciples. "Lord, how is it that you will reveal yourself to us, and not to the world." The answer seems to be: the disciples are ready for revelation. They meet the requisite conditions. First and foremost, they love Jesus. In the context of John's Gospel, this means they are united to him and receive God's love through him. This reception of divine love allows them to keep Jesus' word. In particular, they are able to love one another. If people are not connected to Jesus (do not love him), they do not have the God-grounded capacity to keep his word. Revelation begins with loving Jesus and keeping his word. But it does not end there.

Once this process of living and acting out of divine love is initiated, an inner development begins to unfold. The disciples realize Jesus and Father are intimately linked, and they are not strangers or even visitors to their lives. They are permanent residents in the house of their being. The Father and the Son are making a home in them. To love Jesus and to keep his word is to be inhabited by his Father. Jesus' word was never his alone. It was always the word he heard from the One who sent him. The revelation of Jesus always cuts two ways. It manifests the love of the Father and it shows how that love indwells in the disciples.

I have said these things to you while I am still with you. But the Advocate, the Holy Spirit, whom the Father will send in my name, will teach you everything, and remind you of all that I have said to you. Peace, I leave with you; my peace I give to you. I do not give to you as the world gives. Do not let your hearts be

139

troubled, and do let them be afraid. You heard me say to you, 'I am going away, and I am coming to you.' If you loved me, you would rejoice that I am going to the Father, because the Father is greater than I. And now I have told you this before it occurs, so that when it does occur, you may believe.

Jesus is preparing his disciples for his death and his departure to the Father. Although there will be loss, his return to the Father will initiate the sending of the Holy Spirit. Therefore, the disciples will never be without a link to Jesus because the Holy Spirit functions as an Advocate for everything Jesus has said and done. This advocacy involves overcoming the most predictable feature of living in time—forgetfulness. But the Holy Spirit will stimulate more than the mere memory of Jesus in the disciples. What Jesus revealed, the Spirit will teach. Teaching implies greater comprehension and more thorough integration. The revelation of the Son naturally evolves into the teaching of the Spirit.

This relationship between Jesus and the Spirit presents Jesus' departure in a positive light. It is not a disruption of God's plan but part of a mysterious providence. Jesus has accomplished his work, revealing the love of the Father for his earthly children. Now it is time to teach the meaning of that love.

But even so, Jesus is departing from this earth and, as every dying person, wishes to leave a gift. However, it is not a bequest of his earthly goods. Rather, it is the spiritual/psychological state that the revelation of his dying makes possible. Therefore, after he names peace as what he wants to leave, he immediately specifies it as *my* peace. It is not like the peace of the world. The peace of the world comes and goes. It is dependent on outer circumstances. Whenever everything is going well, we can manage a certain amount of inner calm. However, when bad times come, calm is replaced by anxiety and fear. We shake with the wind, vacillate with the circumstances.

But the revelation of Jesus' dying brings a peace that is best expressed in Paul's eloquent statement.

> Who will separate us from the love of Christ? Will hardship, or distress, or persecution, or famine, or nakedness, or peril, or sword? . . . No, in all these things we are more than conquerors through him who loved us. For I am convinced that neither death, nor life, nor angels, nor rulers, not things present, nor things to come, nor powers, nor height, nor depth, nor anything else in all creation, will be able to separate us from the love of God in Christ Jesus our Lord. (Rom 8:35, 37-39)

Jesus' peace comes from the conviction that nothing can separate us from the love of God. This non-abandoning presence of God was revealed on the cross of Christ. In this archetypical place of total loss, divine love sustained Jesus and revealed God as a protecting nearness that does not permit final destruction. If this is true, then "Where, O death, where is your sting?" (1 Cor 15:55).

The peace that Jesus leaves is not a vague wish for inner calm and outer harmony. It comes from inhabiting with love the home of human fear. Death is the ultimate fear that generates all our lesser fears. Whenever we let this ultimate fear into our consciousness, we become anxious and frantic. We sense we are being separated from life, and the separation makes us quake. Therefore, Jesus enters the place of separation, death, with his full and loving communion with the Father. In doing this, he turns irretrievable loss into a transition into a new form of closeness to God and others.

Peace begins to rise in us and replace fear when we realize the revelation of Jesus' dying. We are in an unbreakable relationship with the transcendent Source. As we allow this foundational relationship to reach out and repair all our earthly relationships, we grow in peace and it stabilizes our lives. When Jesus leaves his disciples peace, he is leaving them both the revelation of the non-abandoning love of God and the task of restoring peace on the war-torn earth. These two dimensions of peace are intimately related. As the beatitude says, "Blessed are the peacemakers, for they will be called children of God" (Matt 5:9).

Besides the gift of peace which could only be established by Jesus dying and departing from his disciples, another consolation is the fact that he is coming back to them. However, it is intimated that the way he is coming back to them will be greater than the way he is among them now. He is going to the Father and the Father is greater than he is and out of this greatness is designing a new form of presence. Therefore, the disciples should not be paralyzed with grief and loss. They should rejoice in eager expectation of a greater presence of God through Jesus than they have previously experienced. "Very truly, I tell you, the one who believes in me will also do the works that I do and, in fact, will do greater works than these, because I am going to the Father" (John 14:12). Jesus tells them these things so that they may believe and attend to the greater reality that is coming about through Jesus' death and departure to the Father.

Teaching

I have been at the bedsides of dying people who have regretted they did not have more wealth to leave their heirs. They saw their contribution to the future solely in terms of the financial benefits they would leave behind. Conversely, I have been at dinners where the lucky heirs were at each others' throats over a perceived unfair will. Inherited money is dangerous. It is meant to help, but it can divide.

> Someone in the crowd said to him [Jesus], "Teacher, tell my brother to divide the family inheritance with me."
>
> But he said to him, "Friend, who set me to be a judge or arbitrator over you?" (Luke 12:13-14)

Jesus will not divide this man from his brother over the issue of inheritance. But the man is ready and willing to break the relationship for the sake of the money.

Jesus' last will and testament in the Gospel of John values relationships above all else. Therefore, his bequest to his disciples is something that will not break them apart, but something that will be an active force in keeping them together. He leaves peace, the only truly generative gift to the future. Peace, by its nature, does not divide people but restores them to one another.

If we rummage among the gifts of our ancestors, we may find the gift of peace in some of their stories. If we were bequeathed money, we would spend it. If we are left a story of peace, we are meant to remember it and act on it. If Jesus is correct, the Holy Spirit not only helps us remember peace but, through remembering, teaches us the way of peace. So I remember and hope that I learn. The following story is one of those strange combinations of fact and fiction that is meant to instruct and give hope.

"Why bother?" is what Marie Margaret Mulligan told her husband, John Thomas Mulligan, in June of 1948 when, upon his retirement from Sears & Roebuck after thirty years, he proposed they take their granddaughter, who had just graduated from grammar school, and go back to Ireland to see his older brother. Marie, as was her custom, repeated what she said for emphasis, "Why bother?"

But when he told his granddaughter, she was delighted and asked, "Pop, are you and Gram going to go back to Ireland to live?"

"Why should I?" he said, without ever taking the pipe out of his mouth. "I starved there."

And indeed he had. John Thomas Mulligan was the second son of four sons and three daughters. The farm would go to his older brother. That was the way it was. There was not much for him to do but move along. And the sooner the better. What food there was would go further with one less. So, as he likes to tell it, he threw his shoes over his shoulder to save the wear and tear, walked over the mountain, and got on a boat for America. That was May 1908.

In New York there was a series of jobs—stock boy, wagon driver, a humiliating stint as a servant, "Hey, Paddy, get the dog." Then he went to Chicago and with the help of his cousin's friend landed a job at Sears. There he met Marie O'Malley, got married, had three children, made some money, lost most of it in the depression, got back on his feet, and just as he was standing up, he looked around to find out he was old. At his retirement party, Steve O'Donnell asked Marie to say a few words. She stood, looked at John, and in a voice filled with surprise asked, "O John, where did it all go? Where did it all go?"

Over the years, John Thomas Mulligan did not lose touch with his older brother. Every year at Christmastime he wrote a letter. More often than not it would begin with, "Not much new here." But he always sent a check. After the first of the year, a return letter would arrive. More often than not it began, "Not much new here either." The check was never mentioned.

But in June of 1948 John Thomas Mulligan wrote a letter out of season. "Marie, I, and our granddaughter are coming to Ireland. Would you be home on July 11th in the evening?" One day before they were to take the train to New York and four days before they were to take the ship to Ireland, a return letter arrived. It read: "We would. Come for dinner."

On July 11th John Thomas Mulligan, the second son of four sons and three daughters, rented the newest model Packard he could find, put on his three-piece, broad-lapelled, broad-striped suit, placed his large gold watch in the pocket of his vest, looked approvingly at his wife in her best hat and dress, and told his granddaughter in an uncharacteristically stern voice, "No pedal pushers. I want you to wear a dress." John Thomas Mulligan was on his way to see his older brother.

The stone and thatch cottage was much farther from the main road than he remembered, and by the time they got there the car was covered with mud. Gerald Michael Mulligan and his wife stood at the door of the cottage. "Jerry," said the younger brother with his hand extended. "John," said the older brother taking it. Their eyes never met. Inside the table was already set.

The dinner was plain and good. The talk was general—the brothers and sisters, America, children, Ireland, the war. As soon as she could, the granddaughter escaped to the room where she was to sleep. When she found out it was the same room in which her grandparents were going to sleep, she rolled her eyes but said nothing. Not much later the wives, sensing they should, said goodnight. That left the two brothers alone in the kitchen.

After some time the older brother spoke, "You a rich yank now?"

"I am not," said the younger brother. "You a prosperous land owner now?"

"I am not," said the older brother.

The older brother stood up, moved to the cabinet, got a large loaf of fresh bread and a knife, and sat down. The younger brother stood up and went to the back bedroom. Marie lay on one side of a double bed and his granddaughter was on a cot under the window, reading a Nancy Drew mystery.

"Is it alright with him?" Marie immediately asked in an anxious voice.

John Thomas Mulligan opened the suitcase and rummaged under the neatly folded clothes. His hand brought out a fifth of Kentucky Bourbon.

"Is it alright with him?" said Marie a second time, repeating for emphasis as was her custom.

"Get some rest," her husband said and smiled at her.

"I will now," she said and crossed herself.

In the kitchen sat the two brothers and between them the bread the older brother has wrested from the stubborn land and the bottle the younger brother had brought back from the far country.

The first up in the morning was the granddaughter. She tiptoed out of the room without waking her grandmother. The kitchen table was filled with crumbs. On it was a knife and an almost empty bottle. The door to the cottage was open. She took it as an invitation and went outside.

The new day had just begun. The sun was climbing into the clear sky. It shimmered off the ocean in the distance and lit the land all the way up to the cottage. In the middle of the field stood the two brothers, pipes in their mouths, inspecting the earth the way a mother checks a newborn baby.

They must have stayed up all night, the granddaughter thought to herself.

Then the brothers turned, saw her, and waved. And side by side, stride by stride, step by step they came toward her. As she watched them come toward her, she knew that although she had never had to stay up through the long night to beat back the darkness with her love, when her time came she would be able to do it. And when they came within earshot, she shouted out to them, "O wow! You made it all the way to morning."

Peace, the restoration of relationships, is the only real inheritance.

Seventh Sunday of Easter

John 17:20-26

🔥

Practicing Spiritual Presence

A Spiritual Commentary

Lifting up his eyes to heaven, Jesus prayed saying:

The context of this prayer is Jesus' final supper and his extended last will and testament. Jesus is conversing with his followers and praying to his Father in the light of his upcoming death. There is no simple way to corral the many meanings associated with the death of Jesus in the Gospel of John.

On one level, it signifies physical loss and the corresponding grief and confusion of his followers. The weeping Magdalene seeking his lost body is an unforgettable picture of this sorrow.

On another level, Jesus' death is seen as a departure. He is leaving this world to go to the Father. He came from the Father, completed his work, and now returns to the Father. His death is a transitional event in the providential plan of God.

On still another level, his death is the full revelation of the glory of the Father and the full communication of this glory to his friends. In death the eternal life that is the inner being of Jesus meets and transcends the limits of temporal life. As it does this, his open wounds become rivers of life to his mortal friends and revelations that love is stronger than death.

All these meanings are background to Jesus' prayer. However, the foreground of the prayer, what it explicitly focuses on, is still another level of meaning. The loss of Jesus' physical presence through death unfolds into a new interior, spiritual presence. This spiritual presence was the essence of Jesus' incarnate life. He was always the *Word* Made Flesh. But now that the flesh has faded, the spiritual presence continues among his friends in a profoundly intimate way. Jesus and his Father indwell in them, creating a community of friends who love one another, and inviting an alienated world into this experience of oneness.

Jesus begins this prayer by "lifting his eyes to heaven." This is not a literal instruction in proper liturgical form. "At this point the celebrant will look skyward." It is a symbolic clue that Jesus is contemplating divine reality. He is looking into God and opening himself to the reality he perceives. His entire prayer is going to be under the influence of heaven, directed by divine energy, evaluating the human predicament of loss and presence as it is informed by the power of God. Jesus' rootedness in the Father is going to provide a new possibility for how he will be present to his friends. In this sense, his prayer will be more revelation than entreaty. The Son is so united with the Father that he does not petition the Father. Rather, he discloses their shared intentions for his disciples.

> **"Holy Father, I pray not only for them, but also for those who will believe in me through their word, so that they may all be one, as you, Father, are in me and I in you, that they may also be in us, that the world may believe that you sent me."**

This prayer stretches into the future. Jesus prays not only for those who are with him, his first friends, but also for his second friends, those who will come to believe in him because of the word of his first friends. A chain is envisioned, and the links of the chain is the word about Jesus. This word of the first friends is more than accurate information. It is the expression and communication of their interior relationship to Jesus. This word becomes a seed in the heart of others to enter into the same relationship. A true word about Jesus is always an invitation to share in Jesus' interiority. In this sense the disciples become a first doorway, an opening into the reality of Christ.

However, Christ himself is a doorway into the reality of the Father. The reality of the Father is the flow of life and love into his children. Therefore, multileveled relationships come into being. The first friends gather other people into themselves, and through themselves into Jesus, and through Jesus into the Father. These multiple indwellings result in a unity, a oneness that witnesses to the truth that Jesus is the communication of God to the fractured world. The God-grounded oneness of Jesus' friends among themselves both calls attention to the pervasive condition of human fragmentation and invites it into healing. Therefore, evangelization is an essential component of Jesus' prayer. As Jesus prays for all those who will hear his voice through the voices of others and so enter into unity with himself and the Father, he also prays for all those who need to hear his voice, who live in the world, i.e., in alienation, darkness, and under the power of death. This prayer does not establish a sect; it inaugurates a mission.

And I have given them the glory you gave me, so that they may be one, as we are one, I in them and you in me, that they may be brought to perfection as one, that the world may know that you sent me, and that you loved them even as you loved me.

The prayer continues to circle the same territory, adding perspectives that deepen and reinforce the multileveled relational unity between the Father, Jesus, and believers. The Father's glory is the way his life-giving presence flows into and establishes the identity of Jesus. Jesus does not cling to this life-giving presence as his own privilege. He passes it on to his friends and puts them on a path to perfection, a path of ever-deepening unity. This is entirely appropriated for God's glory and cannot be possessed by anyone, especially by Jesus who is the mediator between the divine and the human. What is given to Jesus is immediately given away to others. It is this action of self-giving that creates unity. In John's Gospel Jesus is the "I am so that others may be." The essence of the being of Jesus is his sharing it with others. Those who receive it from Jesus give it to others. And thus a living chain across time and history is established.

This receiving and giving among the friends of Jesus creates a unity that becomes a message to the non-unified world, a world that lives by taking and holding. The message is: watch love flow between both Jesus and his friends and among his friends. From where does this love come? Is not the source of this unity God? In other words, this way of being human seems so impossible that if it becomes possible, it could only be because God is its ultimate author.

When they asked Gandhi what his message was, he responded, "My life is my message." The same emphasis is attributed to St. Francis who instructed, "Preach the good news. Use words if necessary." In other words, it is the way of being alive, deeper than what is said or claimed, that ultimately attracts people and changes the world. This is the essence of Johannine evangelization: the life-giving love among the followers of Jesus is the invitation to the love-starved world, showing it a possibility it did not think possible.

Father, they are your gift to me. I wish that where I am they also may be with me, that they may see my glory that you gave me, because you loved me before the foundation of the world.

Jesus sees his friends as God's gift to him. This profound insight implies a divine guidance to the whole process of attraction to Jesus. It is reminiscent of what John the Baptist tells his disciples when they complain that people are flocking to Jesus, "No one can receive anything except what has been given from heaven" (John 3:27). The disciples are gifts from heaven.

This providential perspective creates a desire in Jesus. These God-given companions must be with him always. If they are God's gifts, they should be as ever-present as God. They are with him now at this meal. After his physical death, they will be with him through the conferral of his and the Father's Spirit. After their physical death, should they not join him in the house of his Father, in the house of many rooms? This is entirely appropriate for then these gifts of the Father will participate the primordial gift of the Father, the glory of divine life flowing into the Son from before the foundation of the world. The disciples have seen this divine glory in and through Jesus' physical presence while he walked on earth. They have known the Word made flesh. Why should they not see the Word in its eternal form, the Word that left his clothes behind in the tomb as he returned to the Father? Why should not the twin gifts of God—the disciples and the love of the Father—meet? Of course, Jesus, who unites his friends with the love of the Father, will mediate this meeting.

> **Righteous Father, the world does not know you, but I know you, and they know you sent me. I have made known to them your name, and I will make it known, that the love with which you loved me may be in them and I in them.**

The Father is righteous because he is true to his nature, a nature that the alienated world does not know precisely because it is alienated. But Jesus, who is connected to God and to his friends, does know the Righteous Father precisely because he is connected. This connection allows him to bring together divine love and disciples. This effective meeting is characterized as "making known the name of the Father." However, when Jesus does this, he does not disappear. He remains in his disciples as the everlasting bond of meeting, the permanent way the Father enters into the disciples of Jesus as the invitation to the disconnected world.

This profound, mystical prayer is often called the prayer of unity. This title focuses on the goal of the prayer, the multileveled relational communion between the Father, Jesus, his friends, and the world. However, the path to this unity is Jesus' ability to see and practice a form of spiritual presence. Spiritual presence is different from physi-

cal or psychological presence. It is the conscious possibility of being in
God, in ourselves, and in others. It is a way of indwelling.

Teaching

Spiritual presence is one of the consolations that Christian faith offers for physical loss. Therefore, we often turn to it when someone we
love has died. This timing seems to fit well with the prayer of Jesus.
In the face of his upcoming death, he articulates a spiritual indwelling
that is not broken by power of death. William Shannon, in a passage I
often quote, tried to comfort a woman who had recently lost her sister
with this approach.

> I hope you have been able to come to grips a bit more with your feel-
> ing about your sister's death. I realize how very hard this is for you.
> You need to keep reflecting on the fact that, while in one sense death
> separates us from the loved ones, in another and more ultimate sense
> it deepens our spiritual union with them. When there is only that, then
> that becomes most important. And, of course, it should really be most
> important at all times. We are one with one another because whatever of
> us there is that is really worthwhile is from God and in God. And that is
> something that death does not and cannot change—though it appears to
> do so, since we are so accustomed to think of a person solely in terms of
> her empirical ego. Death is the end of the empirical ego, but not of the
> person. We are all eternally one in the love of God. (William Shannon,
> "Thomas Merton and the Quest for Self-Identity," *Cistercian Studies* 22,
> no. 2 [1987] 172. Used with permission.)

Although this vision of spiritual yet disembodied communion is meant
to console us, it often fails to do so. Quite frankly, it seems like wishful
thinking, thinking that will keep us from fully looking into the abyss of
the death.

Shannon targets our difficulty with discerning spiritual presence
". . . we are so accustomed to think of a person solely in terms of her
empirical ego" (172). In short, we are addicted to physical presence. We
want to smell the hair of our children, touch our lover's hand, look into
another's eyes, and hear human laughter. We cannot imagine presence
without the impact of the physical senses. Our consciousness not only
dwells on the physical and psychological, it often stops there. So when
the spiritual is all we have, we cannot confidently discern it and are
highly suspicious of those who say they can. It seems like a fallback

position. We really want what we can no longer have. Spiritual presence is second best, a poor substitute for flesh.

The suggestion of spiritual teachers is to practice spiritual presence now so that when it is all we have, it will not be a total stranger to us. In the Gospel of John the Beloved Disciple discerned the spiritual presence of Jesus while he was in the flesh and when he was no longer in the flesh. Our spiritual presence to one another exists now. It is embedded within our social, psychological, and physical presences. When we become conscious of this dimension of ourselves and learn how to indwell in one another, we develop spiritually. The prayer of Jesus can give us some guidelines for this practice.

The first step is to realize the center of our being is a spiritual reality that is related to yet distinct from the physical, psychological, and social dimensions of who we are. Just as there are practices to help us develop physically, psychologically, and socially, there are practices to help our spiritual capacities develop. The simple recognition that we are a spiritual being capable of development begins the process.

The second step is to pull our consciousness within and down into our spiritual center. When our consciousness rests in this center, we become aware it is receiving its being and love from elsewhere. It is not its own reality. It is dependent on a larger reality that is filling it from within and encouraging it to connect with other spiritual centers and to share its life with them. When this spiritual life is shared, there is more life. On the spiritual level, shared life does not divide and lessen. It multiplies and magnifies.

The third step is to use our imagination to put our spiritual center within the spiritual center of another. In doing so, we will mediate the life and love we are receiving from the Divine Source into another being who is also receiving life and love from the Divine Source. Our spiritual presence to them lessens their aloneness and increases their openness to the Divine Source. This is the essence of spiritual companioning. Within this spiritual act it is important to hold one's intention steady. The only purpose of spiritual centers dwelling within one another is to further realize the love of God. No other agendas are proper to this practice. Spiritual presence is a disciplined act.

The fourth step concerns following spiritual indwelling with physical and psychological presence whenever that is possible. Placing our spiritual presence in another can happen with the living and the dead, with those who are physically present and with those who are physically absent. In some situations this spiritual connection encourages a "follow through." We find an opportunity to be physically and psy-chologically present to the person we have been spiritually indwelling. When this happens, our spiritual indwelling grounds our psychologi-cal sensitivity. We listen more completely, sensing where thoughts are arising from and journeying with them from source to surface. We become companions, not only on the spiritual level but also to the complete person—body, mind, and social relationships.

In the Christian world not a week goes by when we are not asked to pray for somebody. The practice of spiritual presence is one way we might honor this request. Prayer is a capacity of our consciousness to move beyond the physically imposed boundaries of our skin and enter into the spiritual center of another. Since this is a spiritual act on our part, we do not come alone. We bring the love of God from our spir-itual center to this center of the other and, in the process, open them more completely to the love of God that is always waiting to enter. Then we are in them and they are in us, and we are both in Christ, and the Father is in Christ and in us, and the love of God is in and through all, making one out of these many members.

Tenth Sunday in Ordinary Time

Proper 5

Luke 7:11-17

❦

Peddling Choices

A Spiritual Commentary

Soon afterwards, he went to a town called Nain, and his disciples and a large crowd went with him.

As he approached the gate of the town, a man who had died was being carried out. He was his mother's only son, and she was a widow; and with her was a large crowd from the town. When the Lord saw her, he had compassion for her, and said to her, "Do not weep."

Then he came forward and touched the bier, and the bearers stood still. And he said, "Young man, I say to you, rise!"

The dead man sat up and began to speak, and Jesus gave him to his mother.

Fear seized all of them; and they glorified God, saying, "A great prophet has risen among us!" and "God has looked favorably on his people!"

This word about him spread through Judea and the surrounding country.

Miracles steal the show. More than they should. They usurp attention and monopolize the mind. Something extraordinary has happened and nothing else is worth talking about. People speak in exclamation points and spread the news. Even when miracles are played down—and in this tale the miracle of resuscitation is extremely played down—it is hard to get beyond the spectacular. The hunger for the fantastic can never be completely filled. When there is nothing else to feed it, it gorges itself on the technique of the miracle.

When Elijah raised the son of the widow of Zarephath, he stretched himself upon the boy three times and cried to the Lord, "O Lord, my God, let this child's life come into him again." The warm body on

153

the cold one brought the boy to life. The widowed mother of the boy became a believer. "Now I know that you are a man of God" (1 Kgs 17:17-24). The technique is warm on cold three times. Try it.

When Elisha raised the son of the Shunammite woman, he went into the room where the dead boy was, closed the door, got up on the bed, prayed, and "lay upon the child, putting his mouth upon his mouth, his eyes upon his eyes, and his hands upon his hands" (2 Kgs 4:34). Then he got down off the bed, paced around the room, got back on the bed, and bent over the child. "The child sneezed seven times, and the child opened his eyes" (2 Kgs 4:35). The technique is live touching dead, sense for sense. Wait for the sneezes.

The miracles of Elijah and Elisha took some doing—heartfelt prayer and complete body contact. Jesus merely touches the bier, as if to indicate the bearers have been a tad hasty in their judgment of death. They are going away from the village that Jesus is going into. "Not so fast," he seems to be saying. Then Jesus addresses the young man as if he were sleeping (Mark 5:39-42). Instead of body contact, the Lord merely speaks. In fact, he calls attention to the fact that it is he who is speaking, "I say to you." It is his word that does the deed. In fact, the one word, "rise," does it. In response to the word of Jesus the young man begins to speak. No body over body. No seven sneezes. Jesus makes it look easy, a laid-back technique. Very showy, very showy.

It is the details of wonder-working that capture and constrain attention, that become the grist of every conversation, that are prized by the miracle mongers. Even if you do not believe a word of it, you still are caught in checking out the miracle. It may be a fabricated story to sell Jesus as God's prophet in the line of Elijah and Elisha; or it may be the young man was not really dead, a case of a comatose body but not a corpse. But the result is the same. Those who are awed by miracles and those who are offended by miracles are both in the thrall of miracles.

This obsession with the spectacular and how it is accomplished is the downside of miracles. The gospels know the problem only too well. In the temptation stories of Matthew and Luke, the devil is the foremost proponent of miracles (Matt 4:1-11; Luke 4:1-13). He wants Jesus to float down from the pinnacle of the Temple. He knows the people will be mystified. In the Gospel of Mark, the people surrounding the cross give Jesus wine to keep him alive so that they might see Elijah arrive to rescue him in a heavenly chariot (Mark 15:33-39). Ah, true religion! The Gospel of John consistently critiques people who cannot get beyond the surface of miracles (John 6:26). The wow of miracles blinds people. The dazzling surface keeps them from pursuing the meaning of miracles.

But the people in this story of the widow of Nain are not completely mesmerized by the fireworks. They take a first step toward meaning. The risen son means a prophet has risen among them, and this is a sure sign that God is looking favorably upon his people. What Jesus said in his hometown is happening. He is "to proclaim the year of the Lord's favor" (Luke 4:19). But even this correct interpretation of the miracle does not seem to go far enough. It is not enough to say the significance of this risen young man is that a prophet of divine favor has appeared.

The central characters of the story are Jesus and the widow. The dead and risen son is merely the medium of exchange between them. Jesus' compassion is for the widow and his words, "Weep not," reflect the astounding social reversal of the Sermon on the Plain. "Blessed are you who weep now, for you will laugh" (Luke 6:21). But Jesus' compassion extends beyond the fact that this woman has lost her son. She is also a widow who has lost a husband, making her an unprotected woman without husband or son. In the society of Jesus' day, she is completely vulnerable. She does not belong to the house of any man, and so she is without shelter and food. She may be weeping for her lost son, but her tears could legitimately include herself. In truth, Jesus has encountered a burial procession for two. She is leaving the village to be buried with her son. This is a story of how culture and society abandon women without men.

It is this meaning that is a revelation. Once the dust of the miraculous is shaken from our eyes, this story takes us into the compassion of God for the poor and vulnerable. Once the compassion of God for the poor and vulnerable is noted, this story takes us into the cultural conditions that create the poor and vulnerable. The healings and exorcisms of Jesus are as much social critiques as they are stunning miracles. They reveal divine compassion and love and, at the same time, unmask the social conditions that turn people into the poor and vulnerable, invisible and oppressed. But this revelation is resisted. Pander to the miracle. Even ponder the strange compassion of God on the least. But do not bring out of concealment the cultural assumptions and social mechanisms that shape deprivation and death. Too much is at stake.

Teaching

It is difficult to see culture and systems, to put them on the radar screen so they can be directly observed. They are so taken for granted that they are not examined. Yet they are enormously influential. Tracing what we can observe—people's words and action—to the underlying culture and systems in which they participate takes careful detective work. And it is often resisted. It may be we like to think our choices are completely within our conscious control. Pointing out our indebtedness to what we are not aware of goes against our mistaken sense of unfettered freedom. Or it may be that the privilege and power of a few are tied to these hidden cultural assumptions and social mechanisms. In that case, the difficulty to discern the concealed influences would not be an accident. They are deliberately kept out of sight.

So culture and system are "hidden persuaders." But they are hidden in different ways. Culture is a set of assumptions that people have internalized. In highly competitive cultures, these multiple assumptions are unified by a single goal—how do I, as opposed to you, protect and promote myself at all costs. Walter Wink has tried to name some of these delusional assumptions (*Engaging the Powers: Discernment and Resistance in a World of Domination* [Minneapolis: Fortress Press, 1992] 95–6).

- The need to control society and prevent chaos requires some to dominate others.
- Those who dominate may use other people as a means to achieve their goals.
- Men are better equipped by nature to be dominant than women, and some races are naturally suited to dominate others.
- Institutions are more important than people.

A more anecdotal list would include: people on top work harder and so should be paid more; never share information that gives you an edge; never admit mistakes; whatever you do to someone is justified because you can be sure they would do it to you; charity begins at home; wishing people well is enough; some people are just unlucky, but then again everyone gets what they deserve, etc. Since these are assumptions, they may never see the light of day. In fact, if you ask people to clarify their assumptions, they might not be able to do it.

Systems are hidden in a different way. In one sense, they are out in the open, written down as laws, policies, and procedures. This is how healthcare coverage works; these are the rules governing loans; here are the voting regulations; this is how board and management interact with stockholders; here is the formula for incentive pay, etc. But this information is often difficult to obtain, and even more difficult to understand once it is obtained. And, in many circumstances, the most important information is never volunteered or obfuscated with double talk. Most importantly, the system is seen to be independent of the people who created it. Therefore, it is incapable of change.

No better description of a system was ever given than the portrayal of the bank in John Steinbeck's *Grapes of Wrath*.

> If a bank or a finance company owned the land, the owner man said, The Bank—or the Company—needs—wants—insists—must have—as though the Bank of the Company were a monster, with thought and feeling, which had ensnared them. . . . And the owner men explained the working and things of the monster that was stronger than they were. . . . The bank has to have profits all the time. It can't wait. It'll die. When the monster stops growing, it dies. It can't stay one size. . . . The bank is something else than men. It happens that every man in a bank hates what the bank does, and yet the bank does it. The bank is something more than men. Men made it, but they can't control it. (*The Grapes of Wrath* [New York: Viking Press, 1939] 42–5)

People create the systems that eventually turn and imprison them. But they forget this fact and obey the monster made from their own hands.

Cultural assumptions and social systems hide by appearing inevitable. They parade as givens, as natural a part of creation as water, earth, and air. Then the Lord of creation appears in the words and deeds of Jesus and chooses to bestow his mercy on the people that cultural assumptions and social systems oppress. Therefore, these assumptions and systems do not belong to the stuff of creation and, most importantly, they are no longer unseen background. They have been brought out of hiding, exposed, ripe for intervention and change.

Of all the titles for Jesus, one of the most provocative is "peddler of choices." He revealed both the mercy of God and the oppression of people, and this double revelation created a world of choices. People were able to see the assumptions and systems that curtailed their lives, and so they were given the possibility of saying no. I like to think that when the young man sat up on the bier and began to talk, he said what young men are supposed to say. With his resurrected eyes he saw his world clearly and criticized things that should never be. And when Jesus gave him to his mother, his resurrected eyes also saw her clearly. He knew her for the first time. It was only then he was sure he had come back from the dead.

Eleventh Sunday in Ordinary Time

Proper 6

Luke 7:36–8:3

ᶦᶜ

Loving Extravagantly

A Spiritual Commentary

One of the Pharisees asked Jesus to eat with him and he went into the Pharisee's house and took his place at the table.

This story has a larger context that is significant for how it is understood. John the Baptist and Jesus have preached repentance as the initial way to respond to the kingdom of God. The tax collectors have responded positively and undergone John's baptism, but the Pharisees and the lawyers have refused. In doing so, they have "rejected God's purposes for themselves" (Luke 7:29-30). The Pharisees are in a long line of religious elite who have learned to harden their heart to the voice of prophets.

Therefore, this Pharisee who invited Jesus is not seriously interested in his mission and ministry. Although we do not know why Jesus was invited, the presumption is that it is to watch and test him more than it is to sincerely engage him. "On one occasion when Jesus was going to the house of a leader of the Pharisees to eat a meal on the Sabbath, they were watching him closely" (Luke 14:1). Jesus, the preacher of repentance, is in the house of the Pharisee who refuses to repent. Can controversy and confrontation be far behind?

In fact, the Pharisees have done more than merely ignored the call for metanoia (a change of thinking and acting). They have gone on the offensive and attacked the character of the ones calling for repentance. They have vilified John the Baptist as a demon-ridden ascetic and Jesus as a drunk and a glutton who carouses with "tax collectors and sinners" (Luke 7:33-34). These accusations have deftly switched attention from themselves to John and Jesus. They are off the hook to repent; and John and Jesus are on the hook to respond to their charges. Is Jesus really a "friend of tax collectors and sinners"? This story holds the answer; and as the answer unfolds, Jesus is revealed as more than a prophet calling for reform, and the Pharisees are exposed as less than lovers of God.

> **And a woman in the city, who was a sinner, having learned that he was eating at the Pharisee's house, brought an alabaster jar of ointment. She stood behind him at his feet, weeping, and began to bathe his feet with her tears and to dry them with her hair. Then she continued kissing his feet and anointing them with the ointment.**

Although the exact nature of this woman's sin is not known, it is important she is known as a sinner in the city. That information and the fact she has sought out Jesus deliberately makes the Pharisees' accusation credible. He is a "friend of tax collectors and sinners." They follow him around and come looking for him, even when he is in the house of a Pharisee.

But there is more, a mysterious more. The woman is not excessively eating and drinking. Drunks and gluttons are not in the picture. Instead, she is weeping; and her total attention and affection are focused on the feet of Jesus. She is bathing them with her tears, drying them with her hair, kissing them with her mouth, and anointing them with her perfume. Yet she never speaks, explaining why and what she is doing. Therefore, others must interpret these gestures. Since the Pharisee already knows what he thinks, he is quick to see his opinion verified.

> **Now when the Pharisee who had invited him saw it, he said to himself, "If this man were a prophet, he would have known who and what kind of woman this is who is touching him—that she is a sinner."**

What the Pharisee notices is that a "touching" has occurred. The Pharisees are well known to be obsessed with externals, avoiding physical contact with what is impure. Contamination happens by skin on skin. Therefore, what is happening is an unclean woman has touched Jesus and made him unclean. The tears, hair, kisses, ointment, and feet are not mentioned. The Pharisee's mental categories have screened out concrete actuality and reduced it to "mere contact." In fact, he does not even see a concrete individual woman. Rather, he perceives a member of a class, a kind of woman, a sinner. This is a very abstract rendering of what was described in vivid detail.

Also, the fact that Jesus is letting her "touch" him casts doubt on his status as a prophet. A prophet should be able to read the hearts of people. So even if Jesus is a stranger in this city and does not know this woman's reputation, he should see into her heart, know she is a sinner, and flee from contact.

These lightening-fast assessments are happening in the *mind* of the Pharisee. He is saying all these things to himself. Of course, it is in the safety of the inside, in the secret space where we talk to ourselves, that the most damning judgments can be made without fear that they will be challenged. Unless, that is, someone is able to eavesdrop on the heart.

> **Jesus spoke up and said to him, "Simon, I have something to say to you."**
>
> **"Teacher," he replied, "speak."**

In the assessment of the Pharisee, Jesus is not enough of a prophet to know what kind of a woman it is who touches him. But it seems Jesus is enough of a prophet to know what the silent Simon is saying to himself. Jesus, however, does more than read hearts; he also talks to them. He wants to get into Simon's inner monologue and turn it into a dialogue. Jesus' tone may suggest confrontation, but it is probably more in the spirit of instruction. When the Pharisee calls him "Teacher," he realizes he will be on the receiving end of some education. Also, for the first time we know the name of the Pharisee. It is Simon, the same name as the leader of Jesus' disciples. Could this be a teaching for the lurking, unrepentant Pharisee in the heart of every disciple of Christ?

> **"A certain creditor had two debtors; one owed five hundred denarii, and the other fifty. When they could not pay, he canceled the debts for both of them. Now which of them will love him more?"**
>
> **Simon answered, "I suppose the one for whom he canceled the greater debt."**
>
> **And Jesus said to him, "You have judged rightly."**
>
> **Then turning toward the woman, he said to Simon, "Do you see this woman? I entered your house; you gave me no water for my feet, but she has bathed my feet with her tears and dried them with her hair. You gave me no kiss, but from the time I came in she has not stopped kissing my feet. You did not anoint my head with oil, but she has anointed my feet with ointment. Therefore, I tell you, her sins, which were many, have been forgiven; hence she has shown great love. But the one to whom little is forgiven, loves little."**

This is classic prophetic storytelling. Jesus tells Simon a story and concludes with a question about the characters in the story. Simon makes a judgment on the characters without realizing both that he is making a judgment on himself and that he is being given the interpretive key to a deeper understanding of the woman's behavior. Then Jesus makes the connection between the story, Simon, and the woman's behavior. Finally, he articulates the point of the teaching in proverbial language. When Simon said, "Teacher, speak," he did not know what he was in for.

The parable is stark. The characters do not speak; no reasons for their actions are given. If the story is to be grasped, emotional understanding will have to come from the listener's experience of debt. Some debts are difficult but doable; other debts are crushing and undoable. When a doable debt is canceled, we are relieved; when the undoable debt is canceled, we rise from the dead. In both situations we feel gratitude. But with the cancellation of a debt of five hundred denarii gratitude overflows into love, a love as extravagant as the debt that was forgiven.

For those who have been in undoable debt, the question Jesus puts to Simon—"Now which of them will love him more?"—is a no-brainer. Simon gets it right, but he gets it tentatively right. He "supposes" the "one for whom he canceled the greater debt." He is guessing at the obvious math rather than feeling the gut-wrenching recognition of the movement from hopelessness to hope, from deadness to life. It is just this failure of deep living, of never having been pulled from the pit that makes Jesus' second question so difficult, "Do you see this woman?" Although Jesus asks him this question while Jesus is looking at the woman and so wants him to see the woman through his eyes, Simon, who has never known forgiveness so deep it can release extravagant love, does not answer. He may see a "kind of woman." But he cannot see and does not know this overflowing fountain of tears, hair, perfume, and kisses.

Jesus tells him why this woman remains a stranger to him. When a person experiences God's forgiving love in the center of their being, they engage in extravagant gestures of love. If the teachings of Jesus have precipitated this forgiveness, then the feet of Jesus are lavished with attention and affection. It is by becoming a disciple of Jesus, by sitting at his feet and absorbing his words that divine love enters the human heart. Loving the feet of Jesus is just returning the love that has been given. But now it is human love suffused with divine love. Naturally, it brims and spills. The cup is overflowing (Ps 23:5).

But Simon and the Pharisees have not engaged John and Jesus' call for repentance. They remain outside the release of love that this forgiveness makes possible. They have no overflow of tears; all kisses and perfume are withheld; and their hair is braided tight around the brain where a recital of the sins of others rattles on endlessly. Since the teachings of Jesus are resisted, they do not know that extravagant love is a certain sign of divine forgiveness. They are wrapped up in themselves, and this self-enclosed ignorance brings them to their final mistake.

Then he said to her, "Your sins are forgiven."

But those who were at the table with him began to say among themselves, "Who is this who even forgives sins?"

And he said to the woman, "Your faith has saved you; go in peace."

Jesus uncovers the source of the woman's love. Her many sins that had previously constricted her no longer have power over her. They are forgiven. But the Pharisees, who talk among themselves but not to Jesus, are not able to grasp this simple connection between love and forgiveness. They think Jesus is forgiving her sins. But what he is doing is confirming that the woman's love witnesses to the fact of forgiveness. This places the emphasis not on divine forgiveness but on the human openness and courage to respond to it. It is the woman's faith that saved her just as it is the Pharisees lack of faith, their inability to engage the teachings of Jesus, that keeps them from love. The woman goes in peace because peace is the restoration of relationships, and that is precisely what has happened. Is Jesus a friend of tax collectors and sinners? No. He is a friend of God, and everyone who opens to him is restored to God.

Soon afterwards he went on through cities and villages, proclaiming and bringing the good news of the kingdom of God. The twelve were with him, as well as some women who had been cured of evil spirits and infirmities: Mary, called Magdalene, from whom seven demons had gone out, and Joanna, the wife of Herod's steward Chuza, and Susanna, and many others, who provided for them out of their resources.

Jesus continues his mission of preaching, teaching, healing, and exorcising. But he is not alone. Many who have heard him now walk with him. These companions do not include the religious elite. They have too many teachings of their own to hear the teachings of Jesus. But almost everyone else is there, men and women from every strata of society. Many of them have destructive pasts they have left behind. And there are well-connected women who provide resources and organizational skills. What can come of so motley a company?

Teaching

At a major juncture in St. Anselm's classic theological treatise *Cur Deus Homo* (Why God Became Man?), the teacher reminds the student, "You have not yet considered the seriousness of sin." It is the seriousness of sin that lurks in the background of the story of the woman, Simon, and Jesus.

David Steindl-Rast thinks the word "sin" no longer communicates a serious negative condition with disastrous consequences. He suggests the word "alienation." "Alienation is our contemporary word that makes sense to us today. . . . We all know what that is. We know what it feels like; being cut off from everything, from ourselves from anything that has meaning, from all others . . . from ultimate reality, from God" ("Thoughts on Mysticism as Frontier of Consciousness Evolution," in *Human Survival and Consciousness Evolution*, ed. Stanislav Grof [Albany, NY: SUNY, 1988] 98). Other thinkers like the word "separateness." It carries the connotations of being cut off, isolated, radically alone. Dorothy Soelle liked the image of freezing.

> [Sin] . . . is the Ice Age—this slow advance of cold, a freezing process which we experience and try to forget . . . [it is] the absence of warmth, love, caring, trust . . . [it is] the destruction of our capacity for relatedness. . . . [It] means being separated from the ground of life, having a disturbed relationship to ourselves, our neighbor, the creation and the human family. (*The Christian Century* [May 12, 1982] 558)

Each word—alienation, separateness, freezing—expresses with its own nuances what Augustine said about sin. A person in sin was *"incurvatus a se"* (bent over on top of himself or herself).

Christian faith thinks this alienated condition is so pervasive that it is original. Although it does not destroy the good creation, it is coextensive with it. It afflicts everyone. The fact that sin is pervasive is part of its camouflage. It is taken as normal life, just the way things are. Since it is present everywhere, it is difficult to focus on it. As the saying goes, what is everywhere is nowhere. This is why the Pharisees do not see their alienation, their separateness, their frozen life. Although Simon is "bent over" in conversation with himself and the other Pharisees talk only among themselves, their relational poverty never dawns on them. They have learned how to adapt to the small space that their mind has made into a barricaded home.

However, when a flowing, belonging person who is in communion with God and neighbor breaks into human life, sin's cover is blown. In the free life of this one person the prisons of others are exposed. Theologically put, it is in the presence of grace that sin is clearly seen. In this sense, Jesus did not badger people to repent. Repenting was simply what other people found themselves doing in order to participate in the flow of life he was offering. It is also in this sense that Jesus held up the overflowing life of the woman as a mirror to Simon. He wanted him to see himself as he was and himself as he could be. He wanted to lead him to decision's edge. Jesus is not a sad or angry prophet. He is an invitation to fullness.

The seriousness of sin is that it teaches us to believe a lie about ourselves and to defend that lie against the revelation of truth. It tells us we are isolated individuals with scarce resources and meager means who need to oppress others in order to live. But when we turn from this lie, we find ourselves extravagant lovers of God and our neighbor. People uncontrollably burst into glorifying God (Luke 5:25-26; 7:16) and the Samaritan leper praises God in a *loud* voice (Luke 17:18). The Good Samaritan finds himself extending unstinting care to the wounded man (Luke 10:33-35). Zachaeus finds himself giving half his goods to the poor and paying back anyone he has defrauded fourfold (Luke 19:8). Since we have traded communion for separateness, belonging for alienation, and flow for frozen, we are living by a greater life, a life not our own. The alabaster jar is broken and the perfume is pouring out. It is even possible if we take a piece of bread and break it, we can become food for others.

Twelfth Sunday in Ordinary Time
Luke 9:18-24

❦

Singing Our Suffering

A Spiritual Commentary

Once when Jesus was praying alone, with only the disciples near him, he asked them, "Who do the crowds say that I am?"

They answered, "John the Baptist; but others, Elijah; and still others, that one of the ancient prophets has arisen."

He said to then, "But who do you say that I am?"

Peter answered, "The Messiah of God."

He sternly ordered and commanded them not to tell anyone, saying, "The Son of Man must undergo great suffering, and be rejected by the elders, chief priests, and scribes, and be killed, and on the third day be raised." (Luke 9:18-21, NRSV)

In the Gospel of Luke Jesus is portrayed as a person who prays his way into every decision. Prayer is how he maintains his close relationship with the Father, and how he submits everything he says and does to divine direction. Jesus knows himself to be part of a divine plan; but this plan is not preset, sketched out on a heavenly drawing board and authoritatively imposed on him. Jesus is not mindlessly obedient, carrying out orders independent of his understanding and willing. Rather, he prayerfully discerns stage after stage, realizing more deeply what will be required of him as his preaching, teaching, healings, and exorcisms are both received and rejected.

Jesus is praying alone; and the story never says that he stops praying as he engages his disciples in conversation. Therefore, Jesus may not be in his usual role as teacher when he questions his disciples about who the crowds think he is and who they think he is. He is not quizzing them for a right answer he already knows. Instead, he may be casting about for more opinions and observations to fuel his discernment process. He is doing something all seriously spiritual people do: he is testing out in the community the conclusions he is reaching in the solitude of prayer. "Once when Jesus was praying alone . . ."

The crowds' appreciation of Jesus is imprecise. They know his words and deeds make the ancient prophetic traditions come alive. Therefore, they surmise he is one of the prophets come back to life, but they are not sure which one. The picture of them speculating back and forth ("some say . . . others say . . . still others say") gives the impression they are debating within too narrow a framework. They may even be circling around in superstitious conversation. Jesus is not the past resurrected; he is the future arrived. He is not derivative of anyone else.

But the crowd is not completely off the mark. Jesus is in the prophetic tradition and many of his concerns echo those of past prophets. Although he is more than a prophet, he is still a prophet. The crowds represent an outsider perspective. They see something, but they do not see enough.

The disciples represent an insider perspective. They see "prophet," but they also see more. Peter, speaking for all, discerns Jesus as the long-awaited Messiah. While prophets brought judgment and the demand for change, the Messiah brought hope and the fulfillment of dream. With the arrival of the Messiah, the ancient promises would be realized. The Messiah would be surefire victory. He would not be able to be resisted. He would not invite for people to change; he would enforce God's will. In particular, he would free Israel from the bondage to Rome. The title "Messiah" connoted a triumphant warrior king.

It is these connotations that Jesus does not want to endorse; and his injunction to silence is strict and unyielding. Titles are notoriously ambiguous; and if "Messiah" is to be used, it must mean what Jesus is prayerfully discerning it to mean.

In fact, this is not the first time Jesus has had to strip a title of false associations in order to focus on its true meaning. At his baptism, the heavenly voice addressed him as Beloved Son. To make sure he properly understood this title, the Spirit who descended on him drove him into the desert where Satan cleverly suggested three meanings for his new identity. They focused on personal privilege and the rise to political and religious domination. Only when he refused these temptations did the correct path open up.

Now a similar breakthrough in awareness is happening. All the pomp and power around the cultural and religious image of Messiah is dissolving and the reality of the Son of Man is emerging. However, the picture of the Son of Man is a startling departure from the conventional path of the Messiah. The expected messianic scenario was: once the credentials of the Messiah were confirmed, the leaders of Israel would rally behind him. But the Son of Man has to undergo suffering, rejection, and death at the hands of the elders, chief priests, and scribes. The religious elite of Israel will kill this Messiah. God, however, will not abide this negative judgment on the life of Jesus. In God's time and under God's initiative, Jesus will rise to a new life.

But why does it have to be this way? What inevitability of suffering has Jesus discerned in his prayer and conversation?

> **Then he said to them all, "If any want to become my followers, let them deny themselves and take up their cross daily and follow me. For those who want to save their life will lose it, and those who lose their life for my sake will find it." (9:23-24, NRSV)**

Jesus' suffering, rejection, death, and resurrection are not his isolated fate. It is not just an idiosyncratic chain of events that unfolded in first-century Palestine and will never be repeated. Rather, Jesus' destiny reveals a pattern essential to his way of life. As long as people follow Jesus, they will find themselves struggling with the same discernments he has to face and undergoing similar sufferings. What Jesus foresees for himself, he foresees for all his disciples.

The suffering of Jesus is necessary because of two unyielding aspects of the human condition. The first aspect is human ego centeredness. Jesus advocates a way of life dedicated to serving others. But in each person there is a drive to serve oneself, to save one's own life. This drive has the power of a gravitational pull. People instinctively protect and promote themselves and lead a life dedicated to those twin strategies. However, this fierce tendency is to be resisted. Taking "oneself" and "one's life" as absolute must be denied. This struggle to move from an ego-centered to an other-centered way of life, of denying oneself, involves suffering.

The second aspect concerns how other people respond to people who struggle to break the egocentric mold. Jesus taught and lived compassion for all and reconciliation between divided brothers and sisters. This social agenda was grounded in the spiritual energy of God who, through Jesus, was inviting all people into this kind of kingdom activity. However, people, especially leaders committed to the present state of social arrangements, reject this simple and straightforward invitation. Instead, they persecute the ones who offer the invitation. The followers of Jesus will always suffer at the hands of those who curtail compassion and refuse reconciliation.

However, this persecution does not destroy the invitation or the ones who offer it. Their love, just as Jesus' love, will persist in the face of rejection; and when it does, it will be called "taking up the cross." The disciples need to "take up" the cross so the impression will not be given that it is "put on" on them. On one level, the cross is the violent weapon of the persecutors. Yet on another level, the cross is what the disciples have knowingly initiated by pursuing compassion and reconciliation in the midst of people who will not tolerate these efforts at unity. The suffering of the cross is the result of persisting in love in a loveless world. It is so difficult a task that if one moves away from it for a moment, one may move away from it forever. Therefore, the followers of Jesus must take up their cross daily.

Why would anyone chose a life that involves such individual self-denial and such social repercussions? The strange and almost incomprehensible answer is that this is the higher life for which people were made. When life is lost on the physical and social level because of the way of Jesus (for my sake), life is gained on the spiritual level. This is a difficult truth to discern; but once it is discerned, it is a truth that is difficult to ignore. There may be entropy in people to default into self-enclosed, lower levels of human existence. But there is also a call to advance into unseen possibilities. In communion with his Father and in conversation with his disciples, Jesus saw this call into higher possibilities would always be accompanied by suffering. He judged the price acceptable.

Teaching

On April 6, 2006, I was doing a workshop in California when I received an emergency message from my wife. My mother had suffered a stroke and was on her way to the hospital. I caught the next plane to Chicago and finally arrived at the hospital around 10:30 at night. My mother was intermittently conscious. I told her I was here and asked her if she understood. She nodded yes. Then I asked her if she had any pain. She nodded no. I told her we (my wife, sisters, and brother-in-law) were all here with her, so she did not have to be afraid. She did not nod one way or the other. She just closed her eyes.

Contemporary medicine often distinguishes between pain and suffering. Pain is physiological and can be numbed by medications. These medications must be expertly administered because the cost of being pain-free is often the loss of consciousness. Suffering is the mental response to pain and, more generally, the "inner distress associated with events that threaten the intactness of person" (Eric Cassell, *Suffering and the Goals of Medicine* [New York: Oxford University Press, 1991] 33). This inner distress can also be addressed with drugs geared to lessen anxiety. Although my mother had signaled she was not in pain, and we were not sure what level of anxiety might be present, both drugs in moderate amounts were given to her. The medical caregivers were attentive and responding to her pain and suffering. We were grateful. We did not want our mother to experience pain and suffering.

Our mother had suffered the stroke three days before Palm Sunday, and on the first day of Holy Week she took a turn for the worse. She could not be roused. We had her transferred to a hospice bed in the hospital; and we camped around it and watched her labored breathing. As I sat there watching my mother's life come to an end at the same time as the Christian world was remembering the passion, death, and resurrection of Jesus, my mind and heart moved back and forth between the life of my mother and the life of Jesus. In particular, I stumbled over Jesus' insistence that his way of life would involve suffering.

In a conventional sense, pain and suffering is a negative consequence of our physical and social vulnerability. Something befalls us that is beyond our control—an illness, a job loss, a physical injury, the loss of someone we love, etc. We are suddenly at the whim of something we did not choose and responding to it takes the first and immediate form of alleviation. Not wanting ourselves or our loved ones to suffer is a universal human desire. The gospels honor this desire by highlighting Jesus' compassionate outreach to all who suffer and by insisting that Jesus himself did not court suffering. "Father, if you are willing, remove this cup from me" (Luke 22:42).

But the gospels also advocate a larger and nobler view of suffering, a view grounded in the transcendence and finitude of the human person. Each person lives on the border of eternity and time. The eternal dimension of our being stays in continual communion with a Love that Dante said, "moves the sun and the stars." The passion of this Love is to become flesh, to be embodied in the physical and social events of time. As we respond to the call of this inborn Love, our mission in the world unfolds. We undergo adventures. These adventures are our sufferings. Our sufferings are what we endure so Love can enter into the world. Therefore, although we strive to alleviate, accompany, and transform the negative suffering that comes from both finitude and sin, we also sing of the sufferings that are the hidden and strenuous glory of those who choose to love.

That is how it was with Jesus. The love he experienced from the Source of Life drove him into a mission of reconciliation. However, as his mission unfolded, he encountered resistance, a resistance that mobilized into a conspiracy to execute him. But the love that drove him continued to express itself in the face of this resistance. Therefore, as the Gospel of John insists, his glory was not just resurrection on Easter morning but the sufferings he endured on Good Friday so love would enter the world.

As I thought about this noble vision of suffering, what we undergo in the name of love, our mother's life came into focus in a new way. Our mother was gracious, a hostess of other people's souls. She had an art of welcoming that went beyond social politeness. If you were ever at a party with her, you could look across the room and see her engaged and curious, chatting up whomever she was sitting next to. Her presence was a home with the door always open.

But this graciousness was more than a pleasant personality trait. It was born of fierce conviction. A friend of mine told me, "Your mother was so kind to me when I was a squeaky little teenager." But I doubt if our mother ever saw a "squeaky little teenager." She always saw the dignity of a fellow human being. And if people wanted to be more than that, her graciousness deflated them and restored them to this simple joy in being human. And if people forgot and thought they were less than that, her graciousness found them in the bottom of their soul and lifted them up to where she knew they belonged. It was not only that our mother was gracious; it was that she was gracious to everyone.

I knew this, but I never before saw it as her sufferings, the type of initiatory love that struggled to overcome obstacles and better people and situations. But it was true. She took up this cross daily; and as love unfolded in her, it brought her into many adventures. These adventures required her to forge futures from sheer resolve, to endure hardships, to create the conditions where life could flourish. They were her sufferings *and* her glory. What was going on now—the slow collapse of the body's capacities—was nothing compared to the sufferings of love, the suffering that rises into song.

But even as I pondered the type of suffering that could be sung, I worried about the suffering that could break even the best of spirits, the inner distress that accompanies the loss of intactness. Then I remembered something. About nine months after our father's death and four months after our mother's first heart attack, I was driving her somewhere when she suddenly said, "I've decided to give up on fear. It does no good."

I was silent for a few moments and then I said, "I've tried it a few times, Mom. I'm not sure it can be done. I couldn't do it."

"I'm older," she shot back. "I've got a better chance."

Our mother always pushed back, not only toward negative outer circumstances but also, and probably more importantly, toward inner negative states. And she did not pick weak opponents. She took on things like fear and loneliness and loss. And I realized that if she was interiorly alert, she was following the habit of a lifetime and pushing back fear with love. I also suspected there were resources for this struggle with which she was becoming more and more familiar.

She died around 10:00 P.M. on Holy Thursday night, just as Jesus unfolded out of eternity into time, coming down from the consciousness of God ("Jesus, knowing the Father had given all things into his hands and that he had come from God and was going to God" [John 13: 3]) as water flows from a pitcher into a basin, to find a universe of feet waiting for his tenderness.

Sunday between June 19 and June 25 inclusive

Proper 7

Luke 8:26-39

✺

Fearing and Loving God

A Spiritual Commentary

Then they arrived at the country of the Gerasenes, which is op-posite Galilee. As he stepped out on land, a man of the city who had demons met him. For a long time he had worn no clothes, and he did not live in a house but in the tombs.

When he saw Jesus, he fell down before him and shouted at the top of his voice, "What have you to do with me, Jesus, Son of the Most High God? I beg you, do not torment me"—for Jesus had commanded the unclean spirit to come out of the man. (For many times it had seized him; he was kept under guard and bound with chains and shackles, but he would break the bonds and be driven by the demon into the wilds.)

Jesus then asked him, "What is your name?"

He said, "Legion"; for many demons had entered him. They begged him not to order them to go back into the abyss.

Now there on the hillside a large herd of swine was feeding; and the demons begged Jesus to let them enter these. So he gave them permission. Then the demons came out of the man and entered the swine, and the herd rushed down the steep bank into the lake and was drowned.

The inner spiritual world is invisible, but it is the source of either the harmony or disturbance in the visible outer world. If the inner world is inhabited by demons, it manifests itself in chaotic and destructive behavior. If the inner world is inhabited by the Spirit of God, it mani-fests itself in a calm and focused life. In principle, therefore, there can be two parallel worlds with distinct boundaries—the world of demonic possession and the world of communion with the Spirit of God. One strategy of salvation is to avoid the world of demonic possession and stay within the world of communion with the Spirit of God.

However, this is not Jesus' strategy. He is the bearer of God's Spirit and his mission is to cross into the world of demonic possession and reclaim it as God's good creation. Both his courage to engage the demons and his effectiveness in defeating them comes from the superior power of the divine Spirit. This Spirit is the hope of the demon possessed; and, on one level, the possessed seem to know this. So when Jesus steps out of the boat onto the Gentile land of the Gerasenes, "a man of the city who had demons met him."

The demonically possessed man represents the city. He is the symptom-bearer of what the entire population is experiencing. That is why the name of the demon that inhabits him is "Legion; for many demons had entered him." The many demons of the community have gathered together to express their true destructive intent in the body of this one man. The allusion to Roman legions suggests this inner spirit of destruction is tied to the brutal occupation of this territory by Roman soldiers. The demonic power of the Empire has infected every citizen.

As a symptom-bearer, the demon-possessed man acts out what the larger community has managed to repress. In fact, their management of the inner demonic is directly tied to the fact that one of them does not share their defense mechanisms. He becomes the scapegoat, exhibiting in his tortured mind and body what lurks in all. When all the destructiveness is focused in one, the rest can go about leading as normal a life as possible. In a world populated by destructive forces that are more powerful than humans, this is a necessary but reluctant accommodation.

But this way of minimizing the damage of community demon possession is only partly successful. Although they "kept him under guard and bound him with chains and shackles, he would break the bonds and be driven by the demon into the wilds." Their attempt to control the demons who possess them is always threatened by the greater power of the demons. They have strength beyond the community's chains and shackles and can overcome those who guard them. One man, naked and living among the dead, may be acting out the destructiveness, but the entire city is possessed. They know the demons as a superior force, and so they know their constraints can be broken. They lead threatened lives.

In the previous episode, Jesus has stood against the winds and the raging waves of the sea. He rebuked them until they became calm

(Luke 8:22). He now stands against the demons and will rebuke them until the raging man is returned to sanity. There is no doubt about Jesus' ability to do this. The demons know they are outmatched by the "Son of the Most High." They beg him not to torment them the way they torment the possessed man and the possessed city. The demons fear the One who has just set foot on their land.

The demons whine and plead to design their own escape, thinking there might be a place they can flee from the power of the Spirit in Jesus. The abyss is where they came from, but to be sent back would be banishment from the earth. It would be a sign that Jesus completely controls them by keeping them where they belong and where they can do no harm to others. They think the swine might be a habitation where the Spirit of God in Jesus the Jew might be hesitant to approach. The unclean would be hiding among the unclean, but they would still be on earth. Jesus grants them what they wish. But their escape route proves to be their destruction. Like Roman soldiers charging into battle, the swine plunge headlong down the steep bank and drown in the lake. "The waters covered their adversaries; not one of them was left" (Ps 106:11). The Spirit of God is cleansing the earth.

> **When the swineherds saw what had happened, they ran off and told it in the city and in the country. Then people came out to see what had happened, and when they came to Jesus, they found the man from whom the demons had gone sitting at the feet of Jesus, clothed and in his right mind. And they were afraid. Those who had seen it told them how the one who had been possessed by demons had been healed. Then all the people of the surrounding country of the Gerasenes asked Jesus to leave them; for they were seized with a great fear. So he got into a boat and returned.**

Jesus has disrupted the city and the surrounding country's accommodation with demonic forces. Their symptom-bearer is no longer manifesting the outer effect of their possession; the scapegoat is no longer functioning as their surrogate. Rather, he has become a disciple of a greater power, a power that clothes him in dignity and restores him to himself. Through the power of the Spirit in Jesus he has become self-possessed. The sight of this restored man and the story of how he came to be demon free causes the people to be afraid. They ask Jesus to leave. What he has brought among them is not wanted. Jesus honors their request.

It is difficult to surmise why the people were afraid. Some suggest economic reasons. Since it was the swineherds who saw what happened and alerted the city and countryside, they probably told the story from their point of view. Any theological telling would take second place to the dire effects on their business. Transferring the legion of demons from the man to the swine results in product loss. This foreshadows the financial disruption the preaching of the gospels causes in the Acts of the Apostles (Acts 16:16-19; Acts 19:18-27). Although there is nothing in the story to suggest the swineherds were outraged businessmen, the gospel often offends people who profit from the present way things are.

One thing they see and one thing they hear triggers fear in the people of the town and surrounding countryside. The people become afraid when they see their symptom-bearer without symptoms. He is not naked, but clothed; not running wild, but seated; not ranting, but in his right mind. They realize he is no longer bearing the burden of their possession. That leaves them exposed to the demons, and exposure translates into fear.

The people become afraid on a deeper level when they are told how the healing took place. When they hear that the demons cowered before Jesus begging for permission to find another habitation and Jesus let them have what they wanted only to find out that their wish resulted in their complete annihilation, "they were seized by a great fear." The "great fear" usually signifies contact, either directly or indirectly, with the Spirit of the true God. This encounter is overwhelming because it introduces a new and greater power into the equation. The advent of this power changes the hierarchy of fears. The fears that usually dominate ordinary life are dwarfed by the "great fear" (Luke 12:1-4). If they feared what the demons could do to them, will they not be afraid of the One who could do such things to the demons? A new and more terrifying power has arrived to replace the demons. At this stage, that is all they know.

> **The man from whom the demons had gone begged that he might be with him; but Jesus sent him away, saying, "Return to your home, and declare how much God has done for you." So he went away, proclaiming throughout the city how much Jesus had done for him.**

The man whom Jesus has healed is not afraid. He knows the ultimate purpose of Jesus' power, and he never wants to be separated from it. He no longer has any allegiance to his city or country. A new loyalty directs him. He is faithful to the salvation he has experienced. Wherever Jesus is going, he begs that he might go with him.

But Jesus has another mission for him. His healing will be the way the rest of the city, the city that has just asked Jesus to leave, will be evangelized. He is to tell them how much this power that is greater than the power of the demons has done for him. It is not a power that demonstrates its might by destruction. It is a power that demonstrates its might by lifting people into their true status. The people are habituated into fearing power. Anything greater than they are can possibly do them harm. But this is a different type of power. They must learn to welcome the power of God as the energy of their own fulfillment.

So he went back into the city and told them how much *Jesus* had done for him. This is not a contradiction of Jesus' instruction to tell them how much *God* had done for him. Rather, it is the missionary's art of adapting the Good News to the perceptions and sensitivities of the people. For the city people, God is just a power that can cast the powers they are powerless against into the sea. It is the Spirit of God in Jesus who reveals this ultimate power as a transcendent love offering them salvation. When they realize this, they will ask Jesus to return to the city. Or, from a mystical perspective, when they realize this, Jesus will have already returned to their city.

Teaching

There are many paths to the experience of the Good News. This story suggests a path that moves from overwhelming fear to elevating love. It combines the temporal starting point from Proverbs 1:7 that "the fear of the Lord is the beginning of knowledge" with the climactic conclusion of 1 John 4:16 that "God is love." Of course, there are many steps from initial fear to final love. It is a journey of consciousness, a journey mapped out in a two-part teaching from Luke's Gospel.

> **"I tell you, my friends, do not fear those who kill the body, and after that can do nothing more. But I will warn you whom to fear; fear him who, after he has killed, has authority to cast into hell. Yes, I tell you, fear him!"** (Luke 12:4-5)

Jesus is talking to his disciples, but there is a large crowd surrounding the disciples. These people are "trampling on one another," presumably because they are eager to hear what Jesus is saying (Luke 12:1). The teaching is important because Jesus calls his disciples friends.

In the Gospel of John, a friend of Jesus is someone who has been privileged to hear the full revelation. "I do not call you servants any longer, because the servant does not know what the master is doing; but I have called you friends, because I have made known to you everything that I have heard from my Father" (John 15:15). However, this full revelation is not given in a didactic way. Rather, the reflection is structured to gradually lead his friends to the realization of "everything I have heard from my Father."

The first part of the structure is a series of hard-hitting injunctions that are directed to Jesus' listening disciples and, when we read this teaching, directed to us. They are meant to bring us to a proper ordering of our fears. If we are at all familiar with our fears, we know not a day goes by that we do not fret about those possible harms that can come to our bodies. Jesus' command that we stop fearing what can kill the body seems to go well beyond our abilities. Bodily fear is built into biological existence. But the endemic, chronic fear of those powers that kill the body is mentioned only to be put in second place. There is a greater power, a power that can do more than kill the body. This power also rules over the soul, and it can cast the soul into hell after it has killed the body. That is the reality that should be feared; and that reality is easily recognized as God. Jesus throws all his weight behind this command. "Yes, I tell you, fear him!"

At this stage in the teaching, Jesus advocates fearing God as the ultimate power that controls human destiny. Proximate powers can assault and destroy the body. But beyond the body, there is the soul; and that is realm of divine authority. So it is common sense to fear the reality with the biggest stick. Jesus the teacher is hyping the right kind of fear in his disciples. This may not be the usual picture we have of Jesus, but it is how he thinks his friends will receive the revelation he has to give.

I believe this "greater fear" describes the consciousness of the Gerasenes. They have witnessed the power of the demons to harass and terrify their lives. But then a greater power arrives. Whatever the demons have been able to do to the man is nothing like what Jesus can do to the demons. They have met a greater authority and with it comes a greater fear. The fear of the demons is relegated to second place. This teaching presupposes that it is necessary to move from lesser fears to the greatest fear, the fear of God. This is the beginning of wisdom, the proper place for consciousness if it is to take the next step.

Are not five sparrows sold for two pennies? Yet not one of them is forgotten in God's sight. But even the hairs of your head are all counted. Do not be afraid. You are of more value than many sparrows. (Luke 12:6-7)

The teaching moves from injunctions to images. If injunctions whip the mind to move in a certain direction, images coax the mind to explore revelations at the edge of consciousness. Sparrows, pennies, and hairs of the head are invitations to see something that will turn the fear of God into love. They map a sequence of realizations that will take the disciples into the end of wisdom. These realizations do not constitute an argument. Rather, they offer a way of seeing that will bring the disciples, and all who can navigate the images, into the experience that 1 John 4:18 expresses: "perfect love casts out fear."

In the human world, price indicates value. The higher the price is, the greater the value is. Sparrows barely make it on the price scale. Five can be purchased for two pennies. They are cheap, dispensable. But the divine world does not work like the human world. God's care is universal; and its universality is revealed in the fact that it remembers what the human world of selective care would forget. Eminently forgettable sparrows are not forgotten by God. The power of God is the power to care for all creation. This is perfect love.

Now the teaching becomes playful. This love extends even to the hairs of our head. We may be people who are mightily concerned about our well-being, but we do not take the time to count our hairs. This would be more of an effort for some people than for others. But God is a barber and beautician who has collected all the hair that ever was. And as if this were not enough, God does not merely store these hairs in a warehouse. God counts them, and in giving each one a number, gives each one a value, the same value—infinite value. What the human neglects, the divine cherishes.

Therefore, do not be afraid. This injunction goes against all the injunctions of the first part of the teaching. When the greatest power that can do the greatest harm is revealed as infinite care, then the reason for fear has been taken away. In its place is an observation that I think is meant to get a laugh from the disciples. "You are of more value than many sparrows." In a hierarchical order, the animals are below the humans. So how God cares for the animal world is included and transcended in how God cares for the human world. The greatest power is dedicated in an incredibly concrete way to human well-being.

This is what the man from whom the demons were cast out realized as he sat at the feet of Jesus and absorbed his teachings. This is what he must tell other people. Fearing that what is most powerful will harm us seems to come naturally. Knowing that what is most powerful loves us and is committed to our flourishing needs a special revelation. The ones who are able to proclaim it are the ones who have experienced it.

Thirteenth Sunday in Ordinary Time

Proper 8

Luke 9:51-62

❦

Rebuking the Mind

A Spiritual Commentary

When the days drew near for him to be taken up, he set his face to go to Jerusalem.

The life of Jesus is not a series of unforeseen events. There is an over-arching plan, a divine strategy. The goal of Jesus' life is to be "taken up." But ascension can only be reached by walking the road that leads to death and resurrection. This is the road to Jerusalem. Therefore, Jesus summons his courage and determination and moves toward the penultimate events of death and resurrection in the Holy City. These events will bring him to his ultimate destiny of directing his disciples from his "taken up" position in heaven.

> **And he sent messengers ahead of him. On their way they entered a village of the Samaritans to make ready for him; but they did not receive him, because his face was set for Jerusalem.**
>
> **When his disciples James and John saw it, they said, "Lord, do you want us to command fire to come down from heaven and consume them?"**
>
> **But he turned and rebuked them. Then they went on to another village.**

James and John, whom Jesus appropriately named the sons of thunder (Mark 3:17), fulminate. They react to rejection with rejection. They respond in kind, only with a little more muscle. Mere refusal of welcome is met with a scorched-earth policy. The Samaritan village will not welcome Jesus because he is a Jew heading for Jerusalem. Perhaps this is due to the general animosity between Samaritans and Jews. Or perhaps this foreshadows later missionary efforts where people reject the teachings of Jesus because he died as an executed criminal in Jerusalem. Either way, the Samaritans refuse hospitality. This refusal triggers a retaliatory reaction in the sons of thunder. They are ready to call down fire from heaven, to recruit God as the destructive agent of their anger.

Of course, this passion for revenge is the exact opposite of the way of Jesus (Luke 6:27-36). His disciples must be able to return blessing for curse and love for hatred. So Jesus rebukes their overkill proposal. It is interesting that James and John assume they are able to effectively pull God's chain and get the Lord of heaven and earth to do their bidding. But Jesus does not rebuke their presumptuousness. He targets their whole mindset. They are not displaying either love of God or love of neighbor. They are mindlessly escalating simple rejection into catastrophic reprisal. The better and more practical approach is to find a welcoming village.

> **As they were going along the road, someone said to him, "I will follow you wherever you go." And Jesus said to him, "Foxes have holes, and birds of the air have nests; but the Son of Man has nowhere to lay his head."**

Even though the days are drawing near to Jesus' ascension, his disciples need Jesus' instruction in the basic attitudes of what it means to follow him. The same is true for his would-be disciples. A man who is met along the road declares his intent to follow Jesus. His enthusiasm is captured in his absolutist language. He speaks without conditions. He will follow Jesus *wherever* he goes; but, at the moment, Jesus is going to his crucifixion in Jerusalem. Has his unbounded zeal taken that into account?

Jesus' imaginative response injects a note of realism into his romanticism. Although animals (birds and foxes) have a home in this world, the head of the Son of Man (Jesus himself and the new humanity he represents) cannot find a place to rest in the socially constructed world in which he lives. Jesus' way consists in not belonging to the present order of things. It entails a continual struggle to bring about a new understanding of God and neighbor and to create a society based on this new understanding. Any eager desire to follow Jesus must reckon with the difficulties of never belonging to what appears the natural way, the way of creating a home on the earth as it is.

> **To another he said, "Follow me."**

> **But he said, "Lord, first let me go and bury my father."**

> **But Jesus said to him, "Let the dead bury their own dead; but as for you, go and proclaim the kingdom of God."**

One man may come to Jesus because he is attracted; another is directly called. But both need to be corrected. To be directly called by Jesus is considered an absolute demand, a special moment of illumination. But the man does not immediately act on his illumination. Instead, he allows a filial responsibility to take precedence. He will go back and live under the command of his father until the father dies. After he has buried his father—sometime in the indefinite future—his calendar will be cleared for following Jesus.

However, according to Jesus' perspective, this practical plan of fulfilling a past obligation before undertaking a new one will not work. With Jesus' command, "Follow me," a new and vital possibility has entered his life, a possibility that demands immediate and wholehearted response. Loyalty to his past commitments, even to the cultural duties of sonship, should no longer hold him. If he stays in these commitments, he himself will be spiritually dead. He has heard a new call and his rejection of it kills the spirit. He will be in the position of a son who is spiritually dead burying a father who is physically dead. The call of Jesus creates a new situation that must be honored. He is not to go back to father; he is to go forward into proclaiming the kingdom.

> **Another said, "I will follow you, Lord, but let me first say farewell to those at my home."**
>
> **Jesus said to him, "No one who puts a hand to the plow and looks back is fit for the kingdom of God."**

The final would-be disciple is interested in following Jesus if it is permitted. He does not propose to go back to his family for a final farewell party. He wants to return to his family for their blessing on what he has decided to do. If they do not bless his traipsing after Jesus and he follows Jesus anyway, he will be caught looking over his shoulder. The kingdom is about steadfastly moving into a future that people must desire more than anything else. Seeking permission avoids the question of personal decision. However, it is only sheer individual resolve that will overturn the earth significantly enough for the seed of the gospel to be planted. A determined hand on the plough is Jesus' concern.

Teaching

A spiritual teacher instructs disciples in a variety of ways. In general, there is usually a pattern of affirmation and critique. When disciples express a way of thinking and acting that corresponds to the consciousness of the teacher, they are affirmed. When they express a way of thinking and acting that contradicts the consciousness of the teacher, they are rebuked. Although disciples seek to be complimented by the teacher, the greatest learning often occurs in critique.

During his training with Roberto Assagioli, the major figure in psychosynthesis, Piero Ferrucci was corrected or, what the gospels might call, rebuked. Ferrucci was walking with Assagioli in a small garden whose walls barely kept out the noisy Florence traffic. He had written some ideas for Assagioli to reflect on and comment. These ideas included a reference to "following our feelings."

Assagioli very gently but firmly stated: "but you must *not* follow your feelings." He spoke as if this were perfectly obvious. "Your feelings must follow you." Ferrucci relates how he received this correction.

> I was taken aback by this remark. After all, I thought, weren't we all supposed to be listening more to our feelings, which were so often brutally repressed or maltreated in our over-achieving society, thus accounting for so much of the psychological malaise we see around us? Surely we had to give in fully to the natural demands of our emotional life. That was my credo. And here was this old man telling me my feelings had to follow *me*! How authoritarian, how unfamiliar that sounded! At the same time, the statement—perhaps because of the disarming way it had been uttered—awoke my curiosity. I soon realized the importance of the problem. Should we acknowledge our feelings as the primary factor in deciding what to do in our various life situations? And if not, which part of us *should* determine our course of action? (*What We May Be: Techniques for Psychological and Spiritual Growth Through Psychosynthesis* [New York: Jeremy P. Tarcher/Putnam Books, 1982] 95–6)

Assagioli's simple and direct turnabout correction sent Ferrucci reeling.

This vignette gives us a clue to why rebuke from a more enlightened consciousness is so important. The rebuke often targets things we take for granted, ways of thinking and acting that we assume are correct. Ferrucci takes it for granted that discovering feelings and following them will bring him to greater levels of self-knowledge and, eventually, freedom to be and do in a new way. But Assagioli confronts this assumption and opens up a whole new approach.

The interpersonal style of the teacher contributes to the effectiveness of the rebuke, its ability to change consciousness. Since rebuke always entails a judgment of how we presently think and act, there is a tendency to defend ourselves. Our way has merit and we will not have it summarily dismissed. But this defensive posture is undercut by a "disarming authoritarianism." Assagioli speaks an unfamiliar truth as if it was perfectly obvious. He does this using his authority as the master, but in such a way that it awakens curiosity in Ferrucci and not combativeness. This style has the desired effect. It becomes a memorable teaching moment. Where Ferrucci once had a stale slogan, now he has a living question.

Jesus uses the teaching technique of rebuke consistently in the gospels. He criticizes mindsets that he thinks subvert kingdom living. These mindsets are what disciples and would-be disciples are currently following. In Assagioli's critique, they are feelings they are following. The sons of thunder are following the feeling of anger into petitioning God to kill. The eager would-be disciple is following his own emotional exuberance. The one who delays his response in the name of duty and the one who promises to follow Jesus under the condition of receiving permission are following familial and cultural expectations that have been imposed upon them. But there is a higher self, symbolized by Jesus, that anger, enthusiasm, duty, and permission should heed. "Your feelings should follow you." Jesus' rebuke is essentially a reminder of this higher self and the insistence that everything else be integrated into the direction it sets.

Luke's mini-stories do not tell us how the ones whom Jesus confronted responded. Did the sons of thunder ask Jesus if they should pray for fire in the hope he would say yes; and then grumble all the way to the next village? Did the exuberant follower think Jesus dampened his desire? Was the stinging suggestion that "the dead bury the dead" too much for the man who both loves his father and hears Jesus' call? Did Jesus' insistence that the personal hand on the plow replace the desire for family permission leave the man stalled between the values of blood and the values of spirit? The literary conventions of Luke's style do not include the disciples' response, only the master's intentions.

More importantly, how do *we* receive these rebukes? Do we find defensiveness rising in us when some of our prized ways of thinking and acting are confronted? Do not waste your time on revenge no matter how justified you think it is; seek other opportunities. Do not daydream about glory; face the harshness of the path of love in an unloving world. Do not become committed to a way of life that kills the spirit and cloak it in noble-sounding language; follow what gives you life. Do not always look outside yourself and seek permission from others; find your higher self and commit yourself to its unfolding. We might hear these injunctions as hammer blows on the house of the self we have carefully constructed.

It is here that Ferrucci's comments about Assagioli's style are helpful. There is a tendency to imagine Jesus' voice as a proclamation from on high, dropping bombshells into the natural ways we think and act. His superior wisdom can be imagined as a sword through the crowd, dividing those who had courage to follow him from those whose wimpiness won out. Scatter or gather is good drama. But what if Jesus' authoritative voice was disarming? What if his style was confidential, collegial, intimate, and filled with an obvious concern that the one to whom he was talking would fulfill their reason for being alive? What if he spoke the truth in love, so the context of confrontation was always kindness and invitation?

I suspect Jesus' rebukes did not leave people angry and confused. Rather, his direct words opened a door into a room of light, and together, Jesus and his disciple became curious about entering it.

Fourteenth Sunday in Ordinary Time

Proper 9

Luke 10:1-12, 16-20 *LM* • Luke 10:1-11, 16-20 *RCL*

❧

Handing on the Mission

A Spiritual Commentary

After this the Lord appointed seventy others and sent them on ahead of him in pairs to every town and place where he himself intended to go.

While Jesus was in the flesh, these seventy, a symbolic number indicating the faithful of Israel, went ahead of Jesus to convene people for his coming. This was standard procedure at the time. Whenever important people were going to arrive, messengers were sent ahead to make sure there would be a fitting welcome. But after Jesus' death, these pairs of disciples became "Jesus" in every town and place they visited. They carried the myth (the story of life, death, resurrection, and ascension) and the rituals (baptism, table fellowship, healing, etc.) that continued his revelation of God's purposes for creation. The mission had been handed on.

In fact, his disciples became Jesus to such an extent that the degree to which people received the disciples was the degree to which they received Jesus. And to the extent they received Jesus, they received the One who sent Jesus (Mark). God is the sender of Jesus; Jesus is the sender of the disciples; the disciples eventually become the senders of others. Anything that survives in time does so because of multiple handoffs, commissionings from one generation of people to another.

This sending chain is both discontinuous and continuous with the first sender. It is discontinuous because Jesus is not the first disciples, and the first disciples are not the next generation or any of the succeeding generations. The visible carriers are always changing. But the chain is also continuous with Jesus because it carries the original revelation. Therefore, the original revelation, the core tradition, is not lost. It is reincarnated in each new generation. However, this does not mean the tradition is a message that can be abstracted from the people who carry it. The people who carry the revelation are the revelation. The Christian mission is intensely and essentially interpersonal. Each new generation of carriers becomes the Body of Christ, the visibility of God's presence on earth.

As the Christian mission moved through time, it developed a number of different ways of thinking about this. One interesting twist concerned a reversal of who arrived first in "every town and place." In a physical and social sense, before Jesus' death his disciples went before him. But in a spiritual sense, Jesus was always going before his disciples, both before and after his death. Certain texts provided theological clues for this way of thinking.

During Jesus' life, the disciples walked behind him on the road. "They were on the road, going up to Jerusalem, and Jesus was walking ahead of them; they were amazed, and those who followed were afraid" (Mark 10:32); "He came out and went, as was his custom, to the Mount of Olives; and the disciples followed him" (Luke 22:39). After his death and resurrection, the disciples are still in the same position of following. "But go, tell his disciples and Peter that he is going ahead of you to Galilee; there you will see him, just as he told you" (Mark 16:7); "As they came near the village to which they were going, he walked ahead as if he were going on" (Luke 24:28). Both before and after his death, the master shows the way.

After Jesus' death, this meant more than that the disciples were obeying his command to preach the Good News to all nations. It suggested that Jesus was already active in the lives of the people of "every town and place" before the disciples arrived with his myth and rituals. The myth and rituals brought "explicitness" to what was already going on. But the presence of Jesus was invisible and everywhere. Sometimes this perception was grounded in Jesus' identity as the Eternal Word who was co-present throughout creation, and sometimes it was grounded in Jesus' resurrection that allowed him universal access to God's creation, an access that was not possible when he was particularized in the flesh. But however it was grounded, the missionary perception was that the Christ in the disciples met the Christ in the people of "every town and place." Once again, it was in and through the interpersonal relationships that the original revelation was reenacted in "every town and place."

He said to them, "The harvest is plentiful, but the laborers are few; therefore, ask the Lord of the harvest to send out laborers into his harvest."

A strict interpretation of this image would mean that the harvest is ready and the laborers are those who should gather it in. Someone has already sown the seed and the good earth has produced in abundance. But a wider interpretation sees the laborers as those who sow the seed, wait and watch its growth, and gather the wheat. Then the plentiful harvest becomes food for the world. The disciples have supervised the project from beginning to end.

However, there are few laborers with this combination of skills. It means they must work with people on a number of levels. They must preach and teach in such a way that the word enters the heart to be sown on good earth where it has the possibility of growing. Then once it grows, it will be endangered by lack of depth (it will have no roots) and competition from other interests (thorns) (Luke 8:13-14). The laborers must know how to avoid these destructive possibilities. Finally, when the harvest is ready, the laborers must know how to turn it to the benefit of all. The purpose of all this growth is to feed the world. The harvest is not the end; it is the beginning of another transformation. The final destiny of the seed is to be devoured, giving strength and direction to all who eat it.

The disciples are not simply to pray for numerically more laborers. They are to pray for laborers who have the complex abilities that are needed to turn the seed into food. In short, they are to pray for themselves. This prayer should not be a humble recital of their shortcomings followed by petitioning God to supply what they lack. Prayer is staying in touch with the ultimate sender, the one who made both the seed and the earth. In this way, the disciples will come to self-knowledge. When they know how the seed grew in them, first to harvest and then to food, they will grow in the art of guiding the seed through harvest to food in others. The Lord of the harvest does not arrive at the end. The Spirit has been the source of growth from the beginning.

> "Go on your way. See, I am sending you out like lambs into the midst of wolves. Carry no purse, no bag, no sandals; and greet no one on the road. Whatever house you enter, first say, 'Peace to this house!' And if anyone is there who shares in peace, your peace will rest on that person; but if not, it will return to you. Remain in the same house, eating and drinking whatever they provide, for the laborer deserves to be paid. Do not move about from house to house."

I cannot refrain from reading into these instructions the type of nervous letting go that parents experience when they send their children into the world. Jesus is sending the paired disciples off by reminding them of everything they need to know and do in order to be faithful to their mission. He may have sent them out without purse, bag, and sandals; but he did not send them out without advice.

He simultaneously hopes they are ready and knows they are not. In fact, they are lambs in a world of wolves. This means they are likely to be eaten. But, paradoxically, this is precisely who they should be. Jesus' way is a way of peace and not violence. In fact, peace should be their opening word, and they should evaluate their efforts by whether this word is received or rebuffed. If it is rebuffed, they are not defeated. Their "peace" merely returns to them to await another opportunity to go out.

Also, they must learn to combine single-minded haste with single-minded settlement. When they are "on the road," nothing must deter them from their destination. They are not to be overburdened with purse, bag, or sandals that would slow their journey and give the impression they were like other travelers. Also, they are not to be distracted and waylaid by greeting and meeting with people along the way. They are to keep their attention focused on their ultimate purpose.

But once they have arrived, they are to settle into "one house." Their labors will produce harvest and food and they are to be nourished and satisfied by whatever happens, "eating and drinking whatever is provided." They are not to become restless for more than is given them and wish they were in another house where their labor would produce more harvest and food. They are to be at peace wherever they are. Both the haste to arrive and the settlement once they have arrived are timely expressions of a mission-driven consciousness.

> **Whenever you enter a town and its people welcome you, eat what is set before you; cure the sick who are there, and say to them, 'The kingdom of God has come near to you.' But whenever you enter a town and they do not welcome you, go out into its streets and say, 'Even the dust of your town that clings to our feet, we wipe off in protest against you.' Yet know this: 'the kingdom of God has come near.' I tell you, on that day it will be more tolerable for Sodom than for that town."**

All the disciples can do is what Jesus did. They can offer the kingdom; they cannot make people accept it. In their words and deeds, in fact in their very presence, the kingdom "comes near." But the kingdom only "arrives" when people struggle to understand the meaning of eating and drinking together without any ulterior motive ("eat what is set before you") and what curing the sick symbolizes about God and about them. The Good News is always a meeting of divine word and action with the human heart; and the human heart is always a mixture of readiness and resistance, a combination of waiting flesh and un-yielding stone.

Although people's response will always range along a continuum of acceptance and rejection, the disciples can never become indifferent to how the offer of the kingdom is received. Too much is at stake. This is an offer of salvation and its refusal has serious consequences. Nothing might be left of the Lord's offer to the town that refuses the disciples' welcome. The messengers will not even carry the dust from their streets with them. Everything of that town will be left out of God's final restoration. In fact, in the final assize, Sodom, the biblical city of evil that God burned to the ground, will be more favorably treated. When the gracious offer is refused, it turns to judgment on those who have refused it.

> **The seventy returned with joy, saying, "Lord, in your name even the demons submit to us!"**
>
> **He said to them, "I watched Satan fall from heaven like a flash of lightening. See, I have given you authority to tread on snakes and scorpions, and over all the power of the enemy; and nothing will hurt you. Nevertheless, do not rejoice at this, that the spirits submit to you, but rejoice that your names are written in heaven."**

Jesus sent them out with explicit directions about how they should think and act. However, when they return, they say nothing about his directions. But they tell the story that is lifting their spirits. It is the story Jesus wants to hear. When he hears it, he knows the revelation has been passed on.

What they have learned from Jesus has enabled them to overcome demons. In this context, demons are those forces that destroy human-ity, that subvert God's purposes for creation. Mere humans are usually helpless against their superior negative power. But what Jesus has pro-vided ("in your name") has given the disciples the ability to exorcise these demons. Their joy comes from their discovery of this ability in themselves. The fact that the demons submit to them (*"to us"*) is the first thing they have to say upon returning to the master.

Jesus shares their joy; but he also puts it in a cosmic context that corrects their egocentric focus. In first-century mythology, whatever lives in the sky has power over the earth. Therefore, the ultimate power belongs to "our Father in heaven." But in this exchange Satan has usurped God's position. He lives in the sky, and so his negative power inhabits the earth.

However, when the disciples were offering the kingdom of God to people by preaching, teaching, curing, and exorcising, the power of Satan was lessened. He fell like lightening from the sky, a sudden decrease in his power of domination. This is precisely what Jesus wants. In fact, Jesus begins his debriefing of the returning disciples by reminding them it was he who gave them their power. So they should never be tempted to think it is theirs. "See, *I* have given you authority . . ."

Then he explains what this authority is so the disciples will come to an explicit knowledge of their mission. He does not want them to have had a success and yet remain unappreciative of the depth of what really happened. Jesus' power is to step on the snake and scorpion. The usual way of the human is to walk around the snake and scorpion, to avoid what can harm and kill. Although many people, including disciples, petition Jesus to keep evil away from them, his real mission is to confront evil, to go to those places where the enemy of the human is at work and crush its action.

Of course, this entails risk and danger. But Jesus assures them they will not be injured. "Nothing will hurt you." This is truly a remarkable statement from the one whose engagement with evil forces will lead to his crucifixion and death. He will be hurt. However, the key is in "you." There are many levels in the human person. Some levels are subject to pain and passing. But the level the disciples operated out of when they exorcised the demons is the level where they are connected to God, the real sky-dweller. This level is secured by God and is the real reason the demons submitted. They should never lose consciousness of "who" is doing the exorcising. It is this "you" that is beyond harm.

If they can keep this in mind, they will know the real reason for their joy. They should not rejoice because they have new powers and these powers swell them with a bursting sense of significance. They should rejoice because they are cooperating with God's ongoing creation. Creation is a fragile adventure, always hovering between the chaos of the demons and the order of God. The disciples have restored the order of God and contributed to the building of the kingdom. Therefore, their names, along with the name of Jesus, the one in whose name they have acted, are written in the sky, incorporated into the Divine Love that is luring the earth toward fulfillment. Now that is a real reason to rejoice.

Teaching

At the moment, I work for the Ministry Leadership Center out of Sacramento, California. The center provides programming for the senior leadership of five West Coast Catholic healthcare systems. Along with Larry O'Connell, the executive director, I create and implement a formation program that offers the working knowledge and skills that are necessary to lead the mission and ministry of Catholic healthcare. In short, at the behest of the sponsoring congregations of the five systems, we are trying to hand on a tradition.

The Second Vatican Council (1962–5) warranted this transition when it suggested the laity should be fully included in the apostolic mission of the church. This jump-started a new set of arrangements between the religious congregations who led the healthcare ministry and the laity who worked within the ministry. The shape of these new arrangements has been significantly altered by the declining presence of the sisters. The future of the Catholic healthcare ministry now depends on the transmission of the tradition to an interfaith leadership population.

The challenges in this situation are complex and intertwined. There are cultural, social, medical, financial, organizational, theological, and spiritual considerations. The contemporary situation is so different from the situation of this first-century text that there seems to be no connection at all. Yet both are focused on the same existential situation that arises with the reality of living in time. How do we pass on what is valuable to the next generation in such a way that they will take on the responsibility of passing it on to the generation after them? If we do not find a way, time, the great devourer, will swallow the Catholic healthcare tradition.

Is there any help to be had from this ancient text on how to pass on a tradition that goes all the way back to Jesus? Certainly, there is very little, if any, practical advice. The social contexts and medical practices of the first century are confined to past history. When Jesus gives instructions on how to travel, he does not mention security at the airports. And do the disciples have a license to practice medical curing? But there may be some subtler aspects about passing on a tradition that this first handoff, this transmission at the dawn of Christian faith, reveals.

When we reflect on a tradition, we can abstract from it what we think is essential. When we name its distinctive elements, we feel we know what we want to pass on. This is certainly legitimate, but often it obscures the living sense of the tradition that is embodied in people. In one of our formation sessions, we ask the participants to become aware they are middle people, holding the hands of those in the past and holding the hands of those in the future. When they mention whose hand from the past they hold, they know the tradition lives in interpersonal relationships. It is a stretch; but if we let consciousness off its leash, we will find ourselves in a chain that goes all the way back to the hand of Jesus. This is the apostolic tradition and it has always had the power to thrill Catholics. I suspect it has the power to thrill anyone who can honor the revelation of God in Jesus Christ. Without this cherished sense of historical connection to Jesus, traditions are abandoned and become part of the lost past.

Also, I like the fact that when the disciples return, they return in joy. They do not return with the solemn sense of having fulfilled a weighty obligation. They may be indebted to Jesus, but now they are following their own joy. Jesus is quick to tell them the joy they feel is more than their exaltation in newly found powers. It is because they have cooperated with God in lessening the destructiveness of life. I think this joy is the inner energy of handing on the mission. Teilhard de Chardin knew about this joy and named it in scientific-mystical terms.

> [S]ome sort of essential instinct makes me guess at the joy, as the only worthwhile joy, of co-operating as one individual atom in the final establishment of a world: and *ultimately nothing else can mean anything to me.* To release some infinitesimal quantity of the absolute, to free one fragment of being, for ever—everything else is but intolerable futility. ("How I Believe," in *Christianity and Evolution* [New York: Harcourt Brace Jovanovich, 1971] 111)

Rabindranath Tagore knew this joy when he found its path.

> I slept and dreamt life was joy.
> I awoke and saw life was service.
> I acted and behold service was joy.
> > (Selected Quotations of Rabindranath Tagore,
> > compiled by Alan Smolowe,
> > http://www.schoolofwisdom.com/tagorequotes.html
> > [accessed 27 April 2006])

And Jesus, the lover of the earth, was filled with this joy when he smiled and whispered into the ears of the people who would continue his revelation until the end of time, "Your names are written in heaven."

Fifteenth Sunday in Ordinary Time

Proper 10

Luke 10:25-37

❧

Flowing From and With Love

A Spiritual Commentary

Behold a lawyer stood up to test him, saying, "Teacher, what should I do to inherit everlasting life?"

Jesus answered, "What does the law say? How do you read it?"

The lawyer said, "You should love the Lord your God with all your heart, soul, mind, and might and your neighbor as yourself."

"You have answered rightly," Jesus said. "Do this and live."

At the time of Jesus, Jewish life was thicketed with laws. This multitude of laws was unified by the theory that they all grew out of the greatest commandment, the double commandment to love. "You should love the Lord your God with all your heart, soul, mind, and might and your neighbor as yourself." This double commandment was a combination of Deuteronomy 6:4-9 and Leviticus 19:18. It also reflected the two tablets of the Ten Commandments, the first three commanding love of God and the last seven commanding love of neighbor. When Jesus asked the lawyer, "What does the law say?" he easily recited this legal foundation. In fact, reading his ego between the lines, he could not resist the chance to shine.

At this stage in the story, the lawyer can *read* the law. But his question was" "What should I *do* . . . ?" He is in the position of most people. He can cite what the law is, but he cannot enact it. He has conceptual knowledge, but he does not have realized understanding. Realized understanding leads to doing. Although the lawyer may see his exchange with Jesus as a battle of wits, Jesus, the true teacher, is crafting his responses in service of the lawyer's request. He is trying to give him the ability to *do* the double commandment.

The lawyer is also hampered by "do to get" thinking. He thinks if he does something, what he does will win him the inheritance of everlasting life. His action will only have value because of the reward attached to it. So after he correctly identifies the double commandment of love, Jesus subtly corrects his "do to get" thinking. He tells him, "Do this and live." There is no gap between the present and the future. The action is its own reward. It is not a matter of doing something and then waiting for the reward, presumably after death. It is a matter of participating in everlasting life here and now through loving God and neighbor. When the lawyer combines realized understanding and illumined acting, he will be experiencing the everlasting life he so desires. Everlasting life is in the doing.

> **But the lawyer, wishing to justify himself, said, "Who is my neighbor?"**

> **Jesus replied, "A man was going down from Jerusalem to Jericho, and fell into the hands of robbers, who stripped him, beat him, and went away, leaving him half dead. Now by chance a priest was going down that road; and when he saw him, he passed by on the other side. So likewise a Levite, when he came to the place and saw him, passed by on the other side.**

> **But a Samaritan, while traveling, came near him; and when he saw him, he was moved with pity. He went to him and bandaged his wounds, having poured oil and wine on them. Then he put him on his own animal, brought him to an inn, and took care of him. The next day he took out two denarii, gave them to the innkeeper, and said, 'Take care of him; and when I come back, I will repay you whatever more you spend.'**

The lawyer's initial attitude was to test Jesus. Although he called him a teacher, he was not seeking to be taught. He considered himself the teacher and Jesus the student. His plan was to test how extensive and insightful Jesus' knowledge was. However, Jesus answered a question with a question and the quizzer became the quizzed. Things did not go as planned. Jesus turned the tables and tested him. Although he recited what he was asked to retrieve and passed the test admirably, the exchange ended with Jesus giving him an injunction. He was being told what to do. Although in his mind he was the greater, he looked the lesser. This was not acceptable.

So the lawyer begins the testing process again. His question "Who is my neighbor?" is meant to lead Jesus into a maze of opinions. He wants some legal wrangling about boundaries and obligations. And perhaps when the story begins, he thinks he is going to get what he wants. The Levite and the priest who saw the robbed and beaten man but passed by on the other side may or may not have been justified by the law. They might have been weighing their obligations, entertaining an inner debate about what they had to do or what they were excused from doing. If they touched a bleeding and/or dead body, they would become impure. If the man was not a Jew, there was no obligation. This fine-print thinking is the air that legal minds breathe. But it is the air that suffocates Jesus.

Jesus has a quite different strategy for telling this story. It is meant to sneak past the lawyer's defenses, to circumvent his tangled mind. The story uses the classic device of threes to contrast the refusal of the Levite and the priest with the energy and effectiveness of the Samaritan. Both the Levite and priest, knowledgeable in the law, can recite the double commandment. But, like the lawyer himself, neither of them can do it. In hearing the story, the lawyer does not identify with the robbed and beaten man or with the Samaritan; he is most like the Levite and priest who continue to go their way. As they leave the scene, they take with them the legal contest the lawyer had hoped to initiate.

What is left is the compassion and creativity of the Samaritan, a picture of a man doing "love of God and neighbor." It is crucial to understand that the Samaritan is an enemy of the Jewish man who has been robbed and beaten. In this way he fulfills the criteria Jesus has insisted on. "But I say to you that listen, Love your enemies, do good to those who hate you, bless those who curse you, pray for those who abuse you" (Luke 6:27-28). When people are able to do this, they reveal they have an interior connection to God who provides the strength and direction of their compassion. Without this connection their compassion would be reserved for normal familial and ethnic loyalties. But in sync with the God of all, they love all. "But love your enemies, do good, and lend, expecting nothing in return . . . and you will be children of the Most High; for he is kind to the ungrateful and the wicked. Be merciful, just as your Father is merciful" (Luke 6:35-36). The mercy of the Samaritan is ultimately the mercy of the Most High Father.

Therefore, the inner condition of the Samaritan corresponds to "love the Lord your God with all your heart, soul, mind, and might." He is in complete communion with God and cooperating with God's compassion. Although this inner state is not available to outside observation, it is manifested in the actions of the Samaritan. In communion with God, he knows himself as sustained by divine mercy at every moment and he also knows all people are sustained by this same mercy. Therefore, despite the ethnic hostilities between Samaritans and Jews, he sees a similarity so deep that the one God who loves him also loves the robbed and beaten man. Therefore, his neighbor is himself.

However, his God-grounded response to the robbed and beaten man is not only seen in the fact that he crosses ethnic boundaries. It is also revealed in the creativity and extent of his care. He does not seem to know limits. All his property, his "might," is put to work in his over-riding desire to bring healing. His bandages, oil, wine, animal, money, time, and ability to recruit others are freely and abundantly brought to bear in the project of restoring the man to health. The last line of the story (in a different translation) hints at the unending flow of care that only God can inspire: "I will pay you whatever is needed." The limit-less intent of "whatever is needed" is the sure tip-off that the Samaritan is loving his neighbor through the love of God.

> **"Which of these three, do you think, was a neighbor to the man who fell into the hands of the robbers?"**
>
> **He said, "The one who showed mercy."**
>
> **Jesus said to him, "Go and do likewise."**

Jesus' question is a cognitive restructuring of the lawyer's question. The lawyer asked, "Who is my neighbor?" This phrasing implies the initiative will come from the outside. When a proper object is seen, "neighbor," then the one who knows the law will spring into action. But who qualifies as "neighbor?" Debating that question results in ar-gument replacing action.

Jesus' phrasing implies a different starting place. "Which of these three, do you think, was a neighbor to the man who fell into the hands of the robbers?" places the emphasis on the interiority and action of the three characters in the story. It is not the outside person and his condition that spurs the action. The robbed and beaten man is the oc-casion; he is not the cause. The inspiration and creativity comes from the human compassion of the Samaritan that is grounded in the divine compassion, for how else would he have been able to love his enemy and produce such an abundance of effective care?

The lawyer's simple response shows that he understands the story and its teaching. He describes the neighbor as "the one who shows mercy." The mercy of the Samaritan is a manifestation, a revelation, a showing of divine mercy. The lawyer's question has been answered.

He has gone beyond recitation of the law. He now has a realized understanding of how to do love of God and neighbor. There is only one thing left, the most important thing, and the lawyer is now equipped for its difficult enactment. "Go and do likewise."

Teaching

I know this lawyer only too well. He embodies a mindset that afflicts many religious types. We have a great deal of conceptual knowledge of theology and spirituality, but our ability to integrate it into our daily lives is minimal. Therefore, in the absence of real-life connection, we prefer theological jousting. Arguing in abstract terms about what a theological conviction means masquerades as faith development. Ego games replace actions that flow from and with the soul.

Kenneth Pargament, a psychologist, thinks that connecting religious faith to real life is not easily done. He names the problem as the inability to take the generalities of faith and relate them to the dust of our human trials He quotes the incident between a husband and wife reported by a counselor.

> During one argument, the husband confronted the wife and asked what she thought they should do about the marriage, what direction they should take. She reached for her Bible and turned to Ephesians. "I know what Paul says and I know what Jesus says about marriage," he told her. "What do you say about marriage?" Dumbfounded, she could not say anything. Like so many of us, she could recite the scriptures, but she could not apply them to everyday living. Before the year was out, the husband filed for divorce.

Then Pargament remembers a situation from his own counseling experience. A clergyman had come to see him in distress after being in an accident that had left him paralyzed.

> The accident raised many fundamental questions for this man. Why had it happened? Could he have done anything to prevent it? How could he continue to function with his disability? Could he ever find enjoyment in living now that he truly knew how fragile life is? Yet in all his talk about these very basic issues of meaning, responsibility, and finitude he never mentioned a word about religious faith. . . . When I raised the question of where his religion fit into his struggle, he drew a blank. In spite of the fact that he often worked as a religious counselor to people in dire straits not unlike his own, he himself was unable to move from the generalities of his faith to the specifics of his situation. (*The Psychology of Religion and Coping: Theory, Research, Practice* [New York: Guilford Press, 1997] 163–6)

The woman is "dumbfounded" and the clergyman "draws a blank." When we merely quote the words of others or have our faith in a mental compartment, we cannot bring it forward as a resource for "the dust of our human trials." We cannot "do" love of God and neighbor.

This is a hard saying. If we do not work on our faith, it cannot work for us. It will not be part of who we are, and it will not be able to both motivate and console. The goal of working on our faith is to achieve what the lawyer initially lacks—realized understanding and illumined acting.

Realized understanding entails going beyond recitation of texts and the formal connection of ideas. We can say, "The Lord is my shepherd," but that does not mean the Lord actually is our shepherd. That will only happen through an internal process of realization and integration. Also, we can say, "People cannot justify themselves and they must open to the grace of God," but unless we speak that line from our own experience of the futility of the quest for perfection, it will not be available when we need it. There is no way around personal integrity. The authenticity of our own spiritual struggle is the only path from the generalities of faith to the dust of our human trials.

However, the goal of realized understanding is illumined acting. The Samaritan does not argue from his faith to his obligation. This would be the lawyer's predilection. The Samaritan is riding the river of mercy. His interior communion with the source of compassion is expressing itself in his mind, soul, heart, and might. His love of God made him compassion-ready and the robbed and beaten man triggered what was already in him. Illumined acting is co-acting with God. It is not a strenuous act of the will. Rather, it is an act of cooperation with an abundant source. It happens, and we happen with it. Illumined acting is flowing from and with love.

Although this way of acting may seem exceptional, we have all experienced it. There have been times when compassion has stirred in us before thought could intervene. We feel a spontaneous movement to include someone else. We have not pondered, or argued, or fussed. We have simply moved. This movement feels like the release of something that has been pent up. At a later time, we may be judged as foolish or reckless. But at this moment we are riding a spirit that, on a level deeper than strategic rationality, is "right."

But we also know the opposite experience. We have "stood and watched" and "passed by on the other side." We are numb and indifferent to the plight of another. Our feelings are frozen. Our mind is manufacturing reasons at warp speed, not "right" reasons but "good reasons not to act." An inner voice begins to talk to us as if we were a

very slow student. "It's not your concern. . . What can you do? . . .
He wouldn't help you. . . . It's a shame but . . ." If we have known
the rushing river of compassion, most probably we are also familiar
with the stalling tactics of the mind, how it conjures up ways out and
rationalizes evasions.

I like stories where Jesus' efforts as a teacher meet with success. So
when the lawyer indicates he has penetrated to the truth of the story,
I am pleased with both the art of Jesus' dialogue and the lawyer's advance in consciousness.

But I am not sanguine about the injunction to "go and do likewise."
That demands another step, one that will inevitably combine courage and creativity. The story may have ended, but all is not over. And
that certainly is part of the storyteller plan. Throughout the story we,
the readers, were meant to identify with the lawyer. We can recite the
double commandment to love God and neighbor. It was drummed into
us as children and it has become part of general cultural information.
But we are hard pressed to enact it. The story has showed us how it
works. It has given us instructions that are a preparation for action.
But now our surrogate, the lawyer, is nowhere to be found. He has left
the scene. Our cover has been blown. We are the receivers of the last
injunction: "Go and do likewise." The next step is up to us.

Sixteenth Sunday in Ordinary Time

Proper 11

Luke 10:38-42

❧

Integrating Mary and Martha

A Spiritual Commentary

Now as they went on their way, he [Jesus] entered a certain village, where a woman named Martha welcomed him into her home.

Martha welcomed Jesus into her home. Her home is not merely her house, her physical dwelling. It is her whole way of thinking and acting. When Jesus inhabits a dwelling place, he turns it into the Lord's house. (In this story Jesus is only referred to as the Lord.) In order to make Martha's home the Lord's dwelling, the Lord will have to correct the way Martha thinks and acts. But this correction is not unwanted criticism. She asked the Lord in; and although what follows will not be what she expects, it will be what she invited.

She had a sister named Mary, who sat at the Lord's feet and listened to what he was saying.

In spiritual teaching, sisters symbolize side-by-side realities that are meant to be together. Separating them diminishes both. Therefore, although Christian history is fond of playing Martha and Mary against one another, the real task is to discover their proper relationship. It is not a matter of which one is more important; it is a matter of how they complement each other. The teaching of the text is about discovering their mutuality.

Although Martha has not yet been characterized, Mary is quickly sketched as a contemplative. She is a dedicated disciple (sitting at the Lord's feet) absorbing the teachings of Jesus (listening to his every word). In Luke's Gospel, those who effectively hear the word must "hold it fast, in an honest and good heart, and bear fruit with patient endurance" (Luke 8:15). There is an inner activity (holding the word fast in an honest and good heart) that with steady perseverance overflows into an outer activity (bearing fruit in patient endurance). In this story, Mary is a representative of the inner activity.

> **But Martha was distracted by her many tasks; so she came to him and asked, "Lord, do you not care that my sister has left me to do all the work by myself? Tell her then to help me."**

Martha is a representative of outer activity that has disengaged from its inner grounding and has become scattered in multiple tasks. She speaks in a resentful tone and voices a complaint that resonates with every practical person. From her perspective, the problem is simply sized up. She is frantic and distracted because there are too many tasks. Her problem is the amount of work she has to do. Her mindset is universal. Too much to do and too little time to do it makes her frantic. She is the forerunner of multitasking.

But Martha has a solution. The obvious reason she is overwhelmed is that her sister has left her to do all the work by herself. If Mary would join her, "many hands make light work." This makes immense common sense, and throughout Christian history Martha's observation has been vigorously defended as a legitimate complaint. So she asks the Lord to tell Mary to help her. Of course, this means Jesus should do her bidding and tell Mary to help her on Martha's terms—abandon her inner activity of meditating on the teachings of the Lord and join the outer world of multiple tasks. Martha's strategy is to make the two sisters one, turning Mary into a clone of Martha. She wants to collapse the two-tiered, integrated world of Mary-Martha into the one-dimensional world of Martha-Martha.

> **But the Lord answered her, "Martha, Martha, you are worried and distracted by many things; there is need of only one thing. Mary has chosen the better part, which will not be taken away from her."**

However, the Lord sees things differently. Martha's problem is not that she has a lot to do and no one to help her. This is a skewed perception of Mary-Martha. Her real problem is her inner state of worry and distraction. This inner state undercuts her actions and makes them less effective, not "good." But this inner state is not caused by the multitude of tasks, as Martha thinks. Fewer tasks will not make her less discombobulated. The problem lies elsewhere.

Her anxious and scattered consciousness is the result of ungrounded activity. Martha has engaged the many without being rooted in the one thing necessary. Although the English translates this "one thing" as the "better part," the word in the Greek text is "good." The "good" part is the connection to God who is good, the ground and energy of effective action. Martha should not try to take this away from Mary and drag her into the outer world where Martha already flounders. The solution is not for Mary to become Martha or for Martha to become Mary. The spiritual project is to relate them to one another for the benefit of both. After all, they are sisters. The book of Wisdom knows how they flow into one another. "Although she [Mary] is but one, she can do all things [Martha], and while remaining in herself [Mary], she renews all things [Martha]" (Wis 7:27).

Teaching

In the story before the Mary and Martha episode, Jesus encounters a lawyer who wants to know what to *do* to inherit everlasting life. The lawyer can recite the double commandment to love, but he does not know how to put it into action. Jesus deflects his combative attitude and instructs him, through the story of the Good Samaritan, on how to *do* love of God and love of neighbor. The spiritual teaching is: the interiorly realized love of God is the energy and creativity of the outer action of loving the neighbor.

In the Martha-Mary story, the lesson is similar. But Jesus moves the other way, so to speak. Martha has no trouble doing. In fact, she is doing many things, but she is doing them without the one thing necessary. Her evaluation of the problem is wrongheaded. The very situation she thinks is the problem—Mary's sitting at the Lord's feet to absorb his teaching—is her only hope for productive and peaceful action. Jesus confronts Martha and points out clearly she must rethink the situation. Mary should not join her: she should join Mary. The spiritual teaching is that Mary is the one thing necessary, the interiorly realized love of God that is the energy and creativity of effective action in the world.

This Mary-Martha spiritual teaching also resonates with the stories of other religious traditions. There is an exchange in Sufi literature that points both to the importance and difficulty of embodying the dual consciousness of Mary-Martha.

"Master," said the disciple, "I saw a man who could fly."

"So?" said the master, "a bird can fly."

"Master," said the disciple, "I saw a man who could live under water."

"So?" said the master, "a fish can live under water."

"Master," said the disciple, "I saw a man who, in the twinkling of an eye, could move from one town to another."

"So?" said the master, "Satan can do that."

"If you wish to find something truly extraordinary," the master continued, "find a man who can be among people and keep his thoughts on God."

Superficial religion often gravitates to the spectacular. Men flying, living under water, and instantaneously traveling from one place to another are often considered the supernatural stuff of real religion. This exchange between master and disciple dismisses these accounts as the lower level activity of birds and fish. Then it even goes so far as to suggest that Satan is behind our attraction to these "miracles." The truly extraordinary feat is the Mary-Martha—being in the outer company of people with the inner company of God. This ideal is captured in the Sufi phrase, "in the world but not of the world."

The Hindu tradition also has a story that showcases the Mary-Martha consciousness. There was a king named Akbar who had a brilliant and clever prime minister named Birbal. Akbar was always testing Birbal.

One day Akbar asked Birbal if he could bring him someone who is Here and not There. Birbal brought him a thief, saying, "This thief is only in the world trying to get money and goods to increase his wealth Here."

Then Akbar told Birbal, "Bring me someone who is There and not Here. Birbal responded by bringing a wandering ascetic—a sadhu or mendicant—and said, "He completely neglects all aspects of this world, including his body, and his well being, to focus entirely on the world beyond, There."

"Now," said Akbar, "bring me someone who is neither Here nor There." Birbal thought for a while and returned with a beggar, saying, "This man is not Here for he is always envious of everyone else in the world. He is not participating in the world in any sense. But then, at the same time, he has no concern for spiritual matters. Thus, he is in no way There, either. He is neither Here nor There."

"Now," said Akbar, "is it possible that there is anyone in the world who is both Here and There?"

"Yes, your majesty," answered Birbal, and he brought forth an honest householder couple. "This man and woman work in the world and tend to their family, but do everything with God in their thoughts. Therefore, they are both Here and There."

"Very good," said Akbar, and immediately began to think about the next challenge he would give to Birbal (Adapted from Lorna Catford and Michael Ray, *The Path of the Everyday Hero* [Los Angeles: Jeremy P. Tarcher, Inc., 1991] 10–11).

The fickleness of consciousness is the backdrop of this teaching story. People are capable of many inner states. These states are symbolized by how they live in the world—thief, ascetic, and beggar. They can be here and not there, there and not here, or neither here nor there. But the final pride of place is given to the Mary-Martha ideal of being both here and there. It is this consciousness that is held up as something to be achieved by ordinary working people.

Both stories point to the importance of what in the Christian tradition is often called "recollection in action" or "contemplation in action." However, the phrasing—doing outer tasks with thoughts on God—could suggest a division of consciousness, indeed, even schizophrenia. This split picture is often reinforced by inherited religious rhetoric. In the Greek Orthodox tradition, St. Nicodemus of the Holy Mountain connects the Mary-Martha condition with the Pauline injunction to "pray without ceasing" (1 Thess 5:17).

> When the Apostle commanded us, "Pray without ceasing," he meant that we must pray inwardly with our intellect; and this is something that we can always do. For when we are engaged in manual labor and when we walk or sit down, when we eat and when we drink, we can always pray with our intellect and practice inner prayer, true prayer, pleasing to God. Let us work with our body and pray with our soul. Let our outer self perform physical work, and let the inner self be consecrated wholly and completely to the service of God and never flag in the spiritual work of inner prayer. (Quoted in Bishop Kallistos Ware, *The Inner Kingdom* [Crestwood, NY: St. Vladimir's Seminary Press, 2000] 85)

Talking about Mary-Martha consciousness in dichotomous ways gives the wrong impression. Dual consciousness does not cleave the inner from the outer, or drive a wedge between body and soul. Mary-Martha is an invitation to overcome the perceived division of inner and outer and body and soul. It does not want to make them permanent.

The Christian spiritual tradition is deeply aware of this dualistic problem and has many renditions of how Mary and Martha are integrated. Underlying the best of them is a critical understanding of divine reality. God is not one more object of human contemplation. To say, "work in the world with your thoughts on God" could be heard as setting up a competition. It appears we have to divide our attention between cooking and worship, or alternate between paying attention to the recipe or saying our prayers. But this would only be true if God and human effort were on the same level.

God is the ground or, in another image, the horizon of the finite world. When we are Mary, we realize that we are rooted in the ground of God or that our worldly figure can only be seen correctly against the horizon of God. Creation and Creator are in an intimate and unbroken relationship. Our Mary consciousness has learned this God-relatedness from sitting at the feet of the Lord and pondering his teachings. When this inner Mary consciousness connects with Martha the outer actor, a further revelation occurs. The God who grounds us grounds all things; the horizon against which we know the fullness of ourselves is the horizon that reveals the fullness of all things. And this commonly shared Source and Destiny is not a static object. It is a dynamic reality who calls us to participate in its creative activity.

Therefore, we do not have to interiorly think about God while doing exterior things. We have to use our inner disposition toward the divine to discern the lure of God in every situation and cooperate with it to make that situation all it can be. God is both inside and outside, a power that sustains our personal being and a summons that calls us to cooperate in building a just world. When we wake up to this revelation that all things exists and are suffused by divine life, we simultaneously wake up to our identity as Mary-Martha.

Seventeenth Sunday in Ordinary Time

Proper 12

Luke 11:1-13

❧

Praying Someone Else's Prayer

A Spiritual Commentary

He was praying in a certain place, and after he had finished, one of his disciples said to him, "Lord, teach us to pray, as John taught his disciples."

Jesus was praying by himself. He was not in a prescribed place like the Temple or a prescribed time like sundown; he was just in a *certain* place. Official praying has official places and times. But regular prayer places and times are for regular people. Jesus lives in a rhythm of prayer and action, swimming in both the waters of God and the waters of the world. He knows when he must turn toward God and when he must turn toward the incessant demands of the world. Now was the time to turn toward God.

His disciples must have been watching because they knew when he had finished praying. Whatever they saw when they watched him created desire. But they do not request a disquisition on prayer in general. They want to pray the way Jesus prays. Perhaps after following Jesus for a while and observing him closely, they have surmised that "how to connect with God" is the key to his unpredictable attitudes and behaviors. If they could connect to God as Jesus does, their difficulties in following him might be significantly lessened.

Or perhaps they are claiming an expectation of the master-disciple relationship. Masters were expected not only to instruct disciples but also to share their way of prayer with them. This is what John the Baptist had done. But they are apprenticed to Jesus, and it is time for him to measure up. Jesus is never shy about telling the disciples what it takes to be a disciple. Now the favor is returned. "Lord, teach us to pray, as John taught his disciples."

He said to them, "When you pray, say: 'Father, hallowed be your name, your kingdom come. Give us each day our daily

**bread. And forgive us our sins for we ourselves forgive every-
one indebted to us. And do not bring us to the time of trial.'"**

Jesus gives the disciples words to say. These words lack solemnity.
Jesus does not have a flattering and deferential approach to the awe-
some reality of God. The opening address is familiar and immediate. It
is as if Jesus is talking to someone incredibly close. His simple "Father"
is a forerunner and inspiration of Augustine's classic insight that God is
more intimate to me than I am to myself and of Teresa of Avila's insight
that God resides at the center of the human person. Then this revelation of closeness unfolds into other words that disclose an interlocking
unity between the Father and the ones praying, the children. After all,
this is the way of praying of the beloved Son (Luke 3:22; 9:35).

Jesus' way of praying does not start with human need. The ones
praying do not ask God for something for themselves. Rather, they
unite themselves to the being ("hallowed be your name") and activity
("your kingdom come") of the Father. This complete dedication to the
being of the Father translates into the being of the ones praying ("Give
us this day our daily bread"); and the complete dedication to the activity of the Father translates into the activity of the ones praying ("And
forgive us our sins for we ourselves forgive everyone indebted to us").
The hallowing of God's name becomes the daily bread (sustaining
strength) of the children; and the coming of God's kingdom becomes
the divine-human and interhuman forgiveness that facilitates the new
humanity. This succinct prayer transforms the ones praying and the
Father into a unity of being and doing.

In this way, the prayer brings about a new reality, a God-Person
unity walking the earth. However, the earth is predominately populated by humans who are alienated from God. The ideal interaction
between this God-Person unity and alienated humans would be invitation and response. The God-Person would offer to others what is in
himself or herself, and these others would see the truth and beauty of
this offer and accept it. Jesus' way of praying sows a seed in the ones
praying. This seed is destined to become a tree and attract all the birds
of the air (Mark 4:30-32). All nations will be drawn to them.

But there is another scenario, the scenario that played itself out in
the life of Jesus. The alienated humans will reject the offer and attack
the ones who offer it. The God-Person will be tempted to violent reprisal. But he or she must remain in union with God and return only love
(Luke 6:27-36). This is the test, and it must never be foolishly courted.

It comes about only as a last resort. Even Jesus' prayer in the Garden begins by hoping for an outcome that does not happen. "Father, if you are willing, remove this cup from me" (Luke 22:42). Everything is subordinated to the will of God, but a peaceful, nonviolent path is the hope. So the prayer that Jesus teaches his disciples ends not with the inevitability of trial but with the hope it will not come about. "And do not bring us to the time of trial."

> And he said to them, "Suppose one of you has a friend, and you go to him at midnight and say to him, 'Friend, lend me three loaves of bread; for a friend of mine has arrived, and I have nothing to set before him.' And he answers from within, 'Do not bother me; the door has already been locked, and my children are with me in bed; I cannot get up and give you anything.' I tell you, even though he will not get up and give anything because he is his friend, at least because of his persistence he will get up and give him whatever he needs.
>
> And so I say to you, Ask and it will be given you; search and you will find; knock and the door will be opened for you. For everyone who asks receives, and everyone who searches finds, and for everyone who knocks, the door will be opened.
>
> Is there anyone among you who, if your child asks for a fish, will give a snake instead of a fish? Or if the child asks for an egg, will give a scorpion?
>
> If you then, who are evil, know how to give good gifts to your children, how much more will the heavenly Father give the Holy Spirit to those who ask him!"

The disciples have been taught the words of prayer. But more is needed. They must have the proper interior disposition. This proper interior disposition is based on a correct understanding of who they are and who God the Father is. Jesus provides this understanding by using a combination of story-images and injunctions. These story-images and injunctions connect to his prayer by using the image of Father and children that is the core structure of the prayer. These story-images are geared not merely to inform the disciples but to jolt them into the mindset that will make the words of the prayer effective.

In the first story-image, the disciples are asked to put themselves in the position of going to a friend at the inconvenient hour of midnight to request bread for another friend who has recently arrived in the village. Their friend rebuffs them because at this late hour the doors are locked and he and his children are in bed. Their request, which is not for themselves but for another, meets a locked door. This is not how God the Father and the children who pray to him would respond.

But Jesus assures them this locked door will open. If it will not open for friendship, it will open because with persistent requesting the friend [*sic*] will relent, get out of bed, open the door, and give the bread. Some scholars suggest the word "persistence" should be "shame." The idea is that village hospitality is at stake. If the man does not give the bread, the whole village will be shamed. When word gets around of how he has dishonored the village, he will be ostracized. So a concern for his own well-being will drive him to give the bread. The point is: in the human world even those who are reluctant eventually give bread.

In the second story-image, the disciples are not the ones who ask but the ones who are asked. Their children request food from them. Surprisingly, they give to their children what they request—fish and eggs. They somehow manage to do this even though they are evil and, therefore, would be predisposed to give snakes and scorpions. The point is: in the human world even those who are evil give good sustenance to their children. Both the parent in bed and the evil parents are people who give food despite serious obstacles in their willingness and ability to give. Against all odds, giving happens.

If giving the stuff of physical life happens despite obstacles in the giver, how much more will giving the stuff of spiritual life happen when the Giver has no obstacles? The heavenly Father is completely predisposed to give the Holy Spirit, the reality that connects the human and divine worlds. There is no reluctance, inconvenience, or evil in God. The Father is willing, wanting, and waiting to give the Holy Spirit.

Therefore, the ones praying must not hold back. They are to ask, seek, and knock. These activities will be successful: they will receive, find, and gain entrance. This success is not because they overcome resistance in the Giver, for there is no resistance in the Giver. It is successful because their acts of asking, seeking, and knocking open them to receive what is ready to be given. With an abundant and eager Giver, the key to a meeting between the asker and the Giver is the openness of the ones who ask.

Therefore, the correct inner disposition in praying the prayer of Jesus is to realize you are not petitioning God for something God may or may not be willing to give. You are opening yourself to receive the Holy Spirit whom the Father wants to communicate. Learning how to pray the prayer of Jesus is learning the art of reception. This prayer is about allowing the Holy Spirit to create a bond between the heavenly Father and the earthly children, a bond that will jump-start the adventure of discipleship.

Teaching

When Jesus says, "When you pray, say . . . ," he began a tradition that continues to this day. Christian teachers pass along the Lord's Prayer by instructing people, mostly children, to repeat the phrases. (The rendition of the Lord's Prayer that is used is Matt 6:9-13). These teachers are eager to drill the prayer into the next generation and applaud young minds for perfect recitation. This method of imprinting has been effective. If even a nominal Christian is awakened at three in the morning by a blinding flashlight and a husky voice saying, "Say the Lord's Prayer or suffer the consequences," he or she will speed through it from "our" to "amen."

In fact, the Lord's Prayer has become an all-purpose prayer that the Christian has for every occasion. When we are happy or when we are sad, when we eagerly wait for a child to be born or silently stay as an elder dies, when we hear of a plane going down or attend a church going up, when we stroll alone in the woods or gather together in Christian assembly, when we are filled with gratitude or emptied by grief, when we are driven to praise or dragged to repent, we reach for the Lord's Prayer. It is a prayer we know. The familiar words are on our lips.

However, there is a danger in having memorized the words so effectively. We may mindlessly repeat them. We are able to say them without attending to what we are saying. Consequently, we never quite get into the prayer. It never expresses the thoughts of our minds or the feelings of our hearts. We have not apprenticed ourselves to the meaning of the words and learned to enter into that meaning every time we say them. Instead we have mastered the phrases and rattle them off. This is often the fate of inherited prayers.

Recently, I was at a wedding reception where the minister was asked to say grace before meals. He began abruptly. "A man was being chased by a lion and he came to a cliff. He had no way to escape and looked back to see the lion approaching. He decided to pray. He knelt on the ground, closed his eyes, and prayed with all his heart. After a while he opened his eyes. The lion was fifteen feet away from the man. Much to his surprise, the lion was also kneeling and had his paws piously folded in prayer. The man strained to hear what the lion was saying. The words were familiar, especially to those assembled here tonight. The lion was saying . . ."

At this point, the minister gestured for us to join in. Everyone prayed with gusto and without missing a beat. "Bless us, O Lord, for these your gifts which we are about to receive from your bounty through Christ our Lord." With little or no difficulty, the group was able to draw this traditional prayer out of the bank of memory. God was honored with the lips. But where were the hearts?

The mystical traditions are especially sensitive to this problem of saying established prayers without the corresponding interiority. In a classic Jewish story, "The Shepherd's Pipe," a villager does not take his son to the synagogue services because the boy is too slow to learn the Hebrew prayers. Since he cannot learn the prayers, it is assumed he cannot worship. However, on the feast of the atonement the father brings him along. He is afraid that if he leaves the boy alone, he will inadvertently eat and break the sacred fast. The father does not know that the boy has a shepherd's pipe hidden in the pocket of his jacket.

During the service the boy implores the father to let him play his pipe. The father refuses and finally grasps tightly the pocket that holds the pipe. But the boy, driven by desire, wrests the pipe from his father's grip and lets out a blast. The entire congregation is startled. The Bal Shem Tov, who is officiating at the service, tells the congregation that it was this spontaneous "blast from the pipe of the babe" that brought "all their prayers to the throne of God before the gates of heaven closed" (*Jewish Folktales Selected and Retold by Pinhas Sadeh* [New York: Doubleday, 1989] 396).

One message of this simple yet profound tale is that genuine prayer comes from the center of one's being (symbolized by the shepherd's pipe). The boy does not know the inherited prayers, and so he cannot use them. But he may sense that those who are using them are doing so ineffectively. The prayers are not reaching heaven because they are not coming from the center of the ones praying. There is a split between who they are and what they are saying. The problem is not the inherited Hebrew words themselves, but the disjunction between these words and the interiority of the people using them. The "blast from the pipe of the babe" is a unified action, bringing together inner awareness and outer expression.

One of Leo Tolstoy's mystical short stories illumines the same contrast between genuine spiritual expression and inherited prayers.

A bishop, traveling by ship, is told that three hermits are living on a nearby island. He concludes that they are within his jurisdiction and it is his duty to inspect their orthodoxy. He persuades the captain of the ship to change course and put him ashore on the island.

He finds the hermits and asks them if they are Christian. They wholeheartedly respond, "Yes!" He inquires how they pray and they tell him, "When we pray, we say, "We are three. You are three. Have mercy on us." This unauthorized and perhaps heretical prayer horrifies the bishop. He quickly instructs them in the Lord's Prayer, which he believes is the only proper way to pray if one is Christian. They do their best to learn the words, but they are not quick studies. Finally, the bishop returns to the ship, satisfied he has done his duty.

On another trip of the bishop, the ship is sailing past the island of the three hermits. Looking at the island, the bishop remembers with pleasure his pastoral efforts at instructing them in prayer. Later that evening, while strolling on deck, the bishop sees a ball of light come out of the island and move toward the ship. As the ball of light gets closer to the ship, the bishop sees the three hermits are within it. They speak from within the sphere of light and tell the bishop they have forgotten some of the Lord's Prayer. They need him to reinstruct them. The bishop is jolted into a new level of awareness and awakened to the holiness of the hermits, a holiness more profound than the correct recitation of words. The humbled bishop merely says, "Go home and when you pray, say, 'You are three. We are three. Have mercy on us'" (*Stories of the Spirit, Stories of the Heart: Parables of the Spiritual Path from Around the World*, eds. Christian Feldman and Jack Kornfield [San Francisco: HarperSanFrancsico, 1991] 25-6).

Once again, genuine spiritual illumination is played off against memorized inherited prayer, in this case the central prayer of the Christian tradition. The hermits have found their own way of praying, and it obviously "works." They are enveloped in divine light, even though they cannot remember the Lord's Prayer that the bishop taught them. These two stories use conventional religiosity with its emphasis on correct formulas as a contrast to develop a more complete understanding of prayer. Prayer is not mere mouth material but the inner being of the human person in communion with God.

However, the lesson of these stories is not to abandon the inherited prayer of Jesus because it is prone to rote repetition. The lesson is to learn how to mindfully inhabit the structured words of the transcendent consciousness of Jesus. Even after it was given to the disciples and through them to us, the Lord's Prayer remains the *Lord's* Prayer. It is the expression of a consciousness that is not our own. In saying the words, we are meant to enter into that consciousness and make it our own. Therefore, the saying of the words must be matched by an interior alertness to their meaning. This "alertness" is more than a general orientation of devotion to God. It means directing an interior journey, savoring meanings until they become the atmosphere of our very being. In this way repetition does not lead to mindless mouthing but to an ever deeper integration between the consciousness of Jesus and our consciousness.

I have found alternating between the rendition of the Lord's Prayer in Matthew and the rendition in Luke is a help in this process of interior conversion. In public settings we pray Matthew's version. Circumstances usually dictate that we say it fast and in unison. There is no time for slow meditative work. However, when we say the prayer in private, a slower and deeper process is possible. In this setting, in this certain place, Luke's unfamiliar version can hold our attention. Its potent coupling of phrases cleanly carries the agenda of pouring the self-giving, generative love of God into the empty cup of the human heart. When this happens, the cup is destined to overflow (Ps 23:5).

Eighteenth Sunday in Ordinary Time

Proper 13

Luke 12:13-21

❦

Balancing Trade-Offs

A Spiritual Commentary

Someone in the crowd said to him, "Teacher, tell my brother to divide the family inheritance with me."

But he said to him, "Friend, who set me to be a judge or arbitrator over you?"

And he said to them, "Take care! Be on your guard against all kinds of greed; for one's life does not consist in the abundance of possessions."

Rabbis routinely intervened and settled disputes about family inheritance. Jesus is a rabbi and so "someone in the crowd" calls on him to intervene on his behalf. It seems the man has been shut out. His brother has the whole estate. What he seeks is a division of the assets, and he wants Jesus to do the dividing. However, Jesus does not see it as an issue of justice to be fairly mediated. His question concerns the petitioner's assumption that he would take up the role of judge or arbitrator. This role means he will divide the inheritance and break the bond between the brothers. This is not a role for Jesus, the bringer of peace, the reconciler of divided people (Luke 2:14).

Then Jesus admonishes the petitioner. He is to stay alert and ward off all kinds of greed. Greed takes many forms in the sense that it has many objects. It can covet money, fame, sex, compliments, power, etc. But the appetite of greed is always the same: it eats yet remains hungry. The person cannot be satisfied by the acquisition of the desired objects. They always need more; but when they get more, this more is not enough. So they pursue again. Greed is an endless search for more that always leaves the searcher experiencing lack rather than fulfillment.

Once greed is triggered in a person, its fierce energy is difficult to curb. So Jesus advises not to let it get close. "Be on guard" is an image of watching for an impending danger. It is as if greed is lurking outside on the edges of the person's skin. It is waiting for an opportunity to sneak past lax defenses and seize possession of the house. If he does not "take care," one day he will awake and find himself inhabited by what he did not ward off.

Greed is always self-defeating because of its ultimate goal. It does not merely want more of its object. It has projected onto its object a power the object does not have. The object must give and/or secure life. "Life" can mean physical survival, or it can mean a sense of meaning, or zest, or inner calm. This is the heart of the problem. Life, in any of the above senses, does not consist in accumulating anything. In fact, life cannot be possessed. Since by definition it is more than we are, our fist does not fit around it. Grabbing is not how it is held. And grabbing more and more, "abundant possessions," only compounds the problem. This poor petitioner only wanted Jesus to side with him. Instead, Jesus confronts him, suggesting his desire for equity might mask a foolish greed that will bring him to grief.

> Then he told them a parable: "The land of a rich man produced abundantly. And he thought to himself, 'What should I do for I have no place to store my crops?' Then he said, 'I will do this: I will pull down my barns and build larger ones, and there I will store all my grain and goods. And I will say to my soul, 'Soul, you have ample goods laid up for many years; relax, eat, drink, and be merry.'
>
> But God said to him, 'You fool! This very night your life is being demanded of you. And the things you have prepared, whose will they be?'
>
> 'So it is with those who store up treasures for themselves but are not rich toward God.'"

This parable is a picture of greed in action. The land produces abundantly. Life is always creating more and more. Human effort may always be involved, but the story stresses the preexistent given of the earth, the earth that was not created by the rich man. When faced with this crop excess that the earth provided, the question is: how should we participate in this abundance? This is not a problem for the rich man. His mental life is structured by the habit of possession. At the sight of the abundance his first thought is how to contain it. "What should I do for I have no place to store my crops?"

The physical act of possession is simple enough. He must find a larger container. He talks to himself about his action plan—demolition and construction. But then he goes deeper, to the soul space, where the driving energy of his plans resides. In an ironic observation, he tells his soul to relax and enjoy the good times. What they—he and his soul—now possess will give them a life of sustenance and merriment. However, in classical thought, the soul receives its life from God and gives this life into the mind, body, and world. It lives not by possession but by flow.

Suddenly, God enters the story, the original *deus ex machina*. God declares that the way this man thinks is foolish. "Fools say in their hearts, 'There is no God'" (Ps 14:1). This man has responded to life without any consideration of the inevitability of death. The man had promised his soul ample goods for many years. But this night his soul will go on a journey. There is no way to hold onto life in this world. As for what his soul once possessed? It will not be controlled from the grave, an uncontested inheritance. Who knows? Perhaps one of his sons will grab it all and another son, brother to the grabber, will have to beg a wandering rabbi to intervene? Who knows how the wandering rabbi will respond?

This story, as all moral tales, ends with a lesson. You can store up treasures for yourself, thinking they will give you life. But this way of thinking and acting goes against the grain of the life you want. So it is a self-defeating strategy. However, there is another way. It is called "rich toward God." The story does not spell it out. But I suspect part of being "rich toward God," the psychological part, has something to do with lying on the abundant land and letting the grain grow right through your body without ever thinking of a barn.

Teaching

As a sixty-four-year-old middle-class American in the year 2006 of the Common Era, I find this spiritual teaching about greed both extremely relevant and woefully inadequate.

Family inheritances today have the same destructive potential that they did in the times of Jesus. Brothers and sisters will go to war over the parents' estate, leaving their relationships to one another in tatters. Even when the parents saw this coming and created legal obstacles, it means nothing. The children cheerfully hire lawyers and grab at each other's monopoly chips. Inheritance squabbles happen among the poor and the rich, but the rich seem to take to it with particular verve. It is not a battle over the necessities of life. It is a matter of hand-over-hand excess. When Jesus confronts the petitioner, we do not have to consult first-century culture to sense his disapproval.

Also, the rich man's inner life is no stranger to any of us. The dreams of financial security, a life without work, and round after round of eating and drinking drive us to the lotto every Saturday night. Although we read stories about how sudden wealth has led to personal and professional disaster, we assume we can handle it. God is not going to burst into our banquet shouting, "You fool!" In other words, the dream of riches that will secure life and make us happier than we are now is built into the bones of ordinary people. We are deaf to the warnings of every spiritual tradition that this way of securing life is futile. But the warning remains: beware this false promise that is so wildly attractive.

This is eternally good advice, and not to listen to it is foolishness. However, even when it is heeded, it leaves us facing the contemporary world of work, shelter, relationships, and finances. It has put in place some boundaries but it has not mapped the territory. It seems this spiritual wisdom leads to the contemporary conversation around balance and money sanity, but it does not contribute a lot to it.

Most people make money by working. So we seek out work that will compensate us enough to live the way we want. But, of course, we want work that suits our personalities, work that allows our gifts and talents to be expressed. Unfortunately, there is often a tension between work that will fulfill us and work that will compensate us. What we like to do doesn't pay; and what we don't like to do pays a lot. So a trade-off begins.

This trade-off is complicated by two other drives. We want to work with people we like. If we have a boss that bullies us or coworkers who do not respect us, we begin to look elsewhere. But if we like what we do and the pay is good, we may put up with the boss and coworkers. Also, we want work that contributes to the common good. But often that kind of work is considered its own reward. Compensation is low. So once again, we are engaged in the delicate effort of trade-off or, more positively, balance.

In the world of work we seek a balance among fulfillment, compensation, community, and contribution. As we age and as we encounter different circumstances, we juggle these factors differently. If we have more responsibilities in our relational life outside work, compensation becomes more important. If we lose our work, money occupies our mind. If we are approaching retirement without sufficient funds or medical insurance, money management is our day-in day-out strategy. In these situations, and many more, it is not a matter of fantasizing about how to be perfectly secure. It is a matter of trying to stay afloat.

This is why the spiritual wisdom about greed in this passage is simultaneously relevant and inadequate. We always have to be reminded about our tendency to make something finite infinite. Thinking we can secure life and ward off death by accumulation is always a temptation. And just knowing that may be the grounding for an approach to money sanity. But it does not take us far along the path of balance. It establishes priorities, but it contributes little to the ongoing processes of discernment and action. How will we work in a world where fulfillment, compensation, community, and contribution are now and always will be a trade-off?

Nineteenth Sunday in Ordinary Time

Proper 14

Luke 12:32-48 LM • **Luke 12:32-40** RCL

‮❦‬

Receiving and Giving

A Spiritual Teaching

"Do not be afraid, little flock, for your Father's good pleasure to give you the kingdom. Sell your possessions, and give alms. Make purses for yourselves that do not wear out, an unfailing treasure in heaven, where no thief comes near and no moth destroys. For where your treasure is, there your heart will be also.

This teaching concludes Luke's account of Jesus' famous teaching about the ravens of the air and the lilies of the field (Luke 12:22-31). The little flock is encouraged to adopt the alternative consciousness that is advocated in that teaching. The dominant consciousness sees life as an anxious project for survival, constantly concerned with food, clothing, and shelter. The alternative consciousness proposes considering life as a gift given from beyond itself. This gift is previous to our toil and the Source of Life feeds it. ("Consider the ravens: they neither sow nor reap, they have neither storehouse nor barn, yet God feeds them" [Luke 12:24]). The purpose of this feeding is so that life can unfold from the inside into a beautiful outside. ("Consider the lilies, how they grow: they neither toil nor spin; yet I tell you, even Solomon in all his glory was not clothed like one of these" [Luke 12:27]). Considering life as an anxious project for survival is not completely eliminated. Rather the anxious project is integrated into the gracious gift, and the gracious gift transforms it.

Adopting the consciousness of life as a gracious gift is risky business. It may compromise the struggle to survive. But the little flock is not to be afraid of this strange new way. Their struggle will be grounded in the Father's good pleasure. Giving life is what delights the Father. The generative love of the Source is thrilled to give life (the kingdom) to all who can receive it. Therefore, this way is built into the ultimate structure of reality. Once life is received from a bountiful Giver, whoever receives it naturally gives this life to others. The desire to possess is folded into the desire to give as we have received.

This consciousness of receiving and giving reflects the eternal order of things. In the perpetual perishing of time, physical and social possessions are eaten by moths (finitude) or stolen by thieves (sin). But the receiving and giving of life is beyond both destruction and plunder. If the disciples value (treasure) this, it will gradually enter the center of their being (the heart). The heart is the spiritual core of the person that receives from God and gives into the world. This is the spiritual development that characterizes life in the kingdom.

> **Be dressed for action and have your lamps lit; be like those who are waiting for their master to return from the wedding banquet, so that they may open the door for him as soon as he comes and knocks. Blessed are those slaves whom the master finds alert when he comes; truly I tell you, he will fasten his belt and have them sit down to eat, and he will come and serve them. If he comes during the middle of the night, or near dawn, and finds them so, blessed are those slaves.**

> **But know this: if the owner of the house had known at what hour the thief was coming, he would not have let his house be broken into. You also must be ready, for the Son of Man is coming at an unexpected hour."**

It is difficult to enter into the consciousness of receiving life as a gift. There is a need for vigilance and attentiveness. Although from a theological perspective life is never self-sustaining, we are not always aware of our dependency on the Creator. However, there are special moments when the abiding truth of our condition comes home to us. This is when we recognize the master has arrived from the wedding feast. It is not so much he has come from a wedding feast as he brings the wedding feast with him, allowing his life and our life to flow into each other. This happens because we are alert and open the door when he knocks.

And strangely, the roles of slave and master are reversed. It is the master who feeds us and serves our well-being, filling us abundantly. The most subversive truth is that the master's pleasure is not in being served but in serving. Even more, he is precisely the master because this is his desire. "For who is greater, the one who is at the table or the one who serves? Is it not the one at the table? But I am among you as one who serves" (Luke 22:27).

However, there is no way to predict or prescribe when this consciousness of being fed by God will arrive. It may be anytime—in the middle of the night or at dawn. But, most likely, it will be at an unexpected hour. So the most reasonable preparation is constant alertness. This vigilance signifies a readiness to be blessed by the Reality who is always ready to bless.

> **Peter said, "Lord, are you telling this parable for us or for everyone?"**
>
> **And the Lord said, "Who then is the faithful and prudent manager whom his master will put in charge of his slaves, to give them their allowance of food at the proper time? Blessed is that slave whom the master will find at work when he arrives. Truly, I tell you, he will put that one in charge of all his possessions. But if that slave says to himself, 'My master is delayed in coming,' and if he begins to beat the other slaves, men and women, and to eat and drink and get drunk, the master of that slave will come on a day when he does not expect him and at an hour that he does not know, and will cut him in pieces and put him with the unfaithful. That slave who knew what the master wanted, but did not prepare himself or do what was wanted, will receive a severe beating. But the one who did not know and did what deserved a beating will receive a light beating.** (Luke 12:41-48, NRSV)

Peter wants to know the audience of Jesus' parable. Is this a teaching for disciples, or for all in the community, or even all human beings? But Jesus changes the question (as he is in the habit of doing) and in the process answers Peter's question at a deeper level. Continuing the household metaphors of the first parable, Jesus' question is: who is the faithful and prudent manager who can give food at the proper time?

In the first parable the master has fed the servants. The response of the servants is to feed other servants, to give as they have received. If they are able to do this, they move up from servants to managers who are both faithful to what they have received and prudent in how they give it away. These are the ones who are put in charge of the master's possessions because they know from experience what those possessions really are and how the master distributes them.

In this context the answer to Peter's question seems to be: the parable is for all. But the teaching is necessarily received and enacted along a continuum. Some will receive it and put it to work immediately and by their actions make themselves both faithful and prudent managers. Others will not be able to stay open to the presence of the master, think he is delayed, and go about acting as if he had never been served at table by the master. He will focus food and drink on himself and abuse others. This behavior is self-destructive because it "cuts him in pieces," separating him from his natural communion with God and others. This failure to give as one has received can be triggered in two ways. If someone knows what is required and does not do it, he or she is more responsible than one who does not know what is required and does not do it. Ignorance of receiving life from God lessens the consequences of negative behavior from "a heavy beating" to a "light beating." But there is still a beating. Jesus' teachings stress the human possibility of kingdom living, but they never back off the fact that actions have consequences.

> **From everyone to whom much has been given, much will be required; and to the one to whom much has been entrusted, even more will be demanded.** (12:48, NRSV)

This general maxim concludes the parables. It concerns the proportion, and even the increase, between what has been given and what is required and what has been entrusted and what is demanded. In this sense, it sees the life that flows from the pleasure of the Father as a developmental possibility in the life of the children.

If there has been a profound realization that our life is a gracious gift from God, then we are accountable to give that gift to others. The sense of "givenness" is accompanied by a sense of necessity. We are bound to an unfolding pattern; we are required to play out the spiritual process the Source has initiated. When the requirement aspect appears, the "givenness" is seen more deeply as an entrustment. We have been entrusted with life in order to increase it. This increase means we give it to others, and in the process there is more life for us and for others. The master feeds the slaves and the slaves who realize what is happening become faithful and prudent managers who give the food of life to others at the proper time and in the proper way so they may grow strong on it. This is life in the kingdom and this is how it is transmitted from the graciousness of the Father through the receptiveness of the children and into the world of all who are willing to receive it.

Teaching

Many years ago I had an experience around receiving and giving possessions that prepared me for a deeper experience around receiving and giving life.

I was a young man, fresh on the speaker's circuit. I had just finished a talk in Oklahoma City and people were coming up to ask me questions or point out things I should have said. An old Native American man—a Cherokee I suppose—suddenly stood in front of me. He had a large and elaborate belt buckle in his hands. It was a swirl of multicolored beads. If they formed a pattern, I couldn't detect it.

"Please accept this gift," he said, and he held it out to me.

I was a little taken aback, but I had a quick response.

"Thank you. It's beautiful. But I can't accept it."

"Why not?" he asked with a puzzled look.

I pointed to the expanse beneath my chest. "Well, would you want to call attention to this stomach with a large, impressive belt buckle?" I laughed.

He did not. He simply extended the belt buckle again. "Please accept this," he said again.

"It's too expensive," I said. This was probably closer to the truth of why I said no. On some instinctive level, I was afraid I would be indebted if I took an expensive gift. But the truth was—then and is now—I was not sure why I was resistant.

"You know," the old man said, "you can give it to someone else."

I took the belt buckle. No, better, I received it.

I never wore it. But, eventually, I followed the old man's advice and gave the belt buckle to someone else, a student whom I thought made excellent progress.

When I offered it, the student said he could not accept it. I told him the story of how I had received it, and then he took the belt buckle with a knowing smile. Although we did not discuss it, I am sure the story I told communicated to him the same experience I had years earlier. The belt buckle was not a possession but a gift to be given away. It was a mission in disguise. (This experience was previously told in an essay entitled, "The Belt Buckle," in my book *Elijah at the Wedding Feast and Other Tales: Stories of the Human Spirit* [Chicago: Acta Publications, 1999] 5–9.)

All possessions will eventually be given away or taken from us. The changing nature of life means there is nothing we can permanently hang on to. I see this truth with great clarity every so often, but I do not consistently integrate it into my way of acting. But it prepared me for a more subtle awareness, the realization that life itself was a gift to be given away.

I grew up in a church community that frequently reminded one and all that we were creatures. We did not possess being on our own, and we could not sustain it on our own. It was God's gift, and remembering that truth was the key to salvation. But this was only a theological piece of knowledge, one fact among many. It sat on a shelf in the storehouse of my mind. It was something I knew, but I knew it in the mind alone, as Yeats said, and not in the marrow bone. But a slow process of deepening would turn it into a valuable realization.

When I began to talk in public, friends of my parents would often show up. They were not really interested in theology, but they were loyal to the clan. One man once told me, "You have your uncle's body, but you've got your father's way."

I went back to my father and told him, "He said, I've got Steve's body but your way."

My father pondered that for a moment. "I suppose he's right." Then he paused and sighed, "Thank God, you've got your mother's brains."

I added it up. I had my uncle's body, my father's way, and my mother's brains. Where did I—me, myself, and I—come in? I knew the answer. I had taken all this raw material and whipped it into shape. It was my energy and initiative that was important. I counted my achievements like a miser counting coins in the dark.

Then something happened—you never know when the master will arrive at midnight or at dawn, but probably at an unexpected hour—that plunged me irretrievably into the consciousness of gift. I had accepted an invitation to give a storytelling workshop in Ireland. Halfway over the Atlantic, I had an anxiety attack of major proportions. Who did I think I was? Going to Ireland to give a workshop on storytelling gave new meaning to carrying coals to Newcastle. But the Irish were kind and welcoming to the brash yank.

I gave an evening lecture to the public. Afterward, a man approached and told me he knew the brother of my grandfather. I jumped the gun.

"Tim Shea?" I volunteered.

"Ah, no," the man said. "Jerry Mullarkey. You are the grandson of John Thomas Mullarkey, are you not?"

"Yes, on my mother's side."

"Jerry Mullarkey was a *shenacke*, a storyteller. Like yourself. He lived on a mountain, and he used to ride his bike down the mountain to tell stories at wakes and weddings."

Later that night I sat on the edge of the bed, and once again pondered my own private chain of being. I had my uncle's body, my father's way, my mother's brains; and now it turns out I had my grandfather's brother's psychic structure. For if there would be an imaginative way to say how the physical, social, psychic, and spiritual complex comes together in me, it would be to simply describe me as a man who rides his bicycle down the mountain to tell stories at wakes and weddings. I might have done something with it, but I could no longer ignore that everything was given, from genetic material on up.

But I received this realization differently. Before, I felt vaguely diminished by the serious recognition of gift. Now, once I laughingly gave into it, I felt a rush of liberation and energy. What I felt liberated from was a whole psychological and social superstructure that I had scaffolded around my fragile sense of self. The released energy was direct and simple, simultaneously unspecific and unrelenting. I knew my purpose was to give to others what I had received.

Lo, the Lord had come at an unexpected hour. Although I am not sure I was vigilant and attentive, I was alert enough to open the door. He was in before I knew it. He sat me at table and fed me, all the time whispering to me how true food is prepared and served to others.

Twentieth Sunday in Ordinary Time

Proper 15

Luke 12:49-53 *LM* • Luke 12:49-56 *RCL*

❧

Discovering Fire

A Spiritual Commentary

Jesus said to his disciples: "I have come to set the earth on fire, and how I wish it were already blazing! There is a baptism with which I must be baptized, and how great is my anguish until it is accomplished!" (LM)

These are not the measured words of someone following a game plan. This is an impassioned outburst, the eruption of Jesus' heart that divulges what drives him. He understands himself as a man on a mission, and he is impatient for it to be accomplished. In fact, the drive to finish is causing him inner anguish. It seems the fire he wants to cast on the earth is also inside him as a propelling force.

It recalls the words of Jeremiah, "Then within me there is something like a burning fire shut up in my bones; I am weary with holding it in, and I cannot!" (Jer 20:9). Jeremiah tries to keep the fire inside, but he cannot hold it in. This shows the fire is beyond his control and not of his making. It has been placed there by God for divine purposes. "I am now making my words in your mouth a fire, and this people wood, and the fire shall devour them" (Jer 5:14). The fire in Jesus is also from God, but he is not a reluctant prophet trying to control it. He is the eager Son looking ahead to the blaze of accomplishment.

This image, "casting fire on the earth," is closely connected with the experience of the Spirit. John the Baptist has predicted that the one who is to come will baptize with the Holy Spirit and fire (Luke 3:16). In the Acts of the Apostles the coming of the Holy Spirit upon the gathering of the disciples is symbolized as tongues of fire (Acts 2:1-4). This suggests that their speech will be the way the fire of the Holy Spirit will spread upon the earth. Therefore, in the deepest sense, the casting of fire means releasing the Spirit, purifying people even as it empowers them.

In order for the Spirit to be released, Jesus has to undergo another baptism. In the first baptism the Spirit permeated him and sent him on a mission of forgiveness and reconciliation. This second baptism—his death and resurrection—will bequeath the same Spirit to his disciples and send them on a mission of forgiveness and reconciliation. As important and powerful as Jesus' teaching is, it does not have the revelatory power of his death and resurrection. When the disciples grasp the revelation of Jesus' dying and rising, his fire will pass into them. They will be in the condition of the two disciples on the road to Emmaus, their "hearts burning" within them (Luke 24:32). Then the plan of God will emerge into their consciousness. "Thus it is written, that the Messiah is to suffer and to rise from the dead on the third day, and that repentance and forgiveness of sins is to be proclaimed in his name to all nations" (Luke 24:46-47). The fire that began with Jesus casting it upon the land of Israel will now blaze throughout all nations.

Therefore, Jesus' anguish takes on a double meaning. His impending death certainly causes him trepidation. He is human, and he is not exempt from the natural fears associated with loss and death. But this distress is taken up and transformed by the more profound concern of fulfilling his mission. His sufferings are part of a divine plan that he is eager to take to the next stage. "Was it not necessary that the Messiah should suffer these things and then enter into his glory?" (Luke 24:26). Therefore, he does not shrink from his foreseen passion. He moves toward it, accepting it as the sacrifice that will open up the earth for his revelation. The fire that is in his bones is eager to find the wood of the people of the world.

> **"Do you think that I have come to establish peace on the earth? No, I tell you, but rather division. From now on a household of five will be divided, three against two and two against three; a father will be divided against his son and a son against his father, a mother against her daughter and a daughter against her mother, a mother-in-law against her daughter-in-law and a daughter-in-law against her mother-in-law." (LM)**

The answer to the opening question, "Do you think that I have come to establish peace on the earth?" is "Of course." The song of the angels at Jesus' birth suggested that his mission was peace (Luke 2:14). He made reconciliation and peace the center of his preaching and teaching (Luke 15:11-32; 23:34; 6:27-36). He rode a donkey of peace into Jerusalem, not a war horse (Luke 19:29-38). At his arrest in Gethsemane, he stopped the ear-hacking sword of his disciples with the command, "No more of this!" (Luke 22:51). The overall portrait of Jesus suggests a nonviolent man, walking the way of peace and reconciliation.

Here, however, this text does not focus on the teaching of Jesus but on its effects. Some people accept the teaching and follow Jesus. Other people reject the teaching and walk away. As people decide, they divide. Jesus' offer of peace and reconciliation leads to inevitable division. Therefore, he casts fire on the earth in a second way. This is not the fire of the Spirit, but the fire of judgment. It is the fire that purifies, separating the dross from the gold. It is even the fire that destroys, the "unquenchable fire" where the chaff that has been sifted out of the wheat is burnt (Luke 3:17). At the circumcision of Jesus, the aged seer, Simeon, predicted the child would be a sign of contradiction, someone that would be opposed (Luke 3:24). In the contradiction and opposition is the division.

When this division is played out in a family context, it takes on a specific meaning. The text is precise in showing a two-sided division. Something that was always held together is split down the middle in a complete way. Jesus' presence and teaching precipitates a complete tear. It is not just that the father is separated from the son. The son is also separated from the father. The mother and daughter and mother-in-law and daughter-in-law are also mutually divided. These severed blood and marriage bonds used to be the primary human loyalties. But now they must take second place to the loyalty accorded to Jesus. The revelation of God in Jesus makes an absolute claim on people, and any claims that compete with it must be abandoned. The gentleness of Jesus may not quench the flickering wick or crush the bruised reed (Matt 12:20), but the word of Jesus is a two-edged sword (Heb 4:12).

Jesus' forthright admission of the divisive effect of his presence and message on family life is part of his unflinching approach. He never soft-pedals what is involved in following him. He makes clear the consequences of commitment. A would-be follower once wanted to tend to sacred family obligations before joining his company. "'Lord, first let me go and bury my father.' But Jesus said to him, 'Let the dead bury their own dead; but as for you, go and proclaim the kingdom of God'" (Luke 9:59-60; see the Thirteenth Sunday in Ordinary Time, Cycle C). We can modify this sternness of Jesus' demands in a number of ways. Softened interpretations are always available. The fire can be cooled, but it still burns.

Teaching

As a young man, I was attracted to the ideal of a passionate life. What-ever I would do, I had to be on fire and, even more importantly, I had to stay on fire. I did not want to flame out. I was supported in this desire by the writings of Nikos Kazantzakis, whose most famous novels are *Zorba the Greek* and *The Last Temptation of Christ*. Kazantzakis believed there was a great cry resounding through the universe. It called to each person to stand up and advance, to join the evolutionary march into the future. In order to respond to the call, people had to be vigilant and ready to struggle. In particular, they had to overcome the pull of domesticity, the drag of the sedentary life. Zorba called domesticity the full catastrophe; and the last temptation of Christ, one that he resisted, was to settle down with Mary Magdalene and raise children. Although I was always wary of the spirit-flesh antagonism that haunted Kazantzakis' work, he advo-cated fire; and it was not the soft flames from logs in the hearth.

There was another feature of Kazantzakis' work that appealed to me. In the introduction to *The Last Temptation of Christ*, he wrote:

> I never followed Christ's bloody journey to Golgotha with such terror, I never relived his Life and Passion with such intensity, such under-standing and love as during the days and nights when I wrote *The Last Temptation of Christ*. . . . In order to mount to the Cross, the summit of sacrifice, and to God, the summit of immateriality, Christ passed through all the stages which the man who struggles passes through. That is why his suffering is so familiar to us; that is why we share it, and why his final victory seems to us so much our own future victory. (*The Last Temptation of Christ* [New York: Bantam Books, 1961] 2)

Although I did not agree with how Kazantzakis portrayed Christ's struggle, I was impressed by his desire to enter into Jesus' passion and death. I had read many scholarly books of christology that considered Jesus at arm's length. Professionals had pinned him to a board for ob-servation. I had also read many devotional books on Christ with such an elevated sugar content that one reading could induce diabetes. In Kazantzakis I found at least part of what I wanted—an exchange of consciousness between Christ and a contemporary, a communion of shared fire. I had grown up in a church culture. I did not want a general brand of passion, a routine fire in the belly. I wanted the passion of Jesus, the fire he cast upon the earth.

In my mind, Kazantzakis had two things right. He knew passion was paramount, and that the proper relationship to Christ was to participate in his consciousness and share his struggle. But he had the nature of Christ's fire wrong. For him, the God-enflamed soul was a fire that consumed and left behind everything it loved until it too self-destructed, serenely fading into sun. The passion had turned into a stoicism of loss. It reminded me of Camus' "metaphysical rebellion." People created moments of love and laughter in a benignly indifferent universe. This might be fire, but it was the fire Prometheus stole from the gods. There was another fire, the fire God gave Jesus to cast upon the earth. That was the fire I wanted.

So I passed from the extravagant prose and poetry of Nikos Kazantzakis to the confessional honesty of Pierre Teilhard de Chardin. Once again I found passion and fire. But this time the passion was not ultimately futile, and the fire was not raging out of control. Teilhard wanted to show

> how, starting from the point at which a spark was first struck, a point that was built into me congenitally, the world gradually caught fire for me, burst into flames; how this happened all *during* my life, and *as a result of* my whole life, until it formed a great luminous mass, lit from within, that surrounded me. (*The Heart of Matter* [New York: Harcourt Brace Jovanovich, 1978] 15)

This was fire that illumined everything from within, that backlit creation so its beauty could be seen. Even more, this fire was the energy of love, and it held everything together.

> The day will come when, after harnessing the ether, the winds, the tides, gravitation, we shall harness for God the energies of love. And, on that day, for the second time in the history of the world, human beings will have discovered fire. ("The Evolution of Chastity," in *Toward the Future* [New York: Harcourt Brace Jovanovich, 1974] 87)

But there was still more. This fire was taking creation into ever new and deeper levels of convergence, and it needed human cooperation to create this future. This fire generated a zest for life, a faith in the future of the earth. In "The Mass on the World" Teilhard offers up the work of all humanity.

> This bread, our toil, is of itself, I know, but an immense fragmentation; this wine, our pain, is not more, I know, than a drought that dissolves. Yet in the very depths of this formless mass you have implanted—and this I am sure of, for I sense it—a desire, irresistible, hallowing, which makes us cry out, believer and unbeliever alike: "Lord, make us *one*." ("The Mass on the World," in *The Heart of Matter* [New York: Harcourt Brace Jovanovich, 1978] 121)

Finally, I had found a fire that was going somewhere and was going to take me alone. It was a bush that burned but did not burn out (Exod 3:2).

The year 2005 was the fiftieth anniversary of Teilhard's death. Joyce Quinlan, who gives her age as 86, wrote a letter to the *National Catholic Reporter* (June 17, 2005, 29):

> Shortly before Teilhard's death, I had my heart and soul set on fire by reading his *Divine Milieu*. . . . Teilhard's vision broke open a reality never revealed before in my 30 years of life and Catholic education. It spun me into a transformed world in which the Incarnation soared way beyond the astounding reality that God became human; in fact, the entire cosmos, every being within it, became the body of Christ with a divine mission. . . . Doesn't that make every action worth doing with great reverence and devotion? Doesn't that make getting up each day deeply satisfying?

There is one last thing about this fire that Jesus casts upon the earth. It warms the long loneliness; it is a good companion for the joys and sorrows of life. Although I am not 86 (but well on the road to older age), I was heartened to read this witness. When the fire within all things flares, all things are new in each moment. And so is the one who catches sight of their illumination, the one who has been lit and warmed by the fire Christ cast upon the earth.

Twenty-First Sunday in Ordinary Time

Luke 13:22-30

❦

Striving to Enter

A Spiritual Commentary

Jesus went through one town and village after another, teaching as he made his way to Jerusalem. Someone asked him, "Lord, will only a few be saved?" (Luke 13:22-23, NRSV)

The question is not: "Will I be saved?" or "How will I be saved?" Instead there is emphasis on numbers. Will it be only a few, or will it be many, or will it be all? The background for this question is the belief among some Jews that in the age to come all the people of Israel, by the very fact they belong to Israel, will be seated at God's banquet. The prophetic tradition was not so sanguine. The physical bonding that comes from blood and the social bonding that comes from any number of shared activities determine who is "in" and who is "out" in this age. But in the age to come a different criterion will be used. Jesus belongs to this prophetic tradition.

> **He said to them, "Strive to enter through the narrow door; for many, I tell you, will try to enter and not be able. When once the owner of the house has got up and shut the door, and you begin to stand outside and to knock at the door, saying, 'Lord, open to us,' then in reply he will say to you, 'I do not know where you come from.' Then you will begin to say, 'We ate and drank with you and you taught in our streets.' But he will say, 'I do not know where you come from; go away from me, all you evildoers!' There will be weeping and gnashing of teeth when you see Abraham and Isaac and Jacob and all the prophets in the kingdom of God, and you yourselves thrown out. Then people will come from the east and the west, from north and south, and will eat in the kingdom of God. Indeed, some are last who will be first, and some are first who will be last.** (13:23-30, NRSV)

Jesus puts the petitioner's question into a larger picture of panic and exclusion. There is a door leading into the house where Jesus and

God are holding a banquet in the age to come. Everyone is trying to get in, and there is a traffic jam because the door is narrow. Then the owner "gets up" (the resurrected Jesus arises) and solves the problem by shutting the door.

Needless to say, this does not stop the frantic push for entry. It escalates it. People beg for the door to be opened. "Lord, open to us." The Lord refuses because he does not know where they come from. They reply that he *does know* where they come from. They come from the villages and towns where he taught and the dinner gatherings where he ate and drank. But the Lord still insists he does not know where they come from. "Knowing where you come from" obviously means more than geography and social communing. These people who rely on these superficial contacts with Jesus for entry into the banquet are commanded to depart. They fall into the opposite category of where they thought they belonged. They are not righteous but evildoers.

This picture of exclusion begins with the subtle bias in the petitioner's question, "Lord, will only a few be saved?" It sounds like the petitioner suspects the answer is yes. However, when Jesus urges him to "strive to enter through the narrow door," Jesus rejects the speculation about numbers and focuses on the question of struggle. He is telling him: "Forget the question of how many and put your mind and heart into the disciplined work of striving to enter." This focus will not be easily maintained because so many are trying to be saved in the wrong way. The petitioner will have to contend with the many who think the way into salvation is "who you know" rather than "who you are." However, the door does not open because you are well connected.

The Lord's remarks connect "who you know" and "who you are" in a dynamic process of spiritual recognition. The Lord only recognizes his own. He knows you if you are like him. This likeness is not on the level of shared ethnicity. The Lord knows those who come from the same spiritual place as he comes from. "I do not know where you come from" means there is no spiritual link between the people wanting to be admitted and the one who can open the door. Jesus comes from a heart set on God that cooperates with the divine Spirit to love all people. This is the room where the banquet is being held, and the door to this room is narrow.

Entering through the narrow door begins with striving. It is not easy to center your heart on love of God and neighbor. It is a lifelong discipline that must accompany all other adventures. Most people do not take it seriously and do not engage in it. But in every culture of the world—the east, west, north and south—there are people in the tradition of Abraham, Isaac, and Jacob who eat the food of this kingdom possibility and grow strong. The Lord will know where these people come from and he will open the door.

But there will always be those who want in on their own terms. They want to stride into the feast because of who they know and not strive to enter by making themselves into who they really are. Their fantasies of first will be disappointed. But then there will be those who struggle mightily with loving God and neighbor. They will learn the great lesson of grace—what begins in striving is accomplished in surrender. All salvation comes from God, and every picture of the life to come is simply how we focus on what is essential in the life we are leading in this very place and at this very time. Others might consider these people last because they have no interest in transferring the social competition of first and last into the spiritual domain. But, in truth, they are "first" because they have found in their heart what Jesus knew in his heart— divine love makes brothers and sisters of us all. When we know this, the Lord knows us; and the narrow door becomes the widest of gates.

Teaching

Annie Dillard, the naturalist and writer, was walking in farmlands surrounding her house. ("On a Hill Far Away," in *Teaching a Stone to Talk* [New York: Harper & Row, 1982] 77–83.) She comes upon a fenced horse barn, "around which a dun mare and a new foal were nervously clattering." There was also a small boy of around eight there, and she struck up a conversation with him about the new foal.

Toward the end of the conversation, the boy paused.

> He looked miserably at his shoetops, and I looked at his brown corduroy cap. Suddenly the cap lifted, and the little face said in a rush, "Do you know the Lord as your personal savior?"
> "Not only that," I said. "I know your mother."
> It all came together. She had asked me the same question.

I did not grow up in a Christian tradition that encouraged the brazenness to ask an adult about their personal connection to Jesus and their prospects of salvation. But I did grow up with the question of salvation. I learned it very early. "Who will be saved?" and "How are people saved?" intermingled with other questions like "How late may I stay up?" and "May I have a Good Humor ice cream bar?"

Much later in life a childhood friend of mine commented to me, "My kids are certainly growing up a lot different than we did." His kids, at the time, were about nine through thirteen.

"What do you mean?"

"At their age we were thinking about eternal life and all that sort of stuff. It never darkens their mind."

When he told me that, I thought to myself that it hadn't darkened my mind for awhile either. But he was right. It had an established place in our consciousness when we were nine through thirteen.

My church and school insisted that "wanting to go to heaven" should be the driving force of life. This motivation was bolstered by the usual commonsense arguments about the shortness of this life and the everlastingness and permanence of life after death. "Is an eternity of pain worth a moment of pleasure?" As any thirteen year old facing temptation knows, the answer is yes.

But this concern with afterlife, especially avoiding afterlife damnation (being shut out of the banquet forever), was softened by a strong emphasis on the lovingness of God and the constant practices of sacramental confession to cleanse the soul and prepare it for its heavenly journey. Although I have heard stories and read memoirs about how the fear of hell scared boys and girls of my generation, I was never traumatized by afterlife prospects. Heaven, hell, and purgatory were just an accepted part of my theological universe. The project was to learn how to play the game of salvation.

I remember clearly the day I found out I was losing interest in the game. I was studying for the priesthood; and in order to move from philosophical studies to theological studies, you had to write a letter of intent about why you wanted to be a priest. I prayed, soul-searched, and wrote a chiseled page and a half about where I was at. The spiritual director screened these letters before they went to the rector. So I slid my page and a half across the desk toward him. He read it slowly. Then he slid it back toward me and said, "There are five reasons why you want to be a priest." Then he listed them. The first two were: "To save your soul and the souls of others."

Back in my room with my letter of intent, I was a little embarrassed. Why hadn't I thought of that? It was so obvious. It was what I had been taught from the beginning. I quickly rewrote my letter. I had five reasons for wanting to be a priest.

But the reasons on the paper didn't ring true. I wanted to go to heaven. I wanted everyone to go to heaven. Especially considering the alternative. But these reasons were not driving me. Perhaps they did once, and perhaps they still should have been my foremost motivation. But I could feel some theological shift going on. I was not conscious of exactly what it was and I did not feel I was in control of it. So my first reaction was to be suspicious. Was I becoming lax? Was I losing my religious focus? Was I forgetting what was really important? I took myself to task. But it didn't work. I could not get the love of heaven and the fear of hell back into my soul no matter how hard I tried.

Only much later, with the help of some psychological and mystical literature, did I realize theological ideas were like furniture that could be rearranged in the mind. I hadn't lost my faith. I still believed in the four last things—death, judgment, heaven, and hell. But they no longer were center stage. Something different was claiming my interest and attention. I gained greater understanding of what that was by overhearing a smart-aleck remark and pondering a piece of Buddhist wisdom.

I heard that someone had asked Fritz Pearls, the feisty psychologist associated with the human potential movement, if he was saved. Pearls quickly countered with, "I'm trying to figure out how to be spent." This smart-aleck remark helped me see what was going on in me. I wanted to figure out how to give my life to something larger than ego ambitions and petty schemes. Salvation would flow from a life of self-giving. There was no need to go after it directly. In fact, too much concern about afterlife salvation almost inevitably degenerated into some form of works-righteousness. The gratitude of grace was overshadowed by the triumph of merit.

When I first heard the Buddhist saying, "after you cross the river, you no longer have to carry the canoe," I knew how it could be applied to me. My concern with afterlife salvation was a canoe. When I was paddling it, I had developed a strong interest in the spiritual life and struggled with questions that were necessary to resolve. That I was no longer paddling the afterlife canoe did not mean I was drowning. It had done what it was supposed to do. It led me to the next step of my development. I came to an appreciative appraisal of where I had been and where I was going. The canoe of afterlife salvation had brought me across the river. I no longer needed to carry it.

But what exactly was the other side of the river? Where did it bring me?

I became passionately concerned about how the deeper part of me, my spirit, was expressed and realized through my actions. On the one hand, I had a problem with rational ethics that presumed you could argue people into a certain type of behavior. On the other hand, I had a problem with spirituality that explored the life of the soul with God and then abruptly stopped. I wanted to know how the inner dimension of spirit and outer dimensions of mind, body, and society came together. I wanted to know for myself how love of God and love of neighbor are inseparable.

So I have "strived to enter" the world of dual consciousness, the border of eternity and time, the authentic space from which the steady pressure of mediated grace changes the hardened habits of the mind and the stubborn structures of society into God's willing creatures. The reality of grace and my patient struggle to trust is more central than it has ever been. The question of afterlife salvation will take care of itself if I take care of the spiritual striving in this life. At least that is where I am at for the moment. That is the canoe I am presently paddling.

Sunday between August 21 and August 27 inclusive

Proper 16

Luke 13:10-17

❧

Setting People Free

A Spiritual Commentary

Now he was teaching in one of the synagogues on the sabbath. And just then there appeared a woman with a spirit that had crippled her for eighteen years. She was bent over and was quite unable to stand up straight.

When Jesus saw her, he called her over and said, "Woman, you are set free from your ailment."

When he laid his hands on her, immediately she stood up straight and began praising God.

We live in a medically saturated culture. We trade stories of diseases, surgeries, and the best and worst of physicians. In fact, at one time or another most of us have played amateur doctor and have given a free diagnosis to anyone who made the mistake of asking. Immersed in this culture as a yoke in albumen, we immediately wonder about the exact nature of the crippled woman's ailment. Is it a spinal-cord injury, or disk degeneration, or osteoporosis? This anatomical and physiological interest also makes us wonder about the exact nature of the cure. Even if we believe that God in Jesus is capable of working such miracles, how were the damaged bones, tissues, and nerves repaired? We are people with developed medical minds, and these are the questions that medical minds ask. However, the story is not concerned with the details of diagnosis and cure.

Jesus lived in a theologically saturated culture. The miraculous cure of the bent-over woman at the center of the story is presented as a theological catalyst. It stirs up Jesus' theology of mission, the synagogue's theology of illness and women, and both of their theologies of Sabbath. In particular, the woman's condition is a symbolic rendering of the effect of synagogue theology and the woman's cure is a symbolic render-ing of the effect of Jesus' theology of mission. Both these theologies—the theology of the synagogue and the theology of Jesus—revolve around the Sabbath and, by implication, reveal the intentions and nature of God. All gospel miracles are meant to function as encouragements to ponder God's relationship with people as a guide to how people should relate to one another.

Walter Wink has suggested that in the biblical vision every reality has an inner and outer aspect. (*Naming the Powers: The Language of Power in the New Testament* [Minneapolis: Fortress Press, 1984] 104–48; *Engaging the Powers: Discernment and Resistance in a World of Domination* [Minneapolis: Fortress Press, 1992] 9.) The outer aspect is its material shape and organizational structure. The inner aspect is its spirit that determines the purpose, direction, and meaning of the outer aspects. If a social reality is part of the Domination System, those institutions that oppress people, its inner spirit is evil and is often called Satan. There-fore, evil spirits and Satan are not disembodied spiritual realities who freely roam around looking for prey. They are always embodied in in-dividual and social realities; and they can invade people when people enter the arena in which they are embodied.

The synagogue is a social organizational structure that has an inner spirit. The woman suddenly appears within the synagogue with an inner, oppressive spirit that has kept her crippled for eighteen years. She may have brought this spirit into the synagogue with her. She is one of the unlucky ones whom an evil spirit and/or Satan have chosen to torment. Or, appearing "just then" within the synagogue means she is manifesting what the inner spirit of the synagogue does to women. Her bent-over condition reflects the general tendencies of a religion that uses its theology and laws to oppress people rather than liberate them. "For you load people with burdens hard to bear, and you your-selves do not lift a finger to ease them" (Luke 11:46).

Jesus, through his words and deeds, immediately corrects the im-pact of the spirit of the synagogue. When he sees her and calls her to himself, she becomes visible. One of the latent functions of theological perspectives that subordinate females to males is that it makes women invisible. The bodily symbol of being bent over means the person is never at eye level. They do not see others face to face nor are they seen face to face. When Jesus talks to her, he breaks the custom of men avoiding women in public. His address of "woman" is not simply a gender designation. It is a mark of respect. In the Spirit-driven mission of Jesus, the invisible become visible, the ones at the margins become the center of attention.

Also, when Jesus touches her, he overrides the theologically grounded fears of contamination from her Satan-induced crippled condition or from the possibility she may be menstruating. But Jesus' welcome is not the act of a rebel, ignoring tradition and custom. His actions of calling her out, talking to her, touching her, and healing her are theologically motivated. He is doing what God has done from the beginning—freeing people from what oppresses them. What God told Moses to say to Pharaoh, God says throughout history—"Let my people go!" (Exod 7:16). If no one else in the synagogue knows this, then Jesus and the woman do. When she stands straight, dignified, and whole, she praises God.

> **But the leader of the synagogue, indignant because Jesus had cured on the sabbath, kept saying to the crowd, "There are six days on which work ought to be done; come on those days and be cured, and not on the sabbath day."**
>
> **But the Lord answered him and said, "You hypocrites! Does not each of you on the sabbath untie his ox or his donkey from the manger, and lead it away to give it water? And ought not this woman, a daughter of Abraham whom Satan bound for eighteen long years, be set free from this bondage on the sabbath day?"**
>
> **When he said this, all his opponents were put to shame; and the entire crowd was rejoicing at all the wonderful things that he was doing.**

The leader of the synagogue is clueless. His theology is a boa constrictor that has squeezed all the compassion out of him. Instead of rejoicing at the liberation of the woman, he becomes indignant because his theological understanding of the Sabbath has been violated. He is obviously one of those leaders who is always waiting to be offended. He makes his difficulty sound rational and well considered, as befits the theologically trained.

The leader of the synagogue has no problem with Jesus healing. He has a problem with the timing; and the timing is significant. It carries the full import of the cure as a critique of the Sabbath theology of the synagogue. If Jesus cures on one of the six days, the God who guards the Sabbath is not challenged. But Jesus cures on the Sabbath, and so he forces a question about the nature and intentions of God. Is God really concerned with restricting the activity of people, even healing activity, on the Sabbath? Is not God concerned with freeing people from what bends them over and bringing them to full stature? Is not God actively present, bringing about the divine dream for creation? What Jesus has done is not a random healing. This is the restoration of the goodness of creation, cooperating with the Spirit of God who brought all things into being. As such, it is a revelation profoundly at odds with a God who enforces laws and punishes transgressors. Jesus' God is not the God of the leader of the synagogue.

The leader of synagogue does not confront Jesus directly. He makes his argument to the crowds, hoping to turn them against Jesus. Jesus, however, intervenes and responds to the leader, and through him, to all in the crowd who may share the leader's perception. But Jesus does not engage the leader's argument on the leader's own terms. There is not going to be an esoteric debate on what is and what is not permitted on the Sabbath. Rather, Jesus points out the incredible blindness of synagogical theology and practice. They will relieve an animal's thirst on the Sabbath, but they will not untie a woman who has been bound by Satan, who is an enemy of God's purposes. They do not care for a bent-over daughter of Abraham whom they have burdened, but they will care for the beasts who carry their burdens. They show more compassion to animals than they do to women. Although the episode does not pursue how this hypocritical inconsistency could be tolerated, there is a clue in the symbolic number of eighteen.

In the previous episode (Luke 13:1-6), Jesus corrected the view of the crowds that the eighteen people who were killed when the tower of Siloam fell on them were worse sinners than all other Galileans. The people in the crowds were in the grip of teaching that saw physical disasters as punishments for sin. This teaching puts the blame for all life's accidents in the immoral actions of the one who is suffering. Now the number eighteen appears again. It is the number of years the woman has been held in bondage by Satan, the inner spirit of the false teaching of the synagogue. Her physical malady is presumed to be a punishment for sin. Her ailment puts her outside God's care and outside the concern of people who hold this theology. But for Jesus, who sees God as actively restoring creation and renewing the covenant with Abraham, this daughter of Abraham is the center of God's compassionate care. In the theology of the synagogue, the stooped over woman is invisible; in the theology of Jesus, a beloved daughter of Abraham is the center of attention.

Although the leader of the synagogue has tried to sway the crowd to his way of thinking, he has not been successful. It is not that he has been outwitted and out-argued. Jesus has not captured the crowd with debating tactics. Rather, Jesus' action of guiding the woman from bent over to straight is self-authenticating. It does not need a rationale outside itself to justify it. It is the liberation of the human from demonic oppression. When people's minds are not in bondage to false ideas, they will naturally rejoice. So the crowds rejoice and spread the word. But opponents are inevitably shamed. How could so obvious a revelation of God's love for a daughter of Abraham have eluded them for so long? If they reflect, the answer will be available to them. Their theology blinded them.

Teaching

I would like to paint the leader of the synagogue as an insensitive chauvinist whose compassion is constricted to his own animals. In that way, I could dismiss him, fairly confident that we have nothing in common. But I suspect a fuller appreciation would see him as a victim of his theology. His theologically structured mind only allows him to see the stooped woman as a sinner being punished for her sins. The theologically structured mind of Jesus sees a bent-over daughter of Abraham who needs to stand straight. Different theologies allow us to see different realities.

When theologies are abstractly considered, they are evaluated by their fidelity to Scripture and tradition and their internal consistency. However, when theologies are living in the minds of people, there are other criteria. The question is: how are the theologies functioning? What do they keep us from seeing and what do they make us consider? What inner attitudes do they validate? What outer behaviors do they encourage?

Pursuing how theologies impact the psychological and social lives of people is often called investigating their *latent* functioning. Theologies have manifest objectives, and these are usually high-minded ambitions proclaimed from the housetops. But theologies also have secret influences. These are not easily detected, especially when we try to see them in theologies that we espouse. They are too close to home. We do not look at what type of people we are turning into because of our theologies. Therefore, becoming suspicious of our theologies is appropriate activity.

A theology that emphasizes personal sin may let structural injustice off the hook. A theology that emphasizes God as king may encourage

mindless compliance to authority. A theology that emphasizes the sufferings and death of Christ may sap the joy of creation out of its ad-
herents. A theology that emphasizes afterlife salvation may encourage
apathy toward the struggles of this world. A theology that emphasizes
God as Father may validate treating women as an inferior gender. A
theology that emphasizes the infallibility of the church may tempt
leaders to hide ecclesial flaws. A theology that emphasizes life may shy
away from situations where biological and social life is diminishing.
A theology that emphasizes petitionary prayer may keep people from
developing abilities that are able to respond to difficult situations. A
theology that emphasizes that procreation carries the universality of
original sin may insinuate that sex is necessary but not sacred. A theology that emphasizes that Christ is present in Word and Sacrament
may overlook the presence of Christ throughout creation. A theology
that emphasizes there is only one path to salvation may encourage a
negative evaluation of people on other paths.

When people hold theologies, the theologies also hold them. Therefore, we must be careful of what we put in our mind. The downside of
some theologies is obvious. "God helps those who help themselves" is
quickly spotted as a cover for aggressive instincts that center on looking out for number one. But the latent negative functioning of other
theologies may only gradually come to light. When we emphasize that
theological statements are true because they are in Scripture or proclaimed by the authority of the church, we may diminish the desire to
understand the statement personally. We rely on the scriptural witness
and/or the authority of the church. We relax, even sometimes abandon,
our own efforts to realize and integrate the Christian revelation. Theologies are ideas in the mind; and ideas in the mind can subtly support
attitudes and behaviors we may not want.

The delusion is that we can find and formulate the right theology,
the theology that will only have positive effects on attitudes and behaviors. But we are too psychologically and socially complex for so simple
a solution. Rather, we need to develop the discipline of suspicion. All
our theologies must be investigated in terms of their latent functioning.
When we know the limits of our ideas, we also know their potential. As
spiritual traditions have steadfastly insisted, true wisdom is to know
that we do not know. One way of setting people free is to become suspicious of the theological ideas that hold them in bondage.

Twenty-Second Sunday in Ordinary Time

Proper 17

Luke 14:1, 7-14

❧

Laughing at Ourselves

A Spiritual Commentary

On one occasion when Jesus was going to the house of a leader of the Pharisees to eat a meal on the sabbath, they were watching him closely.

This episode begins with the tense pairing of hospitality and observation. Jesus is invited, but he is invited to be watched. The guests observe him closely. However, Jesus is not only watched, he is set-up. There is a man with dropsy at the dinner. (This part of the Lukan episode [Luke 14:2-6] is omitted from this Sunday's reading.) Although the storyteller does not comment on how or why the man is there, he could have been "placed" there to test Jesus' response. This is what the people are observing. What will Jesus do when he finds a sick social outcast at a Sabbath dinner?

Jesus accepts the challenge, but he also turns the tables. He asks the people, "Is it lawful to heal on the Sabbath or not?" The people give him "no word of response." They are too busy watching to talk. Then Jesus heals the man and sends him away. (The reason Jesus sends him away is that he will be welcomed at a much different feast that will appear at the end of this episode [Luke14:15-24].)

A second time he asks the people a question, "If one of you has a child (some manuscripts read "donkey") or an ox that has fallen into a well, will you not immediately pull it out on the Sabbath day?" And for a second time they "gave him no word of response." They refused to engage him. He accepted their challenge, but they would not accept his challenge. Jesus wanted them to look at their assumptions, a look that almost certainly would be disconcerting.

Jesus' questions reveal what is going on in his unresponsive fellow guests. They are wrapped up in their own world and cannot see themselves clearly. On the surface they may be concerned about what behavior is appropriate on the Sabbath. But the underlying issue is more egocentric: whose "ox or son" is in the pit? If it is *their* ox or son, they will take it out—Sabbath or not. But if it is another man's health, strict Sabbath rules apply. No curing is permitted. The safety of their possessions is more important than the basic bodily health of another human being. Their Sabbath concerns are a mask for their preoccupation with the overriding importance of "me and mine."

They have no intention of talking to Jesus about their Sabbath habits; but Jesus has every intention of talking to them about their ego-centered obsessions. They watched Jesus, but it is now Jesus' turn to watch them. "When he noticed how the guests chose the places of honor . . ." Questioning did not get them to respond. Perhaps a prophetic parable or two might induce insight and participation.

> **When he noticed how the guests chose the places of honor, he told them a parable. "When you are invited by someone to a wedding banquet, do not sit down at the place of honor, in case someone more distinguished than you has been invited by your host; and the host who invited both of you may come and say to you, "Give this person your place," and then in disgrace you would start to take the lowest place. But when you are invited, go and sit down at the lowest place, so that when your host comes, he may say to you, "Friend, move up higher"; then you will be honored in the presence of all who sit at the table with you. For all who exalt themselves will be humbled, and those who humble themselves will be exalted.**

These guests love honor and hate shame, and therefore their life project is to gain honor and avoid shame. However, the greedy quest for honor may push them to engage in a strategy that will bring shame. If they seek the first place, they may have to shamefacedly—before everyone—retire to the last. However, if they take the lowest place, the host will surely raise them—before everyone—higher. The result is they will enjoy the esteem of their table companions. This sure-fire strategy is clinched by connecting it to the proverbial wisdom about those who exalt themselves being humbled and those who humble themselves being exalted.

It seems that Jesus is playing their game, only he is playing it better. They desire esteem in the eyes of others and Jesus has some very clever ideas about how to achieve it. He has an inventive strategy about feigning lower to gain higher. Maybe they should play humble in the hope of winning big in front of everyone. Is Jesus a devotee of one-up-manship?

However, this may not be the conspiracy of honor-hungry minds it appears to be. It is difficult to think that Jesus is accepting the basic ego-centric framework he tried to unmask when he questioned them about healing on the Sabbath. Even if he is using their egos to move them toward humility, this advice is suspect. It leaves their motivational structure, inherited from the culture, intact. However, the overall style of Jesus in the gospel is to challenge cultural assumptions. He seldom complies with them.

Instead of teaching them more deft maneuvers on how to be first, Jesus is challenging their jockeying for position. But he is doing it in an indirect, comic way. He is using language as "skillful means." He suggests a strategy that is sincere but outrageous. At first glance, it promotes the exact opposite of what they desire. Only someone mono-lithically hooked on honor would entertain it. And if they did entertain it, even for a moment, it would surface their single-minded pursuit of esteem. In contemporary parlance, they would be "busted." In ancient formulas, they would come to know themselves, to have self-reflexive knowledge about what drives them.

As the guests pondered the possibilities of this ridiculous plan of false humility, Jesus might have said, "Got ya!" In other words, Jesus' language is designed to catch them in their own thinking, to make visible to them their underlying driving forces. If they gravitate to Jesus' off-the-wall strategy, even for a moment, the humor of their ambitions and the pathetic deceits they are capable of may break through to them. Laughing at ourselves is more than therapeutic. It is the first step toward conversion.

Of course, the story could be extended. The scheming guest finds the lowest place. The host, upon seeing the honor-hungry guest seated at the lowest place awaiting a higher calling, bends over and whispers in his ear, "I see you know your place." Nothing awakens self-knowledge so painfully as a failed strategy.

Or, the scheming guest is ignored by the host and forced to frat-ernize with the bottom. He lets go of his social ambitions and enjoys himself. At the next dinner he takes the lowest place because of the company. When the host appears and asks him to come up higher, he declines. He is having too good of a time.

Outrageous strategies are meant to have outrageous results. They may even become a path to inner change and new vitality.

> **He said also to the one who had invited him, "When you give a luncheon or a dinner, do not invite your friends or your brothers or your relatives or rich neighbors, in case they may invite you in return, and you would be repaid. But when you give a banquet, invite the poor, the crippled, the lame, and the blind. And you will be blessed, because they cannot repay you, for you will be repaid at the resurrection of the righteous."**

Jesus turns his irony from the guests to the host, suggesting a wild way to get a really big payback. First, Jesus makes a suggestion that directly contradicts what the host is about. Jesus does not want the host to invite certain people because they are likely to pay him back. But, of course, this is precisely *why he would invite them*. There is always more at work than a simple dinner party. Social stratification is the backdrop and social climbing is the agenda. Who will be at the banquet is more important than what is served.

In this context, Jesus once again suggests a strategy that on the surface looks like the wrong move, but that ultimately is the right move. Invite the people who cannot repay, because God ultimately repays kindnesses to them. Invite the "poor, crippled, lame, and blind." Remember the man with dropsy who no one would talk about. Invite a room full of those types. They cannot repay in this world but repayment will occur at the resurrection of the righteous. So weigh the repayment this side of death of hobnobbing with wealthy friends and relatives with repayment after death by God on the day of resurrection. What a dilemma! This insidious thought will definitely cause consternation in the quid-pro-quo mind. The consternation is the catalyst that may reveal to them the hierarchical bias of the guest list.

Of course, the story could be extended. The host gets to like the outcast group, and his desire to be part of the resurrected righteous lessens. Or, the host dies and is resurrected with the righteous only to find the righteous are not the social and religious elite of his earthly days, but the outcasts he had come to enjoy. The banquet he had on earth is the same banquet going on in heaven.

Although there are echoes of the real virtues of humility and uncalculating generosity in the twin suggestions that Jesus advocates, more fundamentally Jesus is a storytelling prophet playing a mirror game. He is holding up a mirror to the guests and host so they can see themselves as he sees them. He sees these people caught in games of hypocrisy and social posturing. They are far from the kingdom. What will get through to them? They refuse to answer questions and engage in a dialogue. Perhaps a wildly comic picture of themselves using humility as a secret ploy for self-promotion and using disinterested inviting as a secret ploy for self-interested advancement? In the mirror of the parable they may see the frantic and ludicrous ways they play the game of guests and host.

The sad result is they do not see themselves. "One of the dinner guests, on hearing this, said to him, 'Blessed is anyone who will eat bread in the kingdom of God!'" (Luke 14:15). The drive to be first has attached itself to another object—the kingdom of God. But ego promotion is not the way the kingdom of God works. So Jesus tries one more time. He is the gardener who will hoe around the tree until it bears fruit (Luke 13:6-9). He tells them the story of the great dinner (Luke 14:16-24). The people who are invited refuse to come and their reasons are telling. "The first said to him, 'I have bought a piece of land, and I must go out and see it; please accept my regrets.' Another said, 'I have bought five yoke of oxen, and I am going to try them out; please accept my regrets.' Another said, 'I have just been married, and therefore I cannot come'" (Luke 14:18-20). Their own concerns so preoccupy them they cannot accept the invitation. So others are invited—the poor, the blind, and the crippled. Although it is not in the story, there is a rumor that a man who used to have dropsy also showed up.

Teaching

At large banquets a friend of mine often comments that he is obviously favored by the host because he is invariably seated close to the lavatory. This usually brings a laugh from his table companions. As his wife points out, laughing will only encourage him. It does; and he presents a mock economic analysis that argues waterfront property is always the most valuable. The last place he would want to be, he continues, is at the head table where you are in full sight. People can watch you try to push a pea on your knife with your index finger—like one of the sorry humans up there now. The host and hostess have obviously picked them out for public humiliation. He continues in this vein, mocking our sad expression at finding ourselves so close to flushing and the host's painfully thought-out seating choices.

It is not just the Pharisees who play guests and host. It is the Pharisee in all of us. As far as I am concerned, getting it out in the open is welcome. Spiritual teaching often suggests knowing we are in prison is the first step of getting out of prison. When we see the mental and behavioral straightjackets we have created, we can address our immobilized condition. But if we are unaware of what is controlling our actions and causing our emotional lives to either soar or crash, we are victims of these unconscious influences. Therefore, exposure is the first step.

However, it is difficult to say thank you when you are exposed. It is one thing for the inner lives of the guests to be a game of musical chairs with an eye to winning esteem from others and for second-guessing hosts to be checking the guest list and wondering if they have helped themselves by this gathering. It is quite another thing for all this to be out in the open, for the egocentric workings of the mind to be mercilessly laid bare. That is why the humor helps. It allows us to see what is often too painful to look at.

Flannery O'Connor, the Southern, Christian short-story writer and novelist, was once asked why her characters were so grotesque. She responded that you had to paint large, grotesque figures for the blind to see. Behind this imaginative remark was the firm conviction that people were blind to the assumptive worlds that drove them. She fashioned grotesque characters and violent plots to wake us up to who we were and what we were concerned with. Her stories shock, but they also reveal. She was in the tradition of Jesus, the prophetic comic.

When we can laugh at our inner strategies of self-importance, we are paradoxically just a little bit more than those strategies and a little bit less. We are a little bit more because we can see the bars of our self-created prison and know that it is locked from the inside. We hold the key to our freedom. We are a little bit less because if we follow the lure of our new self-knowledge, we will forego what we think makes us socially more. We will be less socially but more spiritually. But social positioning is so ingrained in us, most likely we will find this new found freedom painful. Our only hope is to laugh at ourselves.

In his book *Touching the Holy: Ordinariness, Self-Esteem, and Friendship*, Robert Wicks names four friends of our spiritual life—the prophet, the cheerleader, the harasser, and the spiritual guide (Notre Dame, IN: Ave Maria Press, 1992, 93–122). He gives a personal example of the harasser. He had just finished teaching a class that had gone terribly. A friend came up to him in the hall.

> "You look depressed. Why is that?"
> "I just gave a presentation and it went terribly from the beginning; it was like a rock in water."
> "But why are you depressed?" he repeated.

"They were so bored that they continually checked their watches to see if their batteries were running!"

Again he asked, "But why are you depressed?"

"I couldn't believe how disinterested they were; they did something that I didn't think was anatomically possible—they actually yawned in unison!"

He steadfastly asked again: "But why are you depressed?"

By then I was not only depressed but also furious at him: "After all I have told you, why shouldn't I be depressed?"

"Because five seconds after you left the room, they probably forgot what your name was."

To this I exclaimed while laughing: "My goodness! Isn't there any easier way we could put this in perspective?"

I am afraid there is not any easier way. When our "negative or positive grandiosity" comes into view, laughter is the way we are restored to the simple joy of being human.

Twenty-Third Sunday in Ordinary Time

Proper 18

Luke 14:25-33

🔥

Hungering to Build and Battle

A Spiritual Commentary

Now large crowds were traveling with him; and he turned and said to them, "Whoever comes to me and does not hate father and mother, wife and children, brothers and sisters, yes, and even life itself, cannot be my disciple. Whoever does not carry the cross and follow me cannot be my disciple."

Jesus does not offer the crowds any fantasies of an easy life. He does not play on their needs or appeal to their prejudices. Instead of mollifying them in any way, he turns and confronts them. If they have come to him, then, make no mistake about it, *they have come to him*. If previously they had found identity and refuge by clinging to their family of origin or family of choice, they must forsake that identity and refuge. If they had loved life itself and let this absolute value guide their every decision and action, they must even forsake that allegiance. Jesus is now their center, and there is no room for competing loyalties.

If Jesus is their center, then the cross is their way. The cross is the symbol of leading a persistent and peaceful life in a violent world. This is not a life of avoiding difficulties; it is a life of stepping on the snake and the scorpion (Luke 10:19). They are to move into those places where no semblance of kingdom living can be found and bring the kingdom possibility. To follow Jesus is to use him as a rock to stand on and then put their shoulder to the wheel of the world. When the world refuses to move, the disciples receive its stubborn refusal into their bodies. "When he was abused, he did not return abuse; when he suffered, he did not threaten; but he entrusted himself to the one who judges justly. He himself bore our sins in his body on the cross, so that, free from sins, we might live for righteousness; by his wounds you have been healed" (1 Pet 2:23-24). Carrying the cross means taking on the healing of the earth in the most radical way.

For which of you, intending to build a tower, does not first sit down and estimate the cost, to see whether he has enough to complete it? Otherwise, when he has laid a foundation and is not able to finish, all who see it will begin to ridicule him, saying, 'This fellow began to build and was not able to finish.'

Or what king, going out to wage war against another king, will not sit down first and consider whether he is able with ten thousand to oppose the one who comes against him with twenty thousand? If he cannot, then, while the other is still far away, he sends a delegation and asks for the terms of peace.

This following of Jesus should not be mindless. The disciples are to think about what it entails. It is like building a tower, constructing a connection between heaven and earth. What will it take to finish it? It is like taking on larger forces with lesser forces, risking battle even though overmatched. How will this uphill battle be sustained? If you cannot see it through and you are certain you will be overwhelmed, it is better not to begin. There is a need to assess your resources and evaluate your resolve. It is not advised to sign up under the flush of inspiration or in secret pursuit of anything other than the project of the Cross. A decision should be made with all the practical wisdom of a cost-conscious builder and a battle-hardened king.

David Rhoads relates a contemporary situation that catches the flavor of these parabolic warnings to aspiring disciples.

> In the late 1980s, a volunteer approached a leader of the Sanctuary Movement in the United States serving refugees from Central America, and she asked to join in the work of the movement. The leader said to her, "Before you say whether you really wish to join us, let me pose some questions: Are you ready to have your telephone tapped by the government? Are you prepared to have your neighbors shun you? Are you strong enough to have your children ridiculed and harassed at school? Are you ready to be arrested and tried, with full media coverage? If you are not prepared for these things, you may not be ready to join the movement. For when push comes to shove, if you fear these things, you will not be ready to do what needs to be done for the refugees." The woman decided to think it over. (*Reading Mark, Engaging the Gospel* [Minneapolis: Fortress Press, 2004] 53)

The two parables take the crowds beyond abstractly considering discipleship. They make them consider questions of readiness and risk.

So therefore, none of you can become my disciple if you do not give up all your possessions.

Possessions are whatever we hold onto that competes with our communion with Jesus and cooperation with his mission. They are substitute absolutes. It is not just a matter of freeing ourselves from material holdings or social positions—an outer-world dispossession. It is also a matter of purging our mind of its security fantasies and its habits of violent domination—an inner-world dispossession. An essential step of discipleship is selling what we have that keeps us from integrating the mind and actions of Christ into our minds and actions.

Teaching

In spiritual philosophy a distinction is often made between choice freedom and creative freedom. (See Beatrice Bruteau, *The Grand Option: Personal Transformation and a New Creation* [Notre Dame, IN: University of Notre Dame Press, 2001] chapters 4, 5, and 8.) In choice freedom, the outer world presents us with options, and we choose. We may choose rightly or wrongly, out of noble reasons or ego-centered motives, well informed about our decision or lacking important information. But we choose and take the first steps on the path we have chosen.

In creative freedom, we do not begin by reacting to what is happening. We gather ourselves in. It is assumed that our energies are dispersed and our unified center is spread out in many pursuits. We have multiple allegiances to our families and to the necessary demands and pleasures of life. Our single ray of light has entered the prism and multiple colors have emerged. However, it is now time to pull ourselves out of these many manifestations and concentrate ourselves into a transcendent center. This self-possession is the precondition for self-disposal and accepting the offer of discipleship. Choosing discipleship is not one option among many. It is the gathered self freely giving itself into the world in a particular way.

The most direct strategy for moving people from choice freedom to creative freedom is to lay out a path of struggle. Choice freedom is the usual way we work and its mechanisms are well established. We pick through possibilities according to what we think is best for us. The necessary skill is to become a good rather than a poor picker. However, when a way of dispossession is proposed to us, choice freedom becomes stalled. It cannot consider this invitation seriously. From the perspective of choice freedom, discipleship is all sacrifice; and sacrifice is defined as giving things up we really want. If we choose a way of dispossession and view it as giving things up, we will always fill the lack, and most likely we will not persevere. The tower will not be built and the larger forces will not be vanquished. Discipleship will always be a way of life that denies us what we interiorly want and think we need.

Coming to Jesus means leaving behind the normal world of choice freedom and stepping into the rare air of creative freedom. Jesus is the way into the transcendent self that is the starting point for the creative freedom needed for discipleship. The transcendent self is grounded in God. It is beyond the vicissitudes of time and yet capable of shaping history according to divine purposes. This is the identity Jesus provides, and without it, disciples would not be able to pay the price of building and battling. From the perspective of the transcendent self and creative freedom, the sacrifices of discipleship look radically different. Sacrifice is the act of self-giving that makes life holy, that fashions a future that has never been seen before. It is the overflow of a fullness that develops from being attuned to the self-giving of God. Sacrifice is the energy the sons and daughters of the Holy One bring to building the tower and opposing the forces.

But what types of people are ready to engage these rigorous demands of Jesus? What types of people can sustain the spiritual dynamic of in-gathering and out-flowing that characterizes the commitment to discipleship?

Jesus confronted the crowds who were traveling with him with these rigorous demands. Maybe some of the crowds were thinking about moving from traveling with him to following him, from casual companions to disciples. Then these hard words would sort out the serious from the curious. The simple hunger for religious meaning may be in all people. But the drive to discipleship is definitely not in all people. Traveling with Jesus but not following him is a real option. It may not signal lack of faith, or cowardice, or moral failure. It may be that some people, perhaps most people, are not capable of continued strenuous acts of creative freedom. They cannot sustain the long-haul commitment that Jesus insists is necessary.

But those who are ready to build and battle probably have a sensibility close to what Teilhard de Chardin describes. "I shall begin by describing the *fundamental tendency*, the natural cast of my mind. . . . However far back I go into my memories (even before the age of ten) I can distinguish in myself the presence of a strictly dominating passion: the passion for the Absolute" (Pierre Teilhard de Chardin, "My Universe," in *The Heart of Matter* [New York: Harcourt Brace Jovanovich, 1978] 196). In the young Teilhard, this passion for the Absolute took the form of contemplating iron objects—the lock-pin of a plough, the head of a bolt, etc. These objects had to be as thick and massive as possible. In this way there was a plentitude to them, a concentrated fullness. In particular, the "cherished substance should be resistant, impervious to attack, and *hard!*" (*The Heart of Matter*, 19).

This names the raw stuff of disciples. They are consumed by an Archimedean hunger to find a place that is "impervious to attack and hard," a place to stand in order to move the world. They want to feel in themselves a "cherished substance" that can be resistant to what is in order to create what must be. This "cherished substance" was the house built on rock that Jesus promised to people who could hear his words and put them into action (Matt 7:24-27). Disciples desire this rock identity because they are tired of going along. They want to change what they see more than they want to live. When they hear Jesus offer them a concentrated plentitude that will be able to transform the earth, their desire is fulfilled. They have always hungered to build and battle, and now the food to feed this hunger has arrived. Jesus is walking toward Jerusalem and they fall in line behind him, forgetting to say goodbye to normal life.

Twenty-Fourth Sunday in Ordinary Time

Proper 19

Luke 15:1-32 *LM* • **Luke 15:1-10** *RCL*

❧

Getting Back What We Lose

A Spiritual Commentary

Now all the tax collectors and sinners were coming near to listen to him. And the Pharisees and the scribes were grumbling and saying, "This fellow welcomes sinners and eats with them."

"Tax collectors and sinners" is a social category for people outside the law, and therefore unrighteous. "Pharisees and scribes" is a social category for those inside the law, and therefore righteous. The righteous are complaining about Jesus' association with the unrighteous. They characterize it as "welcoming sinners and eating with them." This is code for approving of their unrighteousness.

However, it is unlikely that Jesus ever thought he welcomed and ate with sinners. Although the Pharisees and scribes saw him as going over to the other side, he saw himself as bringing the two sides together. He was a man of reconciliation in a world that had accepted, and even gloried in, division. He was struggling to put things back together that other people were struggling to keep apart.

So he told them this parable: "Which one of you, having a hundred sheep and losing one of them, does not leave the ninety-nine in the wilderness and go after the one that is lost until he finds it? When he has found it, he lays it on his shoulders and rejoices. And when he comes home, he calls together his friends and neighbors, saying to them, 'Rejoice with me, for I have found my sheep that was lost.' Just so, I tell you, there will be more joy in heaven over one sinner who repents than over ninety-nine righteous persons who need no repentance.

"Or what woman having ten silver coins, if she loses one of them, does not light a lamp, sweep the house, and search carefully until she finds it? When she has found it, she calls together

her friends and neighbors, saying, 'Rejoice with me, for I have found the coin that I had lost.' Just so, I tell you, there is joy in the presence of the angels of God over one sinner who repents."

Jesus does not condone sinful behavior. He sees himself as seeking the lost, finding them, including them among the already found, and inviting everyone to a communal feast of rejoicing. Moreover, what he is doing is subtly portrayed as the deepest instinct of every man and woman, even the Pharisees and scribes to whom he is talking. "Which one of you . . . ?" "What woman . . . ?" If anyone were in these circumstances, they would do the same thing. Why is Jesus so sure that what the shepherd and the woman are doing is universal behavior?

Both one hundred and ten are symbolic numbers. They connote wholeness, completeness, fullness. There is a drive in each person for wholeness on every level. We want physical, psychological, social, and spiritual completeness. The story of the shepherd and the woman are about social completeness which, when it happens, also triggers a spiritual wholeness, an integration of heaven and earth. Israel is split into two camps—tax collectors/sinners and righteous. They must become one people, the one people under the covenant of the one God. So the shepherd seeks the one sheep to add him to the ninety-nine; and the woman seeks the one coin to add it to the nine. In this way a divided people become whole.

This drive to find the missing one is not the anxious activity of anal-retentive people, or the expression of an underlying greed that always wants one more, or just a general quirkiness. It represents an alignment between God and creation. God desires this reconciled unity. So the angels rejoice more when a whole is approached by the inclusion of what was formerly excluded than when an incompleteness, even when it is a righteous incompleteness, remains one short. The simultaneous rejoicing of heaven and earth means that they are in sync. The sheep are reunited; the coins are reunited; heaven and earth are reunited. What unites them is joy in the realization that things are the way they were meant to be. Creation is fulfilled.

Yet, from an earthbound perspective, there is something startling in this insistence on wholeness. Our practical minds cannot help but see it as romantic. It does not reckon with the inevitability of loss; it does not settle for realistic assessment of what is possible. Even more, it does not recognize one of religion's most persistent sensibilities. Religious traditions are noted for making people face loss as the key to a correct understanding of the human condition. When we realize the truth of impermanence, we will accept our finitude, establish clear priorities, learn to cherish the present moment, and cultivate a sense of dependence on God. We will also understand the "originality" of our sin. Sin is coextensive with all creation and always a dimension of who we are. Therefore, in this life our finitude and sinfulness conspire to teach us the wilderness claims sheep foolish enough to stray and the coins lay forever unclaimed in the dark corners of houses. Mature consciousness does not fantasize perfection in an imperfect world.

However, this emphasis on necessary losses may have an unintended side effect. It can lead us into a blank-check acceptance of loss as inevitable. We have lost our brothers and sisters, or we have lost a crucial part of our creativity or verge, or we have lost our desire to contribute to the future of the earth, or etc. Impressed by the truth of transience and our own inability to search and retrieve, we may shrug off these losses rather than begin to search and reclaim them. The truth of loss may have impressed us too much and taught us to accommodate too quickly. We become numb to the pain of missing what was once part of our total identity. We accept it as the normal ways of things. But Jesus is not resigned. He is searching the wilderness and sweeping the house. The Son of Man does not settle for loss. "For the Son of Man came to seek out and to save the lost" (Luke 19:10).

He also does not settle for sweet but private reunions. If the finding of the one makes the ninety-nine and the nine whole, then it is not just the good fortune of the shepherd and the woman. The whole community must gather. When all the sheep and coins are together, then the neighbors and friends are brought in. One whole invites another whole. Getting back what we lost, receiving into ourselves what makes us complete, necessarily overflows into communal rejoicing (Luke 15:32). Joy is contagious and the whole community is infected. Making whole translates into making merry with all the people. The angels who are rejoicing in heaven are probably the same crowd who appeared to the shepherds at Jesus' birth and announced "good news of great *joy* for *all* the people" (Luke 2:10).

Teaching

It is great when we find something we have lost, especially when what we have lost is a relationship.

I was told a story about a woman who, when she was growing up, had an estranged relationship with her father. Her father was always on her case. Whatever she did, it was not good enough. He corrected her constantly. She found it so maddening that as soon as she could she left the house and got an apartment. Away from day-in day-out living with her father, she calmed down and was politely distant toward him—whenever she was forced to be with him. One of those times she was forced to be with him was her mother's birthday.

When she went to her mother's birthday party, she was immediately uncomfortable. As soon as she entered the house, the walls started to come in on her. Her sister was there with her husband and their four-year-old son. They had just bought a dog, a puppy, for the boy. So she took her nephew and the dog and went out into the backyard. She took the leash off the dog and the dog ran around. Her mother came out on the porch and told them to come in for dinner and to bring the dog. But when they tried to catch the dog, the dog ran away from them, running under and around their grasp.

Her father comes out in the yard, asks her for the leash, sits calmly on a bench, and tells her and her nephew not to run after the dog. They do not chase the dog, and the dog figures the game is over. He pads up to the father on the bench who clips the leash on his collar. The father turns to his daughter and grandson and says, "That's how you do it."

This infuriates the woman. It is one more time she isn't good enough.

After dinner and before the birthday cake, the woman decides once again she would like to get out of the house. She takes her nephew and the dog outside, only this time in the front of the house. Before she can stop him, the nephew takes the leash off the dog. The dog is running out in the street between the parked cars. They chase the dog, but the puppy is too quick.

Frustrated, she tells her nephew to sit on the curb next to her and not to move. After a while, the dog realizes the running game is over and pads his way toward the woman and her nephew. But the nephew jumps up and tries to grab the dog. The dog is off and running.

The woman scolds her nephew and tells him to sit still. Since the dog is not being chased, he makes a return visit. The woman clips the leash on his collar, stands up, takes her nephew's hand, and turns around. There—in the front window of the house is her father. He has been watching it all. He has a big grin on his face. Then he flashes an OK sign, the forefinger and thumb together and his arm pumping the air.

The woman laughs and gives him an OK sign back.

It seems to me the woman of this story got her father back in the most serendipitous of ways. That series of events could not be planned. But step by unforeseen step grace was leading them to a place of shared laughter. When I think of this story, I remember a story about my father and how I got him back even though I had never lost him.

It was 1959, I was eighteen, and I was sitting in class on a hot September Saturday—when the light bulb lit.

The school I went to was a high school seminary. We went to class on Saturday and we were off on Thursday. The point of this strange schedule was to keep us separated from the shenanigans—from football games to dating—that were sure to happen on Saturday. So as we sat in class on Saturday, we schemed about how to get out of class on Saturday.

The school had ongoing mission activities. Each classroom tried to raise the money for the missions. It was very competitive. And there was a reward for winning. The classroom that raised the most money got a Saturday off.

What the light bulb was about was a surefire plan to win the mission drive and have Saturday off.

The movie *Ben Hur* had just been released. It was getting rave reviews and the Catholic Legion of Decency had not condemned it. Christ even made an appearance in the movie. Perfect for seminarians. It was playing in the evenings, with matinees on Saturdays and Sundays. But there were no scheduled matinees during the week. People were working and kids were in school. There was no one to go.

But there were close to a thousand kids who were not in school on Thursday. Perhaps the Michael Todd theater could be persuaded to have a matinee on Thursday and the high school seminarians could be persuaded to buy tickets. And I could do the persuading.

I could buy the tickets from the theater for, say, one dollar and sell them to all the Thursday-off-with-nothing-to-do-kids for, say, $1.50 and make, with a turnout of 600, $300.00. This would put us over the top. A free Saturday was in the making.

I have been told that some theologians of the Middle Ages thought part of the bliss of heaven was seeing your enemies in hell. This, I am sure, is poor theology. But certainly part of my motivation was knowing my friends and classmates would be in school while I was out in the forbidden territory of a free Saturday.

I went to the theater and was directed to a very small office with a very big man in it. He oozed over the sides of the chair and he was smoking a cigar.

"What do you want, kid? I ain't hiring."

I told him my plan.

"I ain't Catholic. But I'll do it." He paused. "Of course, I'll need six hundred up front. I gotta have some assurance."

I went back to the mission director and told him about my sure-fire plan. Then I came to the punch line. "Father, I need six hundred up front."

He looked at me for a long while. Then he laughed.

"I can't do it. It's too risky."

I went home to my father. My father was a cop. We did not have a lot of money.

I told him my plan. "I need six hundred," I said.

"So do I," said my father.

But he gave me the money. The surefire plan proved sure-fire. I added "wheeler and dealer" to the growing sense of who I was.

I paid my father back in six weeks—no interest.

We won the mission drive. And on a Saturday in early November as I sat in the bleachers of a high school football game, I practiced being in heaven.

*   *   *

It is now 1992. It is my father's eightieth birthday party. There are fifteen of us gathered at a restaurant. I am sitting next to my father. He is lifting a drink to his mouth with both hands. The drink is shaking slightly.

He puts the drink back down. He looks at me and says, "Remember the time I lent you the money."

We had not talked about it since 1959. I am surprised, but I remember. "Yes."

"Back then, before you asked me, did you ever think I wouldn't give it to you?"

"No, Dad. I always knew you would give it to me."

"Funny," my father said, "so did I. I always knew I would give it to you."

And that's how I got my father back, even though I never lost him.

And that is how I think life in time is. We walk with one another, but there is also an ongoing getting lost and returning, of not being there and suddenly being there again. Certainly, it is about physically being with one another. But it is also about meeting spiritually. When spiritual meeting happens, the angels get into the act. They are a giddy group to begin with, but when they mix laughter and tears, merriment and sorrow, all creation goes along for the ride.

Twenty-Fifth Sunday in Ordinary Time

Proper 20

Luke 16:1-13

❧

Surviving Spiritually

A Spiritual Commentary

Then Jesus said to the disciples, "There was a rich man who had a manager, and charges were brought to him that this man was squandering his property.

So he summoned him and said to him, "What is this I hear about you? Give me an accounting of your management, because you cannot be my manager any longer."

Then the manager said to himself, "What will I do, now that my master is taking the position away from me? I am not strong enough to dig and I am ashamed to beg. I have decided what to do so that, when I am dismissed as manager, people may welcome me into their homes."

In the previous story, a younger son took his inheritance and "traveled to a distant country, and there he *squandered his property* in dissolute living" (Luke 15:13). Without property, he hits bottom. He herds swine, and he would "*gladly* have eaten what the swine ate but no one would give him anything." His physical survival is at stake and the possibility of a shameful death opens up before him. He suddenly "comes to himself," does an inner assessment, and develops an action plan. As all Christians know, his action plan will not be carried out as he envisioned. It will be trumped by the wild welcome of his father.

In this story, called the dishonest manager, property is also squandered, and the manager who did the squandering also hits bottom—in his imagination. He is not immediately threatened with starvation, but he is immediately threatened with job loss that will lead to starvation. He engages in an inner assessment and sizes up his situation. It is as dire as that of the Prodigal Son. Since he will never be hired again as a manager, the only paths open to him are physical labor and begging.

He is unsuited for both. A shameful death opens up before him; and just as quickly, what psychologists call "primary narcissism" kicks in.

With his back to the wall, he manufactures an action plan. He is not going gently into that good night. He does not sit back and await his dismissal. He concocts a strategy. However, this New Revised Standard Version translation does not give us the "aha" moment as he moves from the trapped feeling of "no way out" to the liberated feeling of "way out." The New American Version has him say, "I have it!" Brainstorm!

The storyteller withholds the details of the plan, but he does give us its purpose. The manager thinks the plan will keep him alive by making people welcome him into their homes after he has been dismissed. He will move from employment to employment, from house to house. He will not be on the street. The threat to his survival has galvanized him into action.

> **So, summoning his master's debtors, one by one, he asked the first, "How much do you owe my master?"**
>
> **He answered, "A hundred jugs of olive oil."**
>
> **He said to him, "Take your bill, sit down quickly, and make it fifty."**
>
> **Then he asked another, "And how much do you owe?"**
>
> **He replied, "A hundred containers of wheat."**
>
> **He said to him, "Take your bill and make it eighty."**

On the surface it is not clear how this carefully executed plan is going to assure the manager a welcome into the homes of "people." It is presumed "people" are the debtors he has just conspired with to relieve their debt. If the idea is that the debtors now "owe" the manager, and when he is dismissed it will be payback time, events might not go as he envisions. The debtors might reason: if he cheated on his former master for our benefit, most likely he will cheat on us for the benefit of our debtors. The manager has tried to recruit them into his survival scheme, but perhaps he was not as clever as he thought. Once the debtors have benefited from the manager, they might leave him to his impoverished fate. If this is how things unfold, his survival is still in jeopardy.

However, a more subtle scheme might be unfolding. The debtors are called in one by one. There will be no chance for group conversation and the scrutiny and hesitation that group reflection often brings.

Stealth needs privacy. Then the debtors are questioned. *They* must acknowledge how much they owe and *they* must alter the numbers. They do so at the instruction of the steward, but *they* change the debt. It is their handwriting that has doctored the bills. And, in line with all shady undertakings, they must do this quickly.

Now the debtors are not only in the manager's debt, they are in collusion with him. They are full-scale accomplices in a scheme to defraud the rich man. The manager has taught them how to cook the books, and they have cooked them willingly. He is already in their homes because he has made them like himself, people whose behavior has put their survival in jeopardy. The rich man now has the same case against them as he has against the manager.

> **And his master commended the dishonest manager because he acted shrewdly.**

However the plan was intended to work, for those of us with more than a little experience in scheming (i.e., all of us), the plan does not appear foolproof. Nevertheless, the master is surprisingly impressed. Instead of focusing on his lost income and being angry and punishing, he comments on the practical virtue of his manager. If there was ever any doubt that this story was constructed to teach a specific point, there should be none now. If the father of the Prodigal Son does not act like a patriarch, this master does not act like a rich man. In fact, the master is so unrealistic and out-of-character that he does not even get to speak. The readers are simply told about his favorable comments.

Although the dishonesty of the manager is forthrightly acknowledged, the master has seen more than dishonesty. So he commends rather than corrects, decries, or threatens the manager and the debtors. His commendation may be a form of "begrudging admiration." What comes to mind are those scenes in mystery movies where the Scotland Yard detective, with a worldwide reputation for solving crimes, stares into the empty vault where once fifteen million pounds lived a lonely life and says to his nodding associates, "Well, boys, you got to give him credit. He knew what he was doing." In other words, the sentiment is: "I don't agree with what he did. But you have to admit, it was a bold move."

Although the text says the master commended the manager for "acting shrewdly," the Greek word simply means "wise." It is associated with practical actions that ensure survival. At the conclusion of the Sermon on the Mount, Jesus says that those who hear his words and put them into action are like *wise* people who build their house on rock (Matt 7:24-27). Rain, floods, and wind can beat on the house but it will not fall. They will survive. These wise ones are contrasted with the foolish who have heard Jesus' words and have not put them to use. The house of the foolish will collapse under the rain, floods, and wind. They will not survive. The wise are those who can survive storm.

In a similar way, in Matthew's story of the wise and foolish brides-maids, the ones who bring oil for their lamps are wise (Matt 25:1-13). But the bridesmaids who did not bring oil are foolish. When the bride-groom finally arrives, the foolish are told to go to those who sell and buy. The wise accompany the bridegroom into the feast. By the time the foolish get back the door is shut. Their pleading is of no avail. The bridegroom insists from inside the locked door that he does not know them. The wise are those who get into the feast before the door closes.

The wise know how to survive. Even though the rich man's resources are further depleted, he so values the manager's resiliency and effective action that he praises rather than critiques him. The Prodigal Son acts to ensure physical survival and the dishonest servant acts to ensure social survival. But the teachings of Jesus as a whole are about the dimension of spirit. Stories that focus on physical and social dynamics are meant to be applied to spiritual dynamics. Therefore, the take-away from this story is: as the dishonest servant knew his physical and social life was threatened and acted decisively and wisely in order to survive, so the disciples should realize their spiritual life (gospel consciousness) is threatened and act decisively and wisely in order to survive.

The first observation in carrying out this teaching is that the dishon-est manager is more shrewd in his area of life than the disciples are shrewd in their area of life.

> **For the children of this age are more shrewd in dealing with their own generation than are the children of light.**

This is a lament. I consider the children of this age and the children of light to be the same children seen from different perspectives. When our consciousness is immersed in physical and social life, we are chil-dren of this age. As children of this age, we are quick to sense any threat to our physical and social life and we spring into action. We will find food and shelter and we are ingenious in how we do it. Nothing will stand in our way. Our survival is our priority.

But we are also children of light whose consciousness has been illumined by the Good News that Jesus teaches. We are aware that we

have a soul relationship to God that simultaneously makes us brothers
and sisters to one another. However, this consciousness is threatened
on all sides. Powerful internal and external factors seek to overwhelm
it. But we are not alert to them and we do not struggle against them.
Therefore, we are not galvanized into action to save our spiritual life
the way we are galvanized to save our physical and social lives. We are
shrewd in the ways of the world, but we are not shrewd in the ways of
the Spirit. We need to be instructed.

> **And I tell you, make friends for yourselves by means of dishon-
> est wealth so that when it is gone, they may welcome you into
> the eternal homes.**

Here is one instruction about how the children of light might become wise in the ways of spiritual survival. They should not allow
money to become dishonest. Money is promoted as providing social
security and, to some extent, it does that. But it can easily come into
competition with God who ultimately is the only security, the true rock
that can withstand the storm. This makes wealth dishonest because it
promises what it cannot provide. Therefore, a correct use of possibly
dishonest wealth is to use it for honest purposes, i.e., to make friends.
In this way, money will be a medium of establishing relationships. It
will be one way of loving our neighbor.

A bolstering argument for making friends with wealth focuses on
money as a passing commodity of this world. It is not permanent. So
if we try to use it to secure our lives, it will fail us. It cannot protect us
against death. Its only legitimate use is as a resource to bind people
together. If we use it this way, the way that God intended, we will have
used it well and we will be welcomed into the eternal home. Therefore,
if we want to use money to secure our spiritual existence and not just
our physical and social existence, we should share it with others and
make it the cement of relationships and community. This use reflects
how God uses "his wealth." Therefore, our life will be grounded more
deeply in God, more adapted to spiritual survival.

> **"Whoever is faithful in a very little is faithful also in much; and
> whoever is dishonest in a very little is dishonest also in much.
> If then you have not been faithful with dishonest wealth, who
> will entrust to you true riches? And if you have not been faith-
> ful with what belongs to another, who will give you what is
> your own?"**

This spiritual wisdom presupposes different levels that have different evaluations. There is a lesser level and a greater level and they are connected to one another in complex ways. The lesser level is "a very little," "dishonest wealth" and "what belongs to another." The greater level is "a very much" and "true riches" and "what is yours." One way they interact is that the lesser level is symbolic of the greater level. Our trustworthiness in small things reflects and shows our capacity in greater matters. Our trustworthiness with earthly wealth reflects and shows our capacity with spiritual wealth. Our trustworthiness with the property of another reflects and shows our responsibility for our own possessions. If we are doing well on the lesser level, it is because we are doing well on the greater level.

A second way the levels interact is as a developmental stepladder. If we do well on a lesser level, the ones who are teaching us will invite us to experience a greater level. But if we cannot handle money correctly or manage the possessions of another properly, we will not be shown spiritual riches and the deeper possession of our own soul. Spiritual survival, the greater level, is not pursued independent of physical and social reality. The spirit survives and thrives in dynamic relationship with the whole person.

> **No slave can serve two masters. For a slave will either hate the one and love the other, or be devoted to the one and despise the other. You cannot serve God and wealth.**

This is a forced choice typical of spiritual teaching. We have to choose what is most important and make everything else serve that reality. How earthly wealth works to secure existence and how God works to secure existence are two different strategies. Both cannot be embraced on their own terms at the same time. Serving one means using the other in that service.

Serving mammon means trying to manipulate God into that service. We pray for our success and see every material advance as a sign that God is blessing us. God has become the servant of what we truly worship. On the other hand, serving God means learning how to use mammon in that service. If we learn how to do this, mammon is freed from its role as a surrogate god and becomes just money, one of the many servants of God.

This strong contrast sums up the practical wisdom on spiritual survival. We must become as alert and responsive when our spirits are threatened as we are when our social position is threatened. We must be careful not to let money become a rival with God. It has a relative power to provide security, but it seductively parades as an ultimate safety. Its real purpose is to facilitate community. How to use it correctly is a test case for spiritual development. This development is not a path of opposing the spiritual (greater) to the material (lesser). Rather, it is how greater and lesser are integrated with one another. In order to get this integration right, it is necessary to adopt a hierarchical ranking where God is supreme. The first and capstone commandment is the key. "I am the LORD your God, who brought you out of the land of Egypt, out of the house of slavery; you shall have no other gods before me" (Exod 20:2).

Teaching

On the way out of a meeting in a corporate healthcare setting, a man pulled me aside and asked, half in anger and half in jest, "Do you have anything I can read? This 'f- - - - -' materialism is killing my soul."

Often spiritual teachings on the human person distinguish a true and false self. The false self is the ego with its bottomless appetite for pleasures and adventures of physical and social life. The true self is the soul that is grounded in God and in communion with all of creation. The soul is the true self because it does not suffer the collapse that our physical and social dimensions undergo. When we identify with our souls, we are transformed through death. So, from this perspective, it seems incorrect to say our spirit or soul can be killed, especially that it can be seriously threatened by materialism.

Yet I think most people would understand the outburst, "This f- - - - - - materialism is killing my soul." It means that I am so immersed in thinking about the material and social dimensions of life that I can find no time to open my mind to the spiritual. This loss can be quite painful. One of Rachel Remen's patients, a gifted cancer surgeon, told her, "I can barely make myself get out of bed most mornings. I hear the same complaints day after day, I see the same diseases over and over again. I just don't care anymore. I need a new life" (Rachel Remen, *My Grandfather's Blessings* [New York: Riverhead Books, 2000] 116). This is an advanced case of ennui. He is still plodding along, doing work, and sitting up and taking nourishment. But zest for his work has disappeared. He is no longer in conscious contact with his soul.

This surgeon might think that if he changes his circumstances, the new life he needs will be available to him. He might be right, for sometimes changing the outer world can help. If he retires or reduces his surgery schedule or takes three months off, his ennui may recede. But often the old maxim holds true: wherever you go, there you are. He will carry with him his mental conditioning wherever he goes. He has learned a way of life that screens out spirit. The result is he has to keep on going without what spirit provides—pleasure, passion, purpose. Everything goes on according to its own inertia, and this experience is so powerful we give it credit for killing our spirit.

The gospel story and its subsequent reflections think this is where we need help. We are not shrewd at keeping the spirit alive. Our much-vaunted ability to spring into action when threatened does not transfer to the spiritual level. A recent New Yorker cartoon showed two men in a dungeon without windows or doors. They are manacled to the wall by their wrists, ankles, and neck. Both have long beards; they have obviously been there awhile. One is leaning over to the other and whispering "Now here's my plan." But when we are chained to a life that no longer gives us pleasure, passion, or purpose, we have trouble saying, "Now here's my plan." We are not skilled in spiritual survival.

There are some hints in this gospel passage that might help. Picture what a life without spirit is like. A sharp evaluation of options is always a good motivator. If we savor the monotony and boredom of living without spirit, it will stimulate us to seek out interest and excitement. The manager's excruciating contemplation of his inability to beg and dig puts his mind in high gear to find another way. As one person said, "The more I thought about it, the more I became determined not to live an unlived life." A *commitment* to live spiritually is the first step to finding a *way* to live spiritually.

Make friends with people who are not only spiritually surviving but also spiritually thriving. Some people are the right people to hang around. Their rightness consists in their receptivity to our spirit and their eagerness to share their spirits. A community of spiritually serious people can identify the threats to spirit more quickly and support our individual efforts to ward off those threats. Our friends often see the warning signs before we do. They also often know the remedy before we do. Spiritually surviving often means keeping the right company and heeding what they have to say.

Invest attention in what you enjoy and are good at. Although our spirit is imaged as an inner resource, its drive is to move outside and enliven what we are doing. Therefore, we should seek out what we enjoy and are good at and become intensely curious about it. It is not enough to self-indulgently do what we like, for any activity has the potential of deadening spirit. We must take up a "first time" attitude. This is the first time I have ever seen her; the first time I have ever given a talk; the first time I have ever attended a meeting. In this way we will maximize attention, notice new features of our situations, and act in a way that is more aligned with what is happening. When we invest attention, our spirit flows into what we are doing and returns to us with more spirit. Spirit is the reality that when it is given away, there is more of it. Paradoxically, spending spirit is the best way to enhance spirit.

A while back, my doctor sat me down for a serious chat. "Jack," he said, "think of yourself as a car. What you don't want to happen is to lose a bumper here and a highlight there as you go along the road of life. What you want to do—sometime in the future—is to pull up to a stop sign and," he paused, "er . . . disassemble." I got the idea, but I was not quite sure I could execute.

If a spiritual doctor would volunteer the same advice, it might sound like, "Jack, what you don't want to do is lose your zest for life and keep on going as if nothing were missing, making more and more out of the material and social dimensions as if they could do it for you on their own. What you want to do is to learn how to become alert to what threatens spirit and to act effectively to guard spirit from dissipation. And if you do lose spirit, stop and don't go on until you find it." I get the idea, but I am not quite sure I can execute.

Twenty-Sixth Sunday in Ordinary Time

Proper 21

Luke 16:19-31

❧

Needing Something More

A Spiritual Commentary

Jesus said to the Pharisees: "There was a rich man who dressed in purple garments and fine linen and dined sumptuously each day. And lying at his door was a poor man named Lazarus, covered with sores, who would gladly have eaten the scraps that fell from the rich man's table. Dogs even used to come and lick his sores. (LM)

In spiritual teaching stories a "rich man" is a designation that can go two ways. The rich man might be generous, and then we are prone to understand him either as a symbol for God or a symbol of human righteousness. A famous Sufi story begins, "There was a rich and generous man of Bokhara. Because he held a high rank in the invisible hierarchy, he was known as the President of the World. Every afternoon he gave gold to a different group of people" (Osho, *Journey to the Heart: Discourses on the Sufi Way* [Shaftesbury, Dorset: Element, 1976] 30). In this story, the rich man symbolizes the self-giving God.

In other stories, the rich man might be miserly. A famous Jewish tale begins, "In a town in Greece, there was a rich Jewish merchant who did business all over the world but was a terrible miser" ("The Rich Man Who Sought to Repent," in *Jewish Folktales Selected and Retold by Pinhas Sadeh* [New York: Doubleday, 1989] 177). These stories often revolve around events that invite the rich man to repent. If he does so, the story ends on a comic note. If he refuses, the story ends tragically.

In this story of the rich man and Lazarus, both types of rich men will appear. The story begins with sharp contrasts. The extravagant luxury of the rich man is played off against the utter destitution of Lazarus. This rich man is not a miser, but he is numb to the presence of the poor and inattentive to their needs. He feasts every day while Lazarus starves every day. Luxurious garments cover his body while wounds and the wet tongues of hungry dogs cover the body of Lazarus. Lazarus lies at his door, a door that is never opened. This is the second type of rich man, the numb one that needs to repent.

When the poor man died, he was carried away by angels to the bosom of Abraham. The rich man also died and was buried. (LM)

The contrast that began in life is continued in death—only the reversal of the rich man and Lazarus begins. The rich man is given a proper burial. Beggars are not given proper burials. But instead of saying Lazarus' body was eaten by the dogs that licked his wounds, the story surprisingly has angels carry him to the bosom of Abraham.

Abraham is the first type of rich man. In the Hebrew tradition he is often characterized as a wealthy man who was hospitable to all. No poor man would lay unattended at his door. The door would be opened and the poor man would be clothed and welcomed at his table. Lazarus in the bosom of Abraham symbolizes he is welcomed and accepted into the heart of the patriarch. Nothing less would be expected from the rich and generous Abraham.

. . . from the netherworld, where he was in torment, he raised his eyes and saw Abraham far off and Lazarus at his side. And he cried out, "Father Abraham, have pity on me. Send Lazarus to dip the tip of his finger in water and cool my tongue, for I am suffering torment in these flames."

Abraham replied, "My child, remember that you received what was good during your lifetime while Lazarus likewise received what was bad; but now he is comforted here, whereas you are tormented. Moreover, between us and you a great chasm is established to prevent anyone from crossing who might wish to go from our side to yours or from your side to ours." (LM)

In some teaching stories, when the rich man finds himself in hell, he sees the error of his ways and begs for another chance. Another chance is granted, and the story goes on to explore if change is really possible for this man. When this happens, the story often moves positively. However, this story takes a different tack. It is unrelenting in spelling out the consequences of self-sufficient, isolating riches.

At the sight of Lazarus in the company of the rich and generous Abraham, the rich man does not repent and seek another chance. His main concern is relief, not repentance. He asks for assistance from his Father Abraham who acknowledges this blood connection by calling him "my child." However, reliance on blood connections is not enough in the Christian economy. John the Baptist prophetically slammed those who thought that salvation came through physical descent from Abraham. "God is able from these stones to raise up children to Abraham" (Luke 3:8). The real children of Abraham are those who hold the hungry and sick, like Lazarus, in their bosom. The rich man is not a true child of Abraham and so the appeal to "Father Abraham" will not get him the hearing he wants.

The irony builds with the rich man's request. He wants Lazarus, whom he never gave food or drink to, to come with only a finger of water. Lying at the door of the rich man, Lazarus did not want a meal. He would have eaten the scraps. This showed the depth of his need and the extent of his torment. Now the rich man does not want to quench his thirst with a long drink. He only wants the touch of a cool finger on his tongue. In a similar way, this shows the depth of his need and the extent of his torment.

Abraham's reply has two parts. The first part asks the rich man to remember the way it was on earth—Lazarus in torment and the rich man in comfort. Now it is the opposite. No explanation is given for this reversal. The rich man is not told the attitudes and behaviors that have brought him to his present state of torment. The reversal is just stated as a fact that the rich man should remember and, presumably, ponder.

The second part of Abraham's answer strips the rich man of hope. In the afterlife even if the better-offs wanted to help the less fortunate, they could not. The gulf that exists between the rich and poor on earth can be crossed. But the gulf in the afterworld is fixed. It cannot be crossed. Therefore, the time before death is the time of repentance. The time after death is the time of consequences. The message is clear. Do not procrastinate: repent now.

> He said, "Then I beg you, father, send him to my father's house, for I have five brothers, so that he may warn them, lest they too come to this place of torment."
>
> But Abraham replied, "They have Moses and the prophets. Let them listen to them."
>
> He said, "Oh, no, father Abraham, but if someone from the dead goes to them, they will repent."

Then Abraham said, "If they will not listen to Moses and the prophets, neither will they be persuaded if someone should rise from the dead." (LM)

The rich man's torment cannot be relieved. So he takes another tack. Perhaps he can keep his brothers from this fate. Here is another chance for the story to move positively, but the storyteller has other intentions. The way of change is not to fear future torment but to listen to Moses and the prophets. The rich man does not think that is enough. People only change if something spectacular happens that will frighten them into taking action. If Lazarus would return from the dead with the news of the consequences of unfeeling riches, then his brothers would listen and change.

Abraham does not think so. There has already been a revelation from the heavenly realm. If they will not listen to "Moses and the prophets," a risen man will not persuade them. This is true even if the risen man is Jesus Christ. On the road to Emmaus, the risen, incognito Christ interprets his life, death, and resurrection by opening up the law and prophets (Luke 24:27). "Moses and the prophets" are the key to understanding the life, death, and resurrection of Christ. They are also what the rich man's brothers have to heed. They do not need something more; they need to attend to what they know.

So the story ends. The main character is a hopelessly doomed rich man who has no relief from the consequences of his actions. The ultimate reason for this terrible destiny is that he did not listen to Moses and the prophets. They clearly spelled out that the responsibility of the rich was to care for the poor. Instead, the rich man took his wealth as a personal advantage and numbed himself to the plight of the poor. This isolated him from others and put him at odds with God's purposes. In the last analysis, nothing survives and flourishes that does not cooperate with God's plan for creation.

Teaching

If this story is read as a straightforward prediction of the punishment of the unfeeling rich, it is a wonderful example of trying to scare them into changing their ways. They may dress and eat well for the short span of human life, but they will thirst for eternity. This theme has "high developmental" possibilities; and Christian preachers have rung the changes on the contrast between passing pleasure and everlasting pain.

However, the persuasiveness of this approach is questionable. Does it produce change or only deepen the resolve, as Macbeth put it, "to jump the life to come"? Even the story seems to suggest that firsthand information about future torment from a man recently returned from the dead is not all that persuasive.

But the story is more than a scare tactic. Religious traditions create many stories of heaven and hell. Although they take place in the afterlife, these stories are not meant to convey information about the world beyond death. Their real target is the assumptions and attitudes of this world. In these stories the afterlife is often portrayed as a "fixed" place. The purpose of this "fixity" is that it provides a focus on something essential that is not easily grasped in the flow of time. In this way the stories of heaven and hell make clear truths that are murky and ambiguous in the earthly realm.

The story of the rich man and Lazarus begins this side of death and continues on the other side of death. What happens on the other side of death reveals the truth of what is happening on this side of death. In particular, there is one thing the afterlife segment of the story clarifies that is not all that clear in the short pre-death segment. The way the world works is not how God works. The social arrangements of time are not sanctioned by eternity. The theology that sees earthly riches as a sign of God's blessing and earthly poverty and sickness as a sign of God's displeasure is mistaken. Furthermore, when this theology is used as a rationale for maintaining the gulf between the rich and the poor, it is particularly insidious. The real energy of God strives to rearrange the goods of the earth so all the people of the earth share in them. It does not support a status quo of inequality. Leaving behind the theology of rich-blessing and poor-curse is the first step toward new social configurations.

Although this heaven-hell story makes the discrepancy between the kingdom of God and the way of the earth clear to readers, Abraham thinks the rich man should have known this all along. Abraham is polite, even solicitous, to the rich a man. But he never once seriously considers relieving his torments or acting on his suggestions. Rather, he seems to be giving him a refresher course in prophetic Jewish theology. In contemporary parlance, he is saying:

> "What is it you don't understand about this? Let me rehearse the basics. You lived a life of luxury, deafened yourselves to Moses and the prophets, and numbed yourself to the needs of the poor. So now you are on the other side where the consequences of actions reach fulfillment. You find

yourself isolated and tormented. Is this a surprise? Our entire people began as poor and exploited. Everything in our history has urged us to welcome the poor and exploited. You have not done this. Do you really think you can ignore and resist God's purposes and succeed? Did you miss that teaching at synagogue? Now you want a spectacular sign for your brothers. Is this an excuse? Are you saying there wasn't enough evidence for you? If you just had a little more certainty, your self-interest would have kicked in and you would have "anted up." I don't think so. That's not the problem. If your brothers, like yourself, do not heed the whole history of their people, they will not listen to a man come back from the dead. The problem is not that they didn't know, but that they knew and didn't care. They hardened their heart and drank their wine. Nothing gets to them, and this self-imposed isolation is their destiny."

There are no excuses. Something more is not needed. There is enough already.

But perhaps there is one more thing that is needed. The directive to bridge the gap between the rich and poor is clear; and today many think we have the material resources to bring it about. But exactly how society as a whole and individuals in particular should go about bringing Abraham and Lazarus together is not clear. The path of advance must be discovered by people who have heard this powerful word from the story of the rich man and Lazarus and asked how it could be put into action. The Christian message always searches for creative disciples who can translate spiritual truths into social facts. On one side of the door, the rich man feasts; on the other side of the door, Lazarus starves. Who holds the key to open the door? The answer to that question begins with the universally recognized truth that doors are locked from the inside.

Twenty-Seventh Sunday
in Ordinary Time

Proper 22

Luke 17:5-10

❦

Accessing What We Have

A Spiritual Commentary

The apostles said to the Lord, "Increase our faith!"

Today we would call this request a cry for help. What triggered the outcry were Jesus' strong instructions on how his followers are to behave toward one another. He told them the "little ones" should not be made to stumble. The "little ones" are those who have just begun their spiritual development and are not yet mature in the faith. They are the weakest; and they must be attended to in such a way that they grow and become strong. They should not be stepped on or stepped over. As if this deference toward "little ones" were not enough, Jesus also told them they must be endlessly ready to forgive whoever offends them.

This must have shocked them to the core. It is social foolishness and goes against the primal instinct to protect and defend oneself. Revenge and retaliation are the accepted way. These new behaviors of deference and forgiveness may be hallmarks of the kingdom of God, but they are unrealistic fantasies in the world where most people live.

The apostles are not ready for this way of life, and they do not think they can carry it out. Whatever resources they have are not sufficient for the task. So they ask for more. They need a power that will enhance their ability to be sensitive to the weak and to live without harming others and to forgive whatever harm is done to them. In their minds they need an increase of faith.

> **The Lord replied, "If you had faith the size of a mustard seed, you could say to this mulberry tree, 'Be uprooted and planted in the sea,' and it would obey you.**

Jesus agrees they need faith. However, he does not support their assumption that a greater quantity of faith will help them. They do not need more faith. They need to be reminded about what faith is and assured they have all they need to do what Jesus has enjoined them to do. Faith results from people opening to and responding to God's initiating action. This allows them to cooperate with divine energy and to bring about the world God envisions. Therefore, faith is not about unaided human powers. It is about human abilities in league with divine intentions and activity.

Earlier, Jesus had told them a parable about the kingdom of God. "It is like a mustard seed that someone took and sowed in the garden; it grew and became a tree, and the birds of the air made nests in its branches" (Luke 13:18-19). Once the mustard seed is sown in the garden—in the human heart where God can nurture it—it grows into a tree of welcome. All people can nest in its branches. That is what Jesus has proposed to them. They must make a home for the human continuum, from the weakest who must not be offended to the strongest who must not elicit from them actions as violent as the ones they perform. Jesus' followers must be a tree of welcome, and their mustard seed faith is eminently qualified for the task. They have all they need.

These tasks of care and forgiveness entail changing what is perceived as intransigent. The extensive roots of the mulberry tree are embedded in the earth, and it grows in that soil. This is an unyielding fact of nature. But in the image that is meant to reveal and convey faith to the apostles, the mulberry tree is uprooted from where it has always been planted and replanted in a place where it has never been, a place where no one would ever suspect it could grow. The impossible has suddenly become possible because "nothing will be impossible with God" (Luke 1:37). Faith is the way humans cooperate with divine creative energy to make obdurate situations obey new commands.

In a similar way, human relationships have always been characterized by the strong trampling on the weak and the first aggression calling forth another aggression until the only way imaginable is reciprocal aggression. The oppression of the weak and the spiral of violence is the ever-present underside of human history. Just as the roots of a mulberry tree are deep in the earth, the roots of this way of human behavior are deep in both the human psyche and social structures.

But faith gives people access to a different way, a way that overturns how it has always been. "Now I have put my words in your mouth. See, today, I appoint you over nations and over kingdoms, to pluck up and to pull down, to destroy and to overthrow, to build and to plant" (Jer 1:10). What looks unmovable is not. Oppression and violence will obey the higher level of faith that is present in Jesus' followers. The apostles must believe that this is possible; and that is precisely what Jesus' rhetoric of a small-sized seed and an outsized uprooting and replanting is meant to supply—confidence.

> **"Who among you would say to your slave who has just come in from plowing or tending sheep in the field, 'Come here at once and take your place at the table?' Would you not rather say to him, 'Prepare supper for me, put on your apron and serve me while I eat and drink, later you may eat and drink'? Do you thank the slave for doing what was commanded?**
>
> **So you also, when you have done all that you were ordered to do, say, 'We are worthless slaves: we have done only what we ought to have done.'"**

Through this story and teaching, Jesus tries to further strengthen and support the apostles' confidence. He has told them that they do not need an increase of faith because they already have the ability to cooperate with God in changing the enduring negative patterns of human behavior. They have what they need to live in the kingdom. Now he tells them this "impossible possibility" is so much within the scope of their identities as servants of God, they should not expect any over-and-above gratitude or special reward. Even though by social standards they might seem to be engaged in double duty, or in multitasking, or in going beyond what is expected, from the perspective of faith it is all in a day's work.

In order to help the apostles understand, Jesus asks them to reflect on their own experience. If they only had one slave and he came in from the field after plowing or tending sheep, they would not allow him to eat until he had also performed the duties of a house slave. A slave is a slave is a slave. Their be-all and end-all is service. In some settings there may be a field slave and a house slave, and so each does only their respective duties. But if there is only one slave, both sets of chores become his. There is no need for special mention because the nature of the slave is to serve. That is how they would treat a slave of their own.

They must treat themselves in a similar way. They are under the orders of God to bring about the kingdom. Even more, they are in touch with the Order-Giver who directs and sustains their actions. Their nature is to serve, and they must be diligent about it. Looking for reward and thanks is not appropriate because it will continue the false consciousness that they are doing something so far beyond the ordinary that they have to be specially acknowledged. In the kingdom of God abundant service is not extraordinary. It is just how things are.

From one point of view, what Jesus tells his apostles may seem quite harsh, even unfeeling. He is not pandering to their request; he is confronting their evaluation of what they need. But his powerful imagery is far from dismissing their concern. In fact, it is geared to counteract their panic. It wants to assure them that what they perceive as requiring extravagant effort is within their reach. They do not need more; they need confidence in what they have. They should not portray Jesus' new possibilities of human behavior as only available to heroic efforts they cannot accomplish. It is simply service as usual.

Teaching

There is a scene in the Gospel of Mark (Mark 6:30-44) that parallels the psychological dynamics of this exchange between Jesus and his apostles. Jesus has had compassion on the crowds because they are like sheep without shepherds, and he has taught them many things. As night descends, his disciples perceive a problem. A situation is arising they do not know how to meet. They say to Jesus, "This is a deserted place, and the hour is now very late; send them away so they may go into the surrounding country and villages and buy something for themselves to eat." Jesus sharply responds, "You give them something to eat." The disciples' immediate response is to focus on their lack. "Are we to go and buy two hundred denarii worth of bread and give it to them to eat?" If the disciples are to feed people, they need more than they have. They must go and buy from others. They perceive the situation as impossible unless they bring in something from the outside.

When the disciples confront new situations and are asked to respond out of their personal resources, they immediately sense they lack what they need and look outside themselves for help. Jesus does not honor this instinctive move. Instead, he directs them inside and asks them to reappraise what they might bring to the situation. Jesus sees more in his followers than they see in themselves. He is continually urging them to reconceive who they are and what they can do. They must include faith among the resources they have and be able to access it.

The disciples are not alone in their failure to know what they have and be able to access it. Kenneth Pargament thinks that every person brings an orienting system into each new situation, especially situations that are challenging and call for creative responses (*The Psychology of Religion and Coping: Theory, Research, Practice* [New York: The Guilford Press, 1997] 99–105). An orienting system is comprised of habits, beliefs, relationships, personality traits, previous experiences, etc. Some of these features are resources and others are burdens. They exist within people as a potential waiting to be actualized. They are like holdings in a bank waiting to be withdrawn. When certain events arise, both the resources and burdens of the orienting system may be called into action. Bringing forward burdens makes responding to the situation more difficult. Bringing forward resources enhances the ability to negotiate the situation creatively.

Of course, to bring forward the resources, you have to know they are there. Pargament tells the story of a man who had resources but did not know it.

> I remember one client who described himself as "a wimp." A midlevel bank manager, he felt pushed around, bullied, and generally ineffectual. In talking about his job, his eyes became glassy, his voice turned to a monotone, and his shoulders drooped. I found myself feeling very tired in therapy. In search of some spark in his life, I shifted the focus to his earlier years and discovered that not only had he put himself through school by working two jobs, he had been on the boxing team in college, and flew airplanes on weekend—hardly the behavior of a wimp. When he talked about flying, he fairly crackled with energy. He seemed surprised when I commented on the difference between his style at work and his style behind the controls of his airplane. The key moment in therapy came when he recognized that his problem was not a "chronically wimpy personality," but a failure to identify and tap into his resources. He pinpointed the solution when he said, "I guess I need to fly at work, huh?" My client illustrated an important point: People cannot cope with tools they do not believe they have. (*The Psychology of Religion and Coping*, 99–105)

If we do not know what we have, we cannot use it to make happen what we want to make happen.

I think Jesus the teacher would have understood this piece of wisdom from contemporary psychology. He kept telling people they had the tools to live in the kingdom of God. The resources were there all the time. But if they did not know they had these resources, they could not access them. So Jesus reached for rhetoric to convince them they were not chronic wimps but people who could fly into the exploration of a new world. We are not told if they soared on this rhetoric or returned to the sniggling world of excuses and impotency. There is such a comfort in being less than who we are.

But also there is such a mistake in thinking we are more than we are. As a man recovering from depression once said, "Now I know I am not Jesus." The gospels are written for people "to take the dare to be more." But how do we take the dare within the realistic limits of our resources? Each person must make this discernment for himself or herself, and discernments are best discerned in a community of discerners (redundancy intended). But even with more moderate appraisals of what we are capable of, the edge of this gospel lesson is not blunted. It is still a matter of not settling for ingrained patterns of oppression and violence. It is still a matter of not being overwhelmed by what we consider impossible. Our faith, minimal as it may be, can uproot old and destructive patterns and replace them with caring and reconciled relationships.

The Sufis have a saying about Jesus. He stands by the river selling river water. He just saw what was there and what was possible, and he struggled mightily with all the art at his command to have other people see what he saw. What he saw were mulberry trees, one after the other, on their way to the sea.

Twenty-Eighth Sunday in Ordinary Time

Proper 23

Luke 17:11-19

\(\text{\textbf{♨}} \)

Seizing Second Chances

A Spiritual Commentary

On the way to Jerusalem Jesus was going through the region between Samaria and Galilee.

In Luke's Gospel, Jesus is always on his way to Jerusalem. The whole gospel is geared to the events of Jesus' death and resurrection in Jerusalem, events that will simultaneously reveal the steady strength of divine love and a vacillating variety of human responses. This episode *on the way* to Jerusalem foreshadows these future events *in* Jerusalem. The steady strength of God's love in Jesus will manifest itself as mercy to the afflicted and humans will respond ambivalently.

The road to this revelation in Jerusalem is through an "in-between" region, the land that is neither Samaria nor Galilee. This geographical preference symbolizes Jesus' mission. Although Jesus is a Jew from Galilee, he is never completely defined by his ethnic identity. He is God's son who has been sent to all people. Therefore, as he walks through this no-man's land, he turns it into everyman's land. It is not a strip of land *between* Galilee and Samaria, but the place where God meets all people, and Jews and Samaritans meet one another. This is the perfect path for Jesus to travel. He is the quintessential border walker.

> **As he entered a village, ten lepers approached him. Keeping their distance, they called out, saying, "Jesus, Master, have mercy on us."**

Jesus can enter the village. He has no disease that makes him unclean. The lepers must keep their distance. Their disease isolates them. They cannot come close to Jesus or enter into community. Their cry for mercy is a plea to cure their body and to admit them back into the company of people.

The fact that there are ten lepers is obviously symbolic, but it is difficult to tell what the symbolism refers to. Eventually, only one of the

ten will be praised by Jesus, and this one will be a foreigner. One out
of ten is reminiscent of the sweeping woman who seeks one lost coin
out of ten, and even the shepherd who searches for one lost sheep out
of a hundred (Luke 15:3-10). However, those stories symbolize the divine passion to seek what is lost. In this story, it is not a matter of the
divine love in Jesus going after one. It is a matter of only one returning
to acknowledge the divine love in Jesus. When these stories are put
together, they reflect Luke's theological vision. God is relentlessly pursuing humans who are relentlessly running away.

> **When he saw them, he said to them, "Go and show yourselves
> to the priests." And as they went, they were made clean. Then
> one of them, when he saw that he was healed, turned back,
> praising God with a loud voice. He prostrated himself at Jesus'
> feet and thanked him. And he was a Samaritan.**

> **Then Jesus asked, "Were not ten made clean? But the other
> nine, where are they? Was none of them found to return and
> give praise to God except this foreigner?"**

> **Then he said to him, "Get up and go on your way; your faith
> has made you well."**

When the storyteller says that Jesus sees them, he does not mean
that Jesus' ears picked up their cry, then he turned and saw them with
his physical eyes. Jesus sees people both in their existential condition
and their essential identity. He sees the lepers in their physical and social isolation and in their relationship to God and through God to the
human community. His sight takes in the seen and the unseen, what is
available to the senses and what is available to the spirit.

The priests are the gatekeepers of the community. Jesus' command
that they go and show themselves to the priests means that they are on
their way back into the community. If the priests declare them clean,
their isolation is over. In this way the story stresses the social consequences of their sickness more than the physical malady itself.

In fact, the physical cure takes place "off camera." As they are going
to show themselves to the priests, they are made clean. Why were the
lepers not made clean immediately and then told to secure priestly
confirmation? This way of telling the story would have highlighted
Jesus' miraculous powers and pushed the religious establishment into
their usual ambivalent stance of refusing to acknowledge Jesus yet

being unable to account for the cures. But the emphasis on the decisions of those who were cured would have been lost.

Ultimately, this is a story about seizing or not seizing second chances. "Being cured on the way" is a literary device that forces the ten to choose. What is more important—organizational approval or praise of God and gratitude to Jesus? What is more important—reentry into the established Jewish community or entry into the company of those who acknowledge God's action in Jesus? What is more important—getting back to life the way it was or getting a whole new life? The second chance unfolds into a second decision.

The Samaritan chooses to return. He praises God and gives thanks to Jesus. Jesus characterizes this response as faith. Faith is the Samaritan's capacity to see the deeper causes of his cure and to acknowledge those causes in praise and thanksgiving. His booming acknowledgment takes him into a life-giving relationship with God through Jesus. This acknowledgment is contrasted with the nine who choose priestly approbation and a return to their old way of life. If there is exuberance in the Samaritan's loud voice, there is poignancy in Jesus the Jew receiving him and looking over his prostrate body down the long and empty road for signs of his fellow countrymen. "Were not ten made clean? But the other nine, where are they? Were none of them found to return and give praise to God except this foreigner?"

When the Samaritan falls at the feet of Jesus, it is more than a profound moment of worship. It symbolizes his commitment to the teachings of Jesus and his desire to follow the way of life Jesus advocates. Praise and gratitude are necessary first responses, acknowledgments that lead to a new life. But more is required. Therefore, Jesus instructs him to "get up and go." It is time to live—not to return to old ways but to find a new way that his faith has begun to forge for him. This new way will be grounded in God's graciousness to him; and as he walks it, he will go beyond cure into healing.

Teaching

The doctor told me I had dodged a bullet. But I really hadn't. My lung x-ray showed a shadow, the possibility of a tumor. But when they retook the x-ray, my lungs were clear. Still the doctor insisted I was a near-dead person who had come back to life. I had never thought that. I always suspected the x-rays were faulty. So it only entailed the inconvenience of a second trip to radiology. I mindlessly went back to business as usual. The truth is I never seriously left business as usual. It was not a second chance, but a blip.

But when people really get second chances, a more serious evaluation may go on. When people emerge unscathed from a car crash, or survive the onset of cancer, or are pulled back from death's door by creative medical interventions, they may take a deep breath and quickly return to business as usual. But they may also have that "stunned deer in the headlights" look. The serious illness and/or close call has had an effect. An inner accounting is going on; tabulations are happening. They have been given a second chance. The question that is growing in their mind is: will they take it?

Many people vow to take it. Their second lease on life is not going to repeat the mistakes of their first lease on life. They make social and spiritual resolutions, revising priorities and focusing on what is truly important. But cynical bystanders predict these resolutions will be short-lived. The cured will return to the mindless lives they have previously led. The "more time" they have been granted is just that—more time. It is not new life, but the same old life prolonged. They may have "gotten lucky," but the odds are against them turning that luck into real life. The twin realizations of the second chance—the time is limited and the time is now—most probably will fade.

In the story only one out of ten seizes the second chance. One out of ten is definitely not a good return, and the sadness of Jesus is palpable. This story laments those lost opportunities. But it ultimately focuses on the power of one and what seizing the second chance entails—praising God, thanking Jesus, and following his way of life. These three aspects are intertwined and together they constitute a transformation of consciousness.

Genuinely praising God involves consistently seeing into the source of life. Our normal sight that takes in discrete persons and objects takes on an added dimension. We become aware of the ultimate mystery that supports and permeates all there is. We sense the creative energies that are always flowing from that mystery. We also become aware that we do not possess that mystery, and so we do not have power over it. Life is on lease, and we are truly tenants who will never be able to claim ownership. Yet the mystery continues to sustain us, freely and abundantly. A gradual trust develops, a trust in the source beyond the vicissitudes. We move into the recognition that the mystery is love, and we may laugh at how obvious it now seems and how necessary it is to say yes to it.

When we realize this spiritual truth in a deep and sustained way, praise arises in us. This emergence of praise is not an act of the will. Rather, it comes from the center of our being, a center that acknowledges complete dependency on God and ultimate trust in divine mercy. This is the beginning of a second lease on life. It qualifies as "second" not only because it is contrasted with a previous consciousness that was not aware of God but also because it recognizes that life itself is always a lease from the landlord God. Praising God properly situates us as human creatures, and it is the first and fundamental step in seizing the second chance.

This seizing continues when we thank Jesus and follow his way. The realization of God's unmerited life and love came to us through Jesus, and so our gratitude naturally flows toward him. He is the medium of mercy, and our thankfulness is how we take a one-time experience of this mercy and turn it into continual happening. In returning to thank Jesus, we establish a relationship with the channel of grace that can sustain us. Staying in touch with this channel of grace naturally unfolds into following Jesus' way of life. We begin to walk with him along the road to Jerusalem. His death and resurrection will not be completely foreign to us. We have already lived in the shadow of death, and we can sense how resurrection is a larger version of the second chance we are now learning how to seize.

In this story of the ten lepers and in our lives we often restrict second chances to escaping from close calls with death and/or being cured from chronic disease. Although these situations are exceptional opportunities, we do not have to wait for close calls with death or miraculous cures. There is nothing stopping us from acting immediately on the twin realizations that the time is limited and the time is now. In this moment, before we finish reading this sentence, we can praise God for the life we do not own, thank Jesus for the revelation of divine mercy that calls us out of isolation, and become more serious about allowing his way of life to have influence on our own. The second chance slumbers in every minute. Will we seize it?

Twenty-Ninth Sunday in Ordinary Time

Proper 24

Luke 18:1-8

❦

Wearing Down Injustice

A Spiritual Commentary

Then Jesus told them a parable about their need to pray always and not to lose heart.

Luke tells us the point of the parable before he tells us the parable. In many storytelling circles, this is not considered a good move. It prejudices the listeners/readers. They already know the prescribed impact of the story before they have heard it or read it. When we know the point the storyteller wants to make, there is a tendency to pay less attention to the story. Also, the upfront meaning might restrict the free range of our imaginations and curtail different interpretations. Whatever the detriments of this approach, the interpretive key to the parable has been leaked.

However, in this case the prelude is a plus. It does not give the story away in any significant way. Rather, it states the fullness of what has to be considered. Knowing the parable is about the connection between praying always to God and not losing heart when it comes to wearing down injustice points us to the spiritual grounding of the quest for justice. Without it, we might interpret the parable either religiously or socially. The parable would be an analogy about how to persevere in prayer to God, or it would be social advice on how to persevere against injustice. The introduction tells us it is both.

He said, "In a certain city there was a judge who neither feared God nor had respect for people. In that city there was a widow who kept coming to him and saying, 'Grant me justice against my opponent.'"

The people in the countryside know the stories about cities. They are impersonal places where hard and cynical people take advantage of the weak. So this city judge is immediately recognized. Appealing to his better side is a waste of time. He doesn't have one. He does not fear God and so no appeal to law or covenant or divine compassion will move him. He does not respect people and so no appeal to human need or decency will have any effect. This is an unmovable object.

But there is also an irresistible force—a widow who is not put off by his putting her off. She cannot count on his adherence to the covenant command to care for the widow and the orphan to help her. Nor can she lay before him the extent of her need. She has only one thing on her side: she is asking for justice and he, being a judge, is supposed to give it to her. But the odds are not in her favor. The Hebrew word for widow means "one who has no voice." Yet her voice is all she has. Her only hope is that she keeps coming. Persistence is not her fallback strategy. It is her only strategy.

> **For a while he refused; but later he said to himself, 'Though I have no fear of God and no respect for anyone, yet because this widow keeps bothering me, I will grant her justice, so that she may not wear me out by continually coming.'"**

At first the judge is unmoved. How could perseverance be advocated if the judge relented immediately? His initial refusal highlights the widow's insistence. Instead of losing heart, she perseveres. Eventually, the judge caves. We are not left in doubt about why. We eavesdrop on his inner monologue, a favorite literary technique of Luke. The judge repeats the description of the storyteller about himself and so reinforces the reason he is "granting justice." It is not because he fears God or respects people. It is because the continual coming of the woman is wearing down his resistance. The justice that should be given because he is a judge is only given because the widow is relentless.

However, more than sheer nagging may be at work. Scholars say "wear me out" is literally translated, "give me a black eye." "Giving a black eye" is an image for tarnishing a reputation. A judge is supposed to give justice and he does not want to be known for not giving justice. This woman's persistence will show him up as an unjust judge. He does not want this. He wants the pretense of justice on the outside even though he is not committed to justice on the inside. He wants to be known as just. This hypocrisy is a key piece of information.

> **And the Lord said, "Listen to what the unjust judge says. And will not God grant justice to his chosen ones who cry to him**

day and night? Will he delay long in helping them? I tell you, he will quickly grant justice to them. And yet, when the Son of Man comes, will he find faith on earth?"

The story is over. Now Jesus himself guides the reflection. Of all the things the Lord could point to in the story, he wants us to listen to the inner monologue of the unjust judge. When we listen to what the unjust judge is saying to himself, we learn one important thing: he can be had. His self-understanding is that he is vulnerable to being exposed for who he is. This is what he most fears and what eventually will drive him to give justice. The relentless widow unmasks injustice until justice is given, even if it is given only reluctantly.

But how are the hearts of widows sustained during this relentless effort? If they pray "day and night," the just God will not "long delay but act quickly" and pour into their hearts divine justice. This is what the just God wants to do, and their knowledge of this divine passion assists them in remaining open in prayer. God suffuses the hearts of those who pray with justice, and then with empowered hearts they bring this justice into the affairs of earth. God does not intervene as a separate agent of activity and bring a justice to the human world that humans themselves cannot bring.

Still, the perseverance to transform the earth is difficult to sustain. Injustice is both an individual habit and an ingrained social structure. It is difficult to wear down something that is so pervasive. It may be exposed and overcome here and there, but it is never unmasked everywhere at once. So the effort is endless, and it leads to the question of endurance. When the Son of Man, whose passion is the transformed earth, comes, will he find the energy of the God-grounded widows unabated or will the opposite of the parable have happened? Will the resistance of those who fear not God and respect not man have worn down the widows? Only those who read this passage and take it seriously have the answer.

Teaching

Conventional religiosity loves to turn this parable into a teaching on perseverance in prayer. It immediately envisions people petitioning God for a specific purpose and not getting what they want. They are tempted to give up. But if they keep importuning, God will relent. So the message is: don't lose heart, turn up the volume. God caves in with persistent petitioning.

This popular interpretation sunders what the parable struggles to keep together. Personal spirituality and social justice are two sides of the same coin. Praying to God is for the purpose of effecting social justice. God answers the cry for justice by giving justice into the hearts of the ones who cry. In this way the ones who pray will endure because they will be grounded in God.

That is, if the ones who pray manage to pray always. "Always praying" means the channel between God and the human person remains open. Divine energy will not periodically spurt and then dry up. Rather, it will be a steady, empowering flow. Therefore, the ultimate source of the energy that wears down injustice will be coming from the boundless source of the passion for justice.

"Praying always" is only possible if the ones praying are widows. As a literary character, the widow in herself is a powerless figure. She has no resources of her own to rely on. If she manages to wear down a hard-as-nails judge, the surmise is that she has had help. When the powerless who seek justice take down the powerful who refuse to give it, a careful investigation will undercover the hidden agency of God. The energy of wearing down is mediated through the widow, but it does not originate with her. It is the result of her communion with God made possible by her continual praying.

This combination of praying always and not losing heart is further developed in the Gethsemani scene (Luke 22:33-53). The injunction, "Pray that you may not come into the time of trial," bookends this episode. In the Garden, Jesus stays awake in prayer, but the disciples fall asleep. As Jesus prays, an angel visits him and takes on the role of a masseuse, strengthening him for the upcoming contest until his sweat becomes as "drops of blood falling down on the ground." This praying is necessary for Jesus to persevere in the mission he has been given.

When the crowd comes to take Jesus away, the disciples, who have not prayed, resort to violence. They cut off the ear of the slave of the high priest. But Jesus, who has prayed, restores the ear. The disciples have yielded to temptation and become as violent as the men who have come to arrest Jesus. But Jesus has not yielded to this temptation and continues to reconcile enemies. The key is that Jesus prayed always, allowing God's peace to suffuse his heart and inform his actions.

This is a significant addition to the "how we are to pray always and not lose heart." Not to lose heart means more than merely persevering in the face of difficulties. It is more than not giving up. It is coming forward with love and being faithful to the ways of peace. The temptation in wearing down injustice is to become more unjust than what we are attempting to wear down. We win on the terms the unjust judge sets. We fear God less and respect people less than he does, and so we can overcome him with more violence than he is able to muster. However, we can resist this temptation when we integrate our hearts into the heart of Jesus. He is the relentless widow who prays always until his heart becomes the heart of God.

Thirtieth Sunday in Ordinary Time

Proper 25

Luke 18:9-14

❦

Checkmating the King

A Spiritual Commentary

He told this parable to some who trusted in themselves that they were righteous and regarded others with contempt: . . .

Luke identifies the audience for the upcoming parable. They are people who have managed to inhabit the relationship between God, self, and others in a twisted way. Instead of trusting in God, an attitude that would establish a right relationship to the Divine Source, they trust in themselves. This mistake earns them the name: the self-righteous. It also results in an excessive focus on the ego that unfolds into contempt for others. Those who are self-righteous need others to look down on. This is how they maintain their elevated sense of themselves. These psychological dynamics result in severing the relational ties between God, self, and others. Therefore, the self-righteous live with a separate sense of self that is neither indebted to God nor connected to neighbor. The parable unmasks this negative state and provides an alternative.

"Two men went up to the temple to pray, one a Pharisee and the other a tax collector. The Pharisee, standing by himself, was praying thus, 'God, I thank you that I am not like the other people: thieves, rogues, adulterers, or even like this tax collector. I fast twice a week; I give a tenth of all my income.'"

The story contrasts two ways of praying. The Pharisee's posture of standing by himself symbolizes his haughty and isolated attitude, an attitude that will permeate his brief but revealing prayer. Although he begins by thanking God, this seems a perfunctory opening to blatant self-promotion rather than a true realization of indebtedness. It is merely polite protocol, something proper praying should include. If there is any real gratitude, it is only appreciation for supplying superiority, making him "not like other men." Although the Pharisee may be addressing God, he is really talking to himself. The pronoun "I" is repeated four times. He is the center of his own prayer.

The Pharisee's recital of his virtues highlights his excessive ego focus. He compliments himself on his over-the-top perfection. He goes well beyond what the law prescribes, fasting and tithing more than is required. In his mind his zealous practice makes him special and separates him from the riff raff. This comparative superiority is available to him at a glance. The far-off tax collector is proof positive he is not like other men. For the Pharisee the real action is between him and the tax collector. God, the focus of all genuine prayer, has receded completely into the background. Just as the introduction to the parable has predicted, the Pharisee is simultaneously trusting in himself and berating others. Both attitudes go hand in hand.

> **"But the tax collector, standing far off, would not even look up to heaven, but was beating his breast and saying, 'God, be merciful to me, a sinner!'"**

The tax collector is a study in contrast. Whatever the Pharisee is, he is not. He does not arrogantly stand by himself, but humbly at a distance. He does not push his own achievements, but bows in reverence and beats his breast in repentance. The words of his prayer acknowledge only the merciful God and his own unworthiness. He takes note of no one else. He simply opens his unworthiness to divine mercy.

> **"I tell you, this man went down to his home justified rather than the other; for all who exalt themselves will be humbled, but all who humble themselves will be exalted."**

Jesus' concluding comment is not the obvious lesson of this parable. Conventional religiosity would see two men praying as befits their station. The Pharisee, who keeps God's law and actually goes beyond it, is grateful to God for his superiority. So what is the problem? Given the measuring stick of the law, the truth is he *is* better than other men. In particular, he is better than a tax collector who works for the Romans, makes his own people suffer, and most probably skims money for extra gain. The tax collector is obviously in a more imperiled situation; and mercy is exactly what he should be praying for. God knows, given his blasphemous life, he needs it. Here is the obvious conclusion: everyone prays according to where they are at. As the story said at the beginning, this is a tale of two men praying. Both are doing it right, given who they are and what they have done.

However, that is not the teaching the Lukan Jesus draws from the parable. The Pharisee has done it wrong and the tax collector has done it right. Prayer is not this way or that way, depending on people and circumstances. Only one type of prayer results in justification, the proper positioning of the self in relationship to God and neighbor. The tax collector represents an ideal form of Christian praying.

Jesus does not give detailed reasons for his choice of the sinfulness-mercy prayer. Instead, he focuses on the contrast between the Pharisee and tax collector by citing a paradoxical maxim about exaltation and humility. This is a proverbial saying that takes on different meanings depending on its context. In this context, it has to go beyond the moral observations that "pride goeth before the fall" or that "the humble are raised up." Rather, it captures a process that transforms the Pharisee and tax collector from contrasting models of prayer into two moments in an unfolding dynamic of spiritual development.

The maxim presupposes the freedom to direct our thinking and acting—"those who exalt themselves" and "those who humble themselves." When we are engaged in ego-centered, self-exalting prayer, a future realization awaits us. Eventually, we will see that this style alienates us from both God and neighbor. It does not significantly acknowledge God as the source of every positive action; and so it cuts us off from the flow of grace that grounds every good work. It also cuts us off from our neighbor because our prized elevated status is only supported by those whom we judge are not as righteous as we are. Putting down others is the necessary corollary of raising ourselves up.

When we realize this, we awaken to the fact that our own thinking has contributed to our sinfulness. How we think and act has broken our relationship to God and neighbor. We have freely engaged in activities that on the surface looked righteous but in the depths were alienating. It is no longer possible to maintain our high estimation of ourselves. In fact, it is our previous high estimation of ourselves that has brought us down. The maxim is correct: those who exalt themselves will eventually be humbled by their own act of self-exaltation.

But this does not end the process. As we chose self-exaltation that proved to be a false way of relating to God and neighbor, now the possibility arises of choosing humility. Humbling may have come about because ungrounded self-exaltation necessarily collapses from the weight of its own wrong-headedness. It tries to establish itself against the metaphysical grain of the unity of God, self, and neighbor. This rebellion cannot be sustained. But the resulting fall should not be dismissed as only the inevitable fate of sinfulness, the crushing of the Pharisee in all of us. Our inability to sustain this wrong direction is the initial moment of metanoia, the conversion of mind and behavior that makes possible the reception of the Good News. We are returned to ground zero and the possibility of a right direction. But we must choose it.

This choosing is shown in a new way of praying. Our prayer will arise from a consciousness of dependency on God and solidarity with our neighbor. This double sensitivity reflects the proper ordering of reality. We know we are a dependent creature, and this makes us one with all others who only live through the creating activity of God. But, more significantly in the light of the parable, we know we are one with all who have lost their way, i.e., everyone. We have just emerged out of a darkness and alienation that was of our own making. As all people do, we tried to establish our worth outside Divine Love. Therefore, mercy is the only prayer that is both authentic to our experience and trusts in the infinite reaches of Divine Love. It is this need *of* and openness *to* mercy that unites us to all people. This humble position of calling on the mercy of God in oneness with all other sinful people paradoxically begins a process of exaltation. God's grace begins to flow into the waiting hearts of all who call, exalting them into a people bound together by a common redemption for the purposes of a common work.

Teaching

There is a take off-on this parable of the Pharisee and the tax collector that has been around for a long time. The Catholic rendition has a priest and a deacon standing before the altar praying together. The priest prays, "Lord, have mercy on me a sinner." The deacon prays, "Lord, have mercy on me, a sinner." Then both hear a voice coming from the back of the church. They turn to see the janitor, head bowed and beating his breast, saying, "Lord, have mercy on me, a sinner." The priest turns to the deacon and haughtily remarks, "Look who thinks he's a sinner!"

Whatever else this clever take-off has to tell us, it highlights our deep-seated need to feel superior. Once we have learned the lesson of the parable, we can parody the prayer of the tax collector. But our Pharisaic heart is still in charge. We turn sinfulness, a negative evaluation that we should eschew, into a competitive asset. We are better sinners than "other men." We will do anything except belong to the mess that is humanity.

We have not been taught the value of "living humbly." We are used to accentuating what makes us different. We value our uniqueness and learn to emphasize it so that it sets us apart. It is a type of self-definition by scarcity. If we have something that no one else has, we think it confers specialness and worth. What is most scarce is most valuable. And if we are pious, we will thank God for it. It is God's way of showing his love for us. This seems to be the ordinary way of the earth. We come down on our edge, what makes us different from other people and, therefore, what makes us stand out among the masses. Our common humanity is the mere backdrop for where the real action is. We are encouraged to make a difference with the advice: if you've got it, flaunt it.

This conventional way of self-valuing is deeply etched in our consciousness. If we are to accept another way of self-valuing, especially the way of self-valuing this parable suggests, a difficult process of inner change must be undertaken. It is easy to facilely identify with all people because none of us can escape the twin universal facts of birth and death. But this banal, intellectual observation does not stand a chance against the passion and intensity of competitive achievement. Shared beginnings and endings are noticed, but they do not play a commanding role in defining us and influencing our decisions. Rather, they become the backdrop for the real drama and adventure of fashioning a difference that is victorious.

There must be some deeper and more personal realization of common humanity if we are to include our sense of uniqueness within a common originality. Uniqueness stays on the surface; and we are driven to define ourselves by how we are separate from others. Originality notes the distinctive way each of us reflects the origin of all of us. The one source is always included in valuing the diversity of its manifestations. When the common gift of a single origin begins to become more valuable than what we individually have done with it, the transition is under way. Our uniqueness is being placed in the context of originality, and so the door is open for a way of valuing both ourselves and others as brothers and sisters. When we cannot escape this larger "way of seeing," we begin a process of authentic inner transformation.

Thomas Merton had a realization of shared common humanity that resituated his sense of uniqueness.

In Louisville, at the corner of Fourth and Walnut, in the center of the shopping district, I was suddenly overwhelmed with the realization that I loved all those people, that they were mine and I theirs, that we could not be alien to one another even though we were total strangers. It was like waking from a dream of separateness, of spurious self-isolation. . . . This sense of liberation from an illusory difference was such a relief and such a joy to me that I almost laughed out loud. And I suppose my happiness could have taken form in the words: "Thank God, thank God that I am like other men, that I am only a man among others." . . . It is glorious destiny to be a member of the human race, though it is a race dedicated to many absurdities and one which makes terrible mistakes; yet, with all that, God Himself gloried in becoming a member of the human race. A member of the human race! (*Conjectures of a Guilty Bystander* [New York: Doubleday, 1966] 156–7)

What Merton realized in an explosive experience, Henri Nouwen realized in quietly reflecting on his fiftieth birthday.

Within a few years (five, ten, twenty, or thirty) I will no longer be on this earth. The thought of this does not frighten me but fills me with a quiet peace. I am a small part of, a human being in the midst of thousands of other human beings. It is good to be young, to grow old, and to die. It is good to live with others, and to die with others. God became flesh to share with us in this simple living and dying and thus made it good. I can feel today that it is good to be and especially to be one of many. What counts are not the special and unique accomplishments in life that make me different from others, but the basic experiences of sadness and joy, pain and healing, which make me part of humanity. The time is indeed growing short for me, but that knowledge sets me free to prevent mourning from depressing me and joy from exciting me. Mourning and joy can now both deepen my quiet desire for the day when I realize that the many kisses and embraces I received today were simple incarnations of the eternal embrace of the Lord himself. (*Gracias!* [San Francisco: Harper & Row, 1983] 120)

At least part of the reason Merton and Nouwen delight in their common humanity is their faith. God chose to become human in Jesus Christ. Therefore basic humanity can be valued more than the "dream of separateness" and "special and unique accomplishments."

But the parable of the Pharisee and the tax collector takes us beyond rejoicing and praying out of common humanity. Merton mentions the human race is "dedicated to many absurdities and . . . makes terrible mistakes." But the parable insists this must be more than a casual observation on human inclinations. We must realize *we* are absurd and *we* make terrible mistakes. If we are united to one another in a common creation, we are also united to one another in a common fall. We do not just belong to humanity, we belong to sinful humanity.

Bede Griffiths, a Benedictine monk who lived in India and worked to connect the mystical traditions of Christianity with those of other religions, practiced the prayer of the pilgrim, "Lord, Jesus Christ have mercy on me, a sinner." This is very close to the recommended prayer of the tax collector. But how could Bede Griffith, a man who sought to love God and neighbor with all his soul, heart, mind, and might identify with being alienated from God?

> I unite myself with all human beings from the beginning of the world who have experienced separation from God, or from the eternal truth. I realize that, as human beings, we are all separated from God, from the source of our being. We are wandering in a world of shadows, mistaking the outward appearance of people and things for reality. But at all times something is pressing us to reach out beyond the shadows, to face the reality, the truth, the inner meaning of our lives, and so to find God, or whatever name we give to the mystery which enfolds us. (Bede Griffiths, "Going Out of Oneself," *Parabola* [Summer 1999] 24–5)

The paradox seems to be: the more we try to open ourselves to God, the more we simultaneously realize our endless wandering in shadows and the endless divine invitation to "reach out beyond the shadows." This is the state that truly defines us and defines all others. There may be varying degrees of lostness and varying degrees of responding to the divine invitation to be found. But on this earth this is the truth of our situation, the bittersweet truth that makes us all brothers and sisters.

It is also the bittersweet truth that finally strips us of our self-justifying defenses. At last we are poor enough in spirit to receive the kingdom (Matt 5:3). And here is the good news. The Divine cannot resist giving it to us; it is God's pleasure (Matt 11:26). The nature of God is to pour grace into any vessel that is empty enough to receive it. Divine unconditional love is released the moment all human justifying conditions are released. Teresa of Avila expressed this truth in metaphor taken from the game of chess. "Humility is the Queen without whom none can checkmate the divine King." (Quoted in Karen Speerstra, *Divine Sparks* [Sandpoint, ID: Morning Light Press, 2005] 206). When we finally come into the consciousness of who we really are, God can really be for us what God truly is. It is humility that checkmates the king.

Thirty-First Sunday in Ordinary Time

Proper 26

Luke 19:1-10

𝕀𝕍

Finding the True Self

A Spiritual Commentary

He [Jesus] entered Jericho and was passing through it.

Jesus is portrayed as passing through Jericho. This "passing through" means he is on a journey and has another destination in mind. The destination is Jerusalem where the important events of his death and resurrection will occur. But the "passing through" also has another meaning. He is making himself available. If anyone in Jericho is interested, they can come out to see him.

A man was there named Zacchaeus; he was a chief tax collector and was rich. He was trying to see who Jesus was, but on account of the crowd he could not, because he was short in stature. So he ran ahead and climbed a sycamore tree to see him, because he was going to pass that way.

Zacchaeus is interested. Although his profession has separated him from the community of righteous in Israel, he is attracted. He wants "to see who Jesus was." This is more than a desire for a simple "sighting." He wants to grasp what Jesus is all about, to know where he is coming from. However, Zacchaeus' desire encounters the obstacle of the crowd. The crowd is a symbol of spiritual obtuseness. They do not understand Jesus, and so they block the true view that Zacchaeus desires.

However, Zacchaeus is not deterred. He runs ahead and climbs a sycamore tree. This gives him a higher perspective, a perspective that connects him with the prophet Amos who was "a herdsman, and dresser of sycamore trees" (Amos 7:14). It indicates a beginning understanding of "who Jesus is." Jesus, like Amos, is a passionate advocate of repentance and social justice.

When Jesus came to the place he looked up and said to him, "Zacchaeus, hurry and come down; for I must stay at your

house today." So he hurried down and was happy to welcome him.

Zacchaeus' perseverance in getting to see Jesus is met by Jesus looking up and seeing him. Zacchaeus has been hurrying, and now Jesus instructs him to continue the rush. "Hurry down. I must stay at your house today." Zacchaeus has been seeking Jesus. Now Jesus is seeking Zacchaeus. Running and hurrying are signs of excitement and happiness at what is occurring.

This dynamic of Zacchaeus seeking Jesus and then Jesus taking the initiative and inviting himself into Zacchaeus' house has theological meaning. The sinner must show enough interest to turn and get to a place where he can be seen. But he does not have to crawl the whole way back, whipping himself in remorse. In the story of the Prodigal Son, the younger son moves toward the house of his father, but while he is still a long way off, the father sees him and begins to run (Luke 15:11-32). Humans must overcome obstacles and get in position, so to speak, but God is an assertive welcome. Once Zacchaeus has managed to climb the tree, it is Jesus who seizes the moment. Grace is always waiting and watching. When the situation presents itself, grace moves quickly and effectively. "Hurry down. I must stay at your house today."

When Jesus says he wants to stay at Zacchaeus' house, it symbolizes he wants to enter into Zacchaeus' consciousness and transform it with his own consciousness. Jesus wants to dwell within him, to shape his mind according to his own. This desire must resonate with Zacchaeus' own reason for seeking out Jesus. He hurries down and happily welcomes him.

All who saw it began to grumble and said, "He has gone to be the guest of one who is a sinner." Zacchaeus stood there and said to the Lord, "Look, half of my possessions, Lord, I will give to the poor; and if I have defrauded anyone of anything, I will pay back four times as much."

The crowd reappears and continues its obfuscation. They misinterpret Jesus' inviting himself to the house of Zacchaeus. They think it means that Jesus is condoning his sinful behavior. However, Zacchaeus, who previously had to see over them, now has to confront them face to face. Although he is talking to the Lord, he is refuting the crowd's estimation of why Jesus is in his house. The presence of Jesus is a catalyst of conversion and not an approval of Roman law and Jewish tax-collecting. In fact, Jesus has put Zacchaeus back in touch with God. This is symbolized by the abundant quality of Zacchaeus' repentance. He gives away and repays more than is required by the law. This overflow is sign of his inner opening to God and the fullness of grace that God bestows on the returning sinner. The repentant sinner passes on this abundance to others.

Then Jesus said to him, "Today salvation has come to this house, because he too is a son of Abraham. For the Son of Man came to seek out and to save the lost."

The story has emphasized that Zacchaeus welcomed Jesus into his house with joy. This is a happy meeting of sinner and Savior. Even though welcoming Jesus means he will have to repent, Zacchaeus is delighted. Repentance is joyous activity because Zacchaeus finds his true nature that Jesus names as a "son of Abraham." Abraham was a rich and generous man. Now the rich and generous Zacchaeus has become his son, not because he has inherited his blood, but because he shares his spirit. In finding this true identity, Zacchaeus returned from the land of the lost. The Son of Man is doing what he came to do.

Teaching

Whenever I let the scrambling and happy Zacchaeus into my imagination, I find myself questioning the conventional wisdom that conversion is filled with pain and anguish. Zacchaeus is smiling as he gives away his ill-gotten gains. The bottom line of conversion is that it is the discovery of our true selves. This coming home to the truth about us is, quite simply, better than any of the substitutes we have embraced. That is why the man who discovers the treasure in the field "in joy . . . goes and sells all that he has and buys that field" (Matt 13:44).

I remember a time "back in the day," as teenagers today would say. I was a camp counselor, new at the job and eager to do well. One of the kids in my cabin, around eleven years old, was sullen and taciturn. He didn't get along with the other kids. He preyed on the weaker ones and picked fights with those who spoke up against him.

I warned him many times and punished him by making him sit out of activities. But what I was doing was not working. There was no change. If anything, things got worse. So I talked to the owner of the camp. He listened carefully, told me not to worry, and simply said, "Send him down to my cabin tomorrow morning."

A week and a half later the sullen kid was happy. He was smiling, playing "nice" with the other campers, and seemingly enjoying himself. I was impressed. When I asked the owner how this change occurred, he told me the story, a story he said that happens over and over again.

When the kid arrived at the owner's cabin, the owner was already in his car. He told him he had to go into town to get some more groceries. He wanted him to come along. On the way into town the owner told him about the problems of keeping the kitchen well stocked. He could never completely predict all that would be needed. So, although he had bought food, he had to periodically go into town to restock what had diminished faster than he thought, or buy something he had just now realized was needed. He ended this analysis of food and campers with something that sounded like, "So I brought you along to help me lug the food, and if you have any ideas about this problem let me know."

After having packed the station wagon with food, on the way back from town, the kid had his first idea.

The owner passed him along to the camp carpenter. He was rebuilding a section of boathouse that had been damaged during the winter. The carpenter had the kid help him and taught him the art of hitting the nail and not the thumb.

The carpenter passed him along to the chef. He had him help prepare the meals and taught him about en-masse cooking.

While the other kids were playing sports, going horseback riding, and doing crafts, the problem kid was hanging out with the owner, the carpenter, and the chef. Then a process known as "reeling him out and reeling him in" was put in place. They would tell the kid to go play basketball with the rest of the kids in his age group. "But be sure you are back here in an hour." A couple times a day he would be "reeled out and reeled in."

Then there came a time when the owner, carpenter, and chef told him thanks for all he had done and "Would it be OK to call on you from time to time?" But they counseled him to use the rest of his time at camp to get involved in other activities. They told him to "be on his way." He came back into the group a changed kid.

The owner explained it to me. "Everyone wants to feel they can add something. But not everyone has the opportunity and encouragement to do something. So we just set it up so the kid could be positively productive. Once he has a taste of that, he won't want to go back to something less. He will want more of doing stuff he is good at and enjoys. When we know we can contribute, we just want to keep on doing it. We're made that way."

In the presence of the Son of Man, people found out what they were made for. And what they were made for was so much better than what they were caught in, they welcomed it with joy. "Then I was beside him, like a master worker; and I was daily his delight, rejoicing before him always, rejoicing in his inhabited world and delighting in the human race" (Prov 8:30-31).

Thirty-Second Sunday in Ordinary Time

Proper 27

Luke 20:27-38

❦

Hoping Without Knowing

A Spiritual Commentary

Some Sadducees, those who say there is no resurrection, came to him and asked him a question, "Teacher, Moses wrote for us that if a man's brother dies, leaving a wife but no children, the man shall marry the widow and raise up children for his brother. Now there were seven brothers; the first married, and died childless; then the second and the third married her, and so in the same way all seven died childless. Finally, the woman also died. In the resurrection, therefore, whose wife will the woman be? For seven had married her."

At the time of this theological duel between the Sadducees and Jesus, explicit belief in a resurrection of the dead was a relatively new feature of Judaism, only a couple hundred years old. The Sadducees were traditionalists, staying within the books that Moses wrote and admitting to little else. One of the reasons they did not believe in the resurrection of dead was that it conflicted with the teachings of Moses. In particular, it could not accommodate the command about levirate (brother-in-law) marriages.

In their minds, this is a serious obstacle. But their reservations are also a touch ludicrous, even prurient. Their argumentation mocks the idea of resurrection as much as it raises insuperable obstacles. They see it as a slippery slope toward polyandry. Another one of their arguments against resurrection has the same flavor. According to the law, if a man comes in contact with a dead body, he has to be purified by sprinkling. So they asked: when the dead are raised, do they have to be sprinkled because they have been in contact with a dead body, namely their own? Mocking other people's beliefs, especially when they seem preposterous, is always fun.

However, underneath their demeaning arguments is a thorough-going materialism. They see the resurrection of the dead as people returning to this space-time continuum and being subject to the laws that are now in effect. The way they characterize resurrection from the dead gives them an opponent they can easily defeat. They set up a straw man and then pick him apart. This trick of defeating a position that nobody holds is a favorite maneuver of theological debates.

> **Jesus said to them, "Those who belong to this age marry and are given in marriage; but those who are considered worthy of a place in that age and in the resurrection from the dead neither marry nor are given in marriage. Indeed, they cannot die any more, because they are like angels and are children of God, being children of the resurrection. And the fact that the dead are raised Moses himself showed in the story about the bush, where he speaks of the Lord as the God of Abraham, the God of Isaac, and the God of Jacob. Now he is God not of the dead, but of the living; for to him all of them are alive."**

Jesus tells them that their assumptions are wrongheaded. The social situation behind the levirate law was the threat of extinction. In the case of the death of the husband before a child had been conceived, the brother had to marry the widow. The continuance of the clan was the overriding value. Marriage equaled procreation. Children had to be raised up, if not by the husband then by the husband's brother. But resurrected people will not die. So there will not be a threat of extinction. Therefore, in the age to come marrying and giving in marriage will not be required. The future of the clan will not be the foremost challenge.

Furthermore, people will be more like angels than like what they are now. They will be children of God, defined by the operations of the Spirit rather than the restrictions of the flesh. Resurrection of the dead does not look to a future time when the dead will rise and go on just as they did when they were alive. It is a whole new order of existence. To speak of "the resurrection of the dead" is to think outside the box.

This understanding of resurrection of the dead is perfectly compatible with the revelation of Moses. In fact, at the center of the revelation, in the episode where God gave Israel his name, God revealed the truth of the resurrection of the dead (Exod 3:6, 15). The Lord said he [sic] is the God of Abraham, Isaac, and Jacob. At the time of Moses when God said that, those patriarchs were dead. Yet we know that God is a God of the living and not the dead. The conclusion is unavoidable: these patriarchs are alive in God. They are living in God even though they had left the earth. This is not some derivative social regulation like the levirate marriage. This is the heart of the faith. Those who read the works of Moses without distinguishing the center from the periphery are caught in trivia. But those who resonate with the heart of Moses discern the revelatory vision in the tenses of the verbs. Jesus, the beloved Son, knows God always "is" and those who are of God always "are." This is what "resurrection of the dead" means.

Teaching

Genuine faith in God always has an element of agnosticism. In classical language, the human creature is capable of the infinite *(capax infiniti)*. We can acknowledge the transcendent reality of God. This acknowledgment includes a degree of authentic knowing. It is more than a blind recognition of Something More. But it is not exhaustive knowledge. We cannot know divine reality in so complete a way that God becomes a mental possession. Our knowledge of God illumines a relationship. But there is always more to the relationship than we know. At the heart of the knowledge of faith is a humble not-knowing. It is this not-knowing that keeps us off-balance and fearful; but it is also this not-knowing that leads us to trust.

This framework of the infinite God and the finite human knower is permanent. It is not changed by revelation. In fact, it is exacerbated. Every revelation of God is simultaneously concealment. The divine-human relationship is an essential mystery. The more we know about it, the more there is to know about. For example, the core Christian revelation that God is love brings light into the darkness. The ultimate reality is gracious toward all who participate in it. But how is this graciousness carried out? How is it manifested in a world of what looks like random destruction? The revelation does not clear up the mystery. It deepens it.

It is difficult to live in this combination of knowing and not knowing, of revelation and concealment. There is a strong drive in people for certitude. As commonsense wisdom puts it: when we know for sure, we know what we are dealing with and we calm down. It is not-knowing that creates sleep-depriving anxiety. This hunger for certitude is particularly evident when we ponder questions of life after death. Does personal consciousness survive the death of the body-mind organism? If so, what awaits us? Can those who have died and those who are still alive communicate with one another? Can they help each other in their respective journeys?

The Christian tradition has not been shy in responding to these questions, and thereby feeding the hunger for certitude that generated them. Precise theological elaborations about afterlife conditions and stories of heaven, hell, and purgatory abound. Whether these theologies and stories are accurate representations of life after death is debated both within the community of faith and outside it. But contemporary concerns often ask different questions: how do these stories and theologies function? What type of sensibilities and attitudes do they create in the people who believe in them?

Many psychological scenarios are proposed. (1) The belief in hell keeps people on the straight and narrow. It is a strong inducement to lead a moral life. (2) The belief in heaven comforts people who have lost loved ones. Knowing they are with God lessens the loss and helps the grieving process. (3) Belief in life after death keeps people from taking life before death seriously. They do not dedicate themselves to justice because they realize this life is short. Improving the earth does not interest them as much as fantasizing about eternity. (4) Belief in life after death keeps people from facing the finality of death. They seem to think they are just going away for the weekend. Therefore, they procrastinate about what has to be done and refuse to prioritize according to what is most important. (5) Afterlife speculations feed the certitude hunger and keep people from cultivating the two attitudes they need most for the transition of death—trust and a capacity for surprise. Although many patterns of how afterlife beliefs function can be imagined, individual persons tend to put together beliefs, attitudes, and behaviors in idiosyncratic ways.

One interesting example is Patricia Monaghan's powerful personal essay, "Physics and Grief" (Patricia Monaghan, "Physics and Grief" in *The Best American Spiritual Writing 2004,* ed. Philip Zaleski [Boston: Houghton Mifflin Company, 2004] 151–67). She has lost her husband and she is deep into the vacillating emotions and behaviors of grief. A friend has also lost his partner, and she asks him what has helped him with his grief. He simply says, "Physics." She is not surprised because physics has also helped her. But before she explains how physics has addressed her grief, she relates her experience with the keys.

She has lost her keys; and she has searched everywhere and cannot find them. In her frustration, she begins to cry. She connects this crying with the crying over the loss of her husband that has been going on for months. Then suddenly she becomes enraged at Bob (her dead husband) for leaving her alone in this sad world of grief.

> I wanted so desperately to believe that Bob, and Bob's love for me, still existed somewhere in the universe, that in my furious pain I flung down a challenge. . . . Find my keys. Find my damned keys! If there's anyone out there, if there's any love left in this universe for me, find my keys!

Once she calms down, she is mortified by her challenge. She has thrown down a gauntlet to the vast universe on the paltry topic of her keys. So, under the guise of housekeeping, she takes apart her home in quest of her keys. She finds no keys.

Now back to physics. She reached for physics when she refused the facile certitudes of religion.

> I adamantly refused to settle for those happy visions that religion held out, of dreamy heavens full of harps, of other lives to come, of eventual reunion in some cosmic void. . . . I had been reading a lot of spiritual literature. But I only grew more isolated, angry at the serenity that seemed forever beyond my grasp, despairing at my continuing inability to find any sense in death's senselessness. It was not that the answers which spiritual literature offered seemed implausible or incorrect; it was simply that I could not believe them, could not make the leap into not-doubting. The more rigidly codified their religious insight, the more it seemed to exclude—even to mock—my anguished confusion.

Religion was not helpful to her because it was so sure of itself and she was so unsure of herself.

Physics, on the other hand, painted a universe of mysterious uncertainty, a universe that could speak to the "wild movements" of her grieving soul. "[U]nlike religion, which seemed hypnotized by its own articulations of the ineffable, physics acknowledged that any picture we hold of the subatomic world is by definition inaccurate, limited, inexact." She immerses herself in the works of de Broglie, Heisenberg, Born, Einstein, Bohm, Schroedinger, Jeans, etc.

> Einstein spoke to me like a voice from a burning bush. I, who lived in a time and space from which my love had disappeared, found respite in considering the ways that time and space were linked. "Any two points in space and time are both separate and not separate," David Bohm said. As incomprehensible as this new space-time was, it was more lively with possibilities than linear and planar realities. My separateness from Bob was real, but in some way, we were also together. In some way—this was most important to me.

When she opens up to a universe of lively possibilities, all of which could not be known, she finds hope in not-knowing, in the indefinite phrase—"in some way."

Then she finds her keys in a most perplexing place—peeking through a hole in a poster that hangs on the inside door of her office. She reenacts all the possible ways the keys could have landed there. Every explanation is "fairly unlikely." So she entertains another "fairly unlikely" scenario.

> Were this a court of law, I would argue that there was no motive for anyone else to hide the keys, and no evidence that I have either before or since gone into a state of mindless fugue. That my beloved Bob had somehow answered my request seems as likely as any of these interpretations. Also: Bob had a unique sense of humor, and he tended to procrastinate. So it would be in character for him to have taken a year to get around to giving me the keys back, and then it would be in a suitably clever fashion.

In an uncertain world uncertain things happen.

However, she resists pouncing on this incident as proof that the man she loves still exists and is coming to her in a time of need. If she did this, she would have been left with "only an odd anecdote which, over time, would have grown less and less vital, would have held less and less consolation." Instead, she uses it to increase her sense of relativity and her growing ability to live with the unresolvability of life's fundamental questions. She sums up her new consciousness. "If there was uncertainty at the basis of the universe, there was also ravishing mystery."

St. Paul urged the Thessalonians to "not grieve as others do who have no hope" (1 Thess 4:13). I take this to mean that we should grieve the loss of the ones we love. When we mortals love, we embrace grief as inevitable. But how is hope sustained during the wild ride of grief? Traditional Christian religion advised us to hold onto the certainty of the resurrection of Christ and the infallible teachings of the church. But a different path may be opening up for some people. When we reconceive the universe as a "ravishing mystery" of possibilities that we can acknowledge but not predict, hope may emerge in a new, agnostic, more humble form.

Perhaps, in the last analysis, this approach to hope may be an ally of Christian faith. This may be what Jesus was arguing for against the literal-minded and blindly certain Sadducees. They were so caught in their rendition of reality that they could not conceive the possibility of something else. It had to be what they already knew or they mocked it, laughing at anything that contradicted their narrow mindset. Jesus' response does not accede to their earthbound worldview. Rather, he overwhelms them with realities that lurk on the edge of conscious-ness—the contrast between this age and one to come, angels and resurrected children, a burning bush and a God in whom everything always lives. They will never be able to stretch into the world of Jesus' consciousness unless they let go, not of their world, but of the absolute way they are using it to evaluate the real. It may be the same for us.

Also, it may be helpful to interpret the resurrection of Jesus as the revelation of uncertainty. The resurrection did more than confirm an already existing belief in life after death. It exploded the way the mind creates impossibilities and then canonizes them as certain. In Luke's Gospel, it is an angel from another world (Luke 1:19) who puts an end to the human pretension to total knowledge by reminding Mary that "nothing will be impossible with God" (Luke 1:37). And it is two "men in dazzling clothes" who tell the woman, who bow their heads to the ground because they know these men are messengers from an-other world, that their certitude about death is unfounded, "Why do you look for the living among the dead?" (Luke 24:4-5). The gospels confront us with the truth that our physical eyes do not see all secrets. The resurrection reveals a world beyond the dictates of the senses, a strange and everlasting connection between human consciousness and the earth. This may come at us only as a mind-boggling piece of infor-mation that does not fit well into what we presently know. But if we let this boundary-breaking revelation sink in, we will be ravished by mystery, thrilled and alert with the consciousness of uncertainty. After the long night of demanding to know everything before we dare hope, Easter morning will have arrived. Christ is risen!

Thirty-Third Sunday in Ordinary Time

Proper 28

Luke 21:5-19

❧

Predicting the Future

A Spiritual Commentary

When some were speaking about the temple, how it was adorned with beautiful stones and gifts dedicated to God, he said, "As for these things that you see, the days will come when not one stone will be left upon another; all will be thrown down."

It is not difficult to distinguish between Divine Reality itself and an earthly building dedicated to Divine Reality. God is eternal and does not suffer the perishing of time. An impressive temple of massive proportions and beautiful stones is still the stuff of both wear and tear and human plunder. Nevertheless, there is always the temptation to think that something of divine imperishability will rub off on the earthly abode. Jesus, a prophet in the line of Jeremiah, calmly states this will not be the case.

The temple will come down; its destruction will be complete. There will not be a shell of a temple left. All the stones will be thrown down; all will lay equally at ground level. If tall buildings symbolize a connection to heaven, then that connection will be broken. Whatever set of arrangements were symbolized and actualized by the temple, they will no longer be operative.

They asked him, "Teacher, when will this be, and what will be the sign that is about to take place?"

And he said, "Beware that you are not led astray; for many will come in my name and say, 'I am he!' and, 'The time is near!' Do not go after them."

"When you hear of wars and insurrections, do not be terrified; for these things must take place first, but the end will not follow immediately."

Then he said to them, "Nation will rise against nation, and kingdom against kingdom; there will be great earthquakes, and

> in various places famines and plagues; and there will be dread-ful portents and great signs from heaven.
>
> But before all this occurs, they will arrest you and persecute you; they will hand you over to synagogues and prisons, and you will be brought before kings and governors because of my name.
>
> This will give you an opportunity to testify. So make up your minds not to prepare your defense in advance; for I will give you words and a wisdom that none of your opponents will be able to withstand or contradict.
>
> You will be betrayed even by parents and brothers, by relatives and friends; and they will put some of you to death. You will be hated by all because of my name. But not a hair of your head will perish. By your endurance you will gain your souls.

The people who have heard Jesus do not question his prediction or ask what it means for Israel. They are more interested in knowing when to expect it. What signs will indicate that it is imminent? This push for more information is not idle curiosity. The more they know the better they will be prepared. Prophets who know the future are always quizzed by people who must face that future.

Jesus' answer unfolds against a backdrop of apocalyptic expectations. In general, apocalyptic sensitivities saw God and people in an increasingly strained relationship. People were supposed to be in a covenant agreement with God, but they were actually in covenant violation. They gave lip service to God's commands, but their hearts were elsewhere. They lived in sinful isolation from God and from one another, breaking the covenant agreement and risking punishment. But God, who is merciful and forgiving, sent prophets to urge the people back to faithfulness. However, the people rejected and killed these messengers. Over time, it became obvious the hearts of the people were going to remain hard. How long would the patience of God last?

Christians placed the life, death, and resurrection of Jesus squarely within this heightening tension between God and people. In a last attempt at reconciliation, God sent Jesus, his Beloved Son. But the people who killed the prophets continued their rejection of God's covenant by killing the Son. Although God reversed their evil actions and raised Jesus from the dead, the murder of this righteous one signaled the end of God's patience. The social order that destroyed the Son, the symbolic center of which was the Temple, would itself be destroyed.

But not all would perish with it. Those who belonged to the Son, who heard his call for repentance and followed his way, would be carried through suffering into glory just as Jesus had been carried through suffering into glory (Luke 24:26). This pattern of suffering and glory is a necessity. The disciples will have to endure trials and persecutions just as Jesus did. However, they will not be alone in this chaos and terror. Jesus will return in the midst of their persecution to help them persevere. Where they are, there he will be.

In this context, Jesus' first piece of advice is not to overreact. Things that might look like signs are not signs. People with placards, "The end is near!" will appear, and many will claim they are Jesus himself risen from the dead. But they are panic peddlers with loud voices who should not be followed. Also when wars and rumors of wars are rife, there is a tendency to think the time has come. But this is still a very preliminary stage, not an immediate harbinger of the cataclysmic end. Panicky prophets claiming to be the risen Christ and routine accounts of political turmoil are not signs to be heeded. They are the usual business of false prophets and wars.

The end itself will be unmistakable. It will entail social and cosmic reverberations. Not only will nations rage, but the earth will be in upheaval and the heavens, which predict and mirror the affairs of earth, will be filled with portents so dreadful they can only signal destruction. This total breakdown will be the result of the continued rejection of the offer of God in Jesus to embrace the ways of the kingdom. Therefore, the real signs that the old order is crumbling will be the disciples' own trials and tribulations. In the world's efforts to destroy God's people, the world itself will come down.

In fact, the disciples' trials and tribulations will continue the passion and death of Jesus. Everything that happened to Jesus will happen to them, and it will happen to them precisely because they bear Jesus' name. They will be arrested (like Jesus in the Garden of Gethsemane), imprisoned and brought before kings (like Jesus was brought before Herod) and governors (like Jesus was arraigned before Pilate). Also, as Jesus was betrayed by Judas and abandoned by his disciples whom he called his brothers and sisters, they will be betrayed by family members and those closest to them.

However, in the midst of this being "handed over" they will be able to witness. During his passion, Jesus forgave his persecutors, offered salvation to the "good thief," and handed his Spirit over to God. There will be similar opportunities for them. But they need not rely on their own powers for this daunting task. Jesus, the one who has been through it before, will be with them and give them words to say. These words, just as Jesus' silence and words during his own trial, will have a wisdom so profound they will not be able to be contradicted. The passion of Jesus is not over; it continues in those who follow him.

However, suffering is not the whole of it. Resurrection is the deeper and more abiding truth. Although their bodies will be brutalized and even put to death, not a hair of their heads will perish (Luke 12:7). God will remember them just as Jesus remembered the "good thief" who repented and requested salvation. Therefore, their response to persecution must be perseverance. They are to endure in the truth of their souls, the truth that Jesus revealed to them. Enduring in this truth, they will be able to endure the sufferings this truth always attracts to itself. "Blessed are you when people hate you, and when they exclude you, revile you, and defame you on account of the Son of Man. Rejoice in that day and leap for joy, for surely your reward is great in heaven; for that is what their ancestors did to the prophets" (Luke 6:22-23).

Teaching

Predicting the future always draws a crowd. We are people who like to be ready for what is coming. It gives us a sense of control. When we know what to expect, we have an edge. When the unknown future becomes known, some of the terror is taken out of it.

It is this need to know the future that urges us, sometimes against our better judgment, to give prophets a hearing. Some thinkers insist that prophets are not people with crystal balls. They are essentially people who speak for God. Through their communion with God, they see into the depth of the present. More often than not what they see is a thoroughgoing incongruity between the divine will and human machinations. Since they are certain that unless God builds the house, those who build it build it in vain, they predict a future of destruction. When human efforts are not grounded in God, they are utterly futile.

Therefore, their ability to see future chaos is really a byproduct of their discernment of the present alienation from a Will that will necessarily prevail. There is no need to posit that prophets are privileged with a supernatural vision of things yet to be. They are simply people with strong convictions and keen psychological and social senses. But whatever their basis for predicting the future is, we listen because knowing what is coming is better than being in the dark.

In today's world prophets are not the people who feed this hunger to know the future. Statisticians are. They give us data on a wide variety of topics, and with this data comes the science of probability. But a recent study by Ellen Langer and her colleagues describes another way the future might come within the province of human control.

Langer and her associates tested two different coping strategies with patients about to undergo major surgery. They provided one group with statistical data about pain and recovery that would help them predict what they were going to experience. With a second group they worked on helping them develop a positive lens, a frame, through which to see their upcoming surgery. Then both groups were tracked with specific measures after their surgery. The second faired significantly better. "These results indicate that although factual preparation and training in reframing both emphasize prediction as the key to an experience of personal control, the type of prediction offered by individual experience is distinct from the prediction offered by group data. Whereas prediction based on statistics assumes some correspondence with reality, prediction based on individual experience enables individuals to give meaning to their own future experience." (Ellen J. Langer, *The Power of Mindful Learning* [New York: Merloyd Lawrence Books, 1997] 128–30.) Knowing the meaning of what will happen may be more important than knowing the statistical details of what will happen.

This way of knowing the meaning of the future is respectful of the future as an unknown reality. But it also brings it into the personal life of the one who is facing that future—a possibility of response that was not previously available. John O'Donohue tells the story of a woman facing limit and loss who, with the help of a priest, prepares herself to bring meaning into her future suffering.

A friend of mine went to the hospital to have a hysterectomy. A priest friend came to visit her on the evening before her operation. She was anxious and vulnerable. He sat down and they began to talk. He suggested to her that she have a conversation with her womb. To talk to her womb as a friend. She could thank her womb for making her a mother. To thank it for all her different children who had begun there. The body, mind and spirit of each child had been tenderly formed in that kind darkness. She could remember the different times in her life when she was acutely aware of her own presence, power and vulnerability as a mother. To thank her womb for the gifts and the difficulties. To explain to it how it had become ill and that it was necessary for her continuing life as a mother to have it removed. She was to undertake this intimate ritual of leave-taking before the surgeons came in the morning to take her womb away. She did this ritual with tenderness and warmth of heart. The operation was a great success. Her conversation with her womb changed the whole experience. The power was not with the doctors or the hospital. The experience did not have the clinical, short-circuit edge of so much mechanical and anonymous hospital efficiency. The experience became totally her own, the leave-taking of her own womb. (John O'Donohue, *Eternal Echoes: Exploring Our Hunger to Belong* [New York: Bantam, 1998] 179–80)

Predicting the future is really about not being victimized by events. It is taking the leverage away from happenstance and fate and placing it in the courage and creativity of the one suffering. It is about making our experience our own.

Of course, when it comes to the unknown future, especially the future of our sufferings, our fears may tell us that this is not enough. What we need are exact timetables and all the details. However, it is in the nature of things that this will not be given. And I do not think the apocalyptic predictions of the Lukan Jesus were meant to be exceptions to the radically unknowable future. Rather, I think he was preparing them to understand the meaning of their sufferings. They were going to suffer the violent night of a way of thinking and acting that was dying and brought to the morning of a way of thinking and acting that was being born. In this terrible transition they are called to witness to and cling to the transcendent love that ultimately holds them. Whatever happens to them, this is really what is happening. There was no one better qualified to tell them this profound truth than Jesus.

Christ the King
Reign of Christ

Luke 23:35-43 *LM* • Luke 23:33-43 *RCL*

🕯️

Testing Life by Dying

A Spiritual Commentary

When they came to the place that is called The Skull, they crucified Jesus there with the criminals, one on his right and one on his left.

At his Last Supper, Jesus insisted the Scripture had to be fulfilled that "he was counted among the lawless" (Luke 22:37). This refers to a passage in Isaiah that puts the fact of being "counted among the lawless" in an illuminating context.

> Therefore I will allot him a portion with the great, and he shall divide the spoil with the strong; because he poured out himself to death, and was numbered with the transgressors; yet he bore the sin of many and made intercession for the transgressors. (Isa 53:12)

This suggests the surface contact with transgressors holds a deeper meaning. Jesus is not one more transgressor. Rather he is among transgressors as a sign that he bears their sins and makes intercession for them. In fact, Jesus is about to make intercession for transgressors, not only those with whom he is crucified but those who are crucifying him.

Then Jesus said, "Father, forgive them; for they do not know what they are doing."

And they cast lots to divide his clothing.

And the people stood by watching; but the rulers scoffed at him, saying, "He saved others; let him save himself if he is the Messiah of God, his chosen one!"

The soldiers also mocked him, coming up and offering him sour wine, and saying, "If you are the King of the Jews, save yourself!" There was also an inscription over him, "This Is the King of the Jews."

> **One of the criminals who were hanged there kept deriding him and saying, "Are you not the Messiah? Save yourself and us!"**

During his life Jesus preached and taught that people should forgive their enemies as a sign that they were sons and daughters of the merciful Father. "But I say to you that listen, Love your enemies, do good to those who hate you, bless those who curse you, pray for those who abuse you. . . . Be merciful just as your Father is merciful" (Luke 6:27-28, 36). However, it is one thing to preach and teach forgiveness; it is quite another thing to do it under circumstances of being hated, cursed, and maltreated by your enemies. Jesus is practicing what he preached; and by forgiving his enemies he is demonstrating that he is the son of the merciful Father.

However, this way of showing that Jesus is God's Son is completely lost on the rulers who are responsible for crucifying him. They do not know that forgiveness of enemies is the key characteristic of God's Son. But their ignorance is more than the simple lack of this theological fact. They are caught in a complex process in which what they think they are doing is not really what they are doing. Their ignorance has an ironic edge to it.

The rulers think they are putting Jesus to the test. If he is the Messiah and King of the Jews, then he will save himself from crucifixion. If he does this, his claims will be true. If he refuses to do this or cannot do this, his claims are false. Their motivation and reasoning is carefully captured in a passage from the book of Wisdom.

> Let us lie in wait for the righteous man, because he is inconvenient to us and opposes our actions; he reproaches us for sins against the law, and accuses us of sins against our training. He professes to have knowledge of God, and calls himself a child of the Lord. He became to us a reproof of our thoughts; the very sight of him is a burden to us, because his manner of life is unlike that of others, and his ways are strange. We are considered by him as something base, and he avoids our ways as unclean; he calls the last end of the righteous happy, and boasts that God is his father. Let us see if his words are true, and let us test what will happen at the end of his life; for if the righteous man is God's child, he will help him, and will deliver him from the hand of his adversaries. Let us test him with insult and torture, so that we may find out how gentle he is, and make trial of his forbearance. Let us condemn him to a shameful death, for, according to what he says, he will be protected. (Wisdom 2:12-20)

They are motivated by personal animosity and their schemes of insult, torture, and death are rationalized as a way "to see if his words are true."

However, this is not what is really going on; and so they "do not know what they are doing." They are involved in something else; and the next line from the book of Wisdom reveals what it is. "Thus they reasoned [to test the righteous man by mockery, torture, and death to see if God will rescue him], but they were led astray, for their wickedness blinded them, and they did not know the secret purposes of God" (Wisdom 2:12-22). Their attempts at disinterested rationality are bogus. They are blinded by wickedness; and they are over-their-heads in the secret purposes of God about which they know nothing.

They prove this ignorance by unwittingly fulfilling a prophecy. They divide his clothing by casting lots. In their minds, this claiming of spoils proves they have been victorious over Jesus. But it also places them squarely in the middle of Psalm 22 that predicts that Jesus will be victorious over them. Psalm 22 painfully recounts the suffering of a just man at the hands of his enemies, his calling upon God, and his final vindication. What looks like a victory for the enemies turns out to be a hymn of praise to divine faithfulness and a victory for God's righteous one. The psalm ends not only with the suffering man's praise of God but with a vision of universal faith. "All the ends of the earth shall remember and turn to the Lord; and all the families of the nations shall worship before him" (Ps 22:27).

The secret purposes of God concern a new embodiment of suffering, vindication, and universal impact. The sufferings of Jesus will be vindicated in the resurrection and become a force for faith throughout the world. The risen Christ indicates this when he asks the two travelers on the road to Emmaus, "Was it not necessary that the Messiah should suffer these things and then enter into his glory?" (Luke 24:26). This connects the sufferings of the Messiah with glory (See the Third Sunday of Easter, Vol. 1, Cycle A). But there is a further connection between glory and the commissioning of the disciples. "[T]he Messiah is to suffer and to rise from the dead on the third day, and . . . repentance and forgiveness of sins is to be proclaimed in his name to all nations. . . . You are witnesses of these things" (Luke 24:46-48). Jesus' persecutors know nothing about this larger divine plan. But, through their actions, they are bringing it about.

The soldiers and the criminal who deride Jesus share the ignorance of the leaders, but they play it out in ways that reflect their situations. The soldiers mock Jesus not because he is a messianic pretender but because he is a kingly pretender. They know nothing of the kingdom of God, but they are very savvy about the kingdom of Caesar. Caesar's legions have put many upstarts in their place, and Jesus is one more. They play cupbearer at court and offer this king wine, appropriately sour, as he sits upon his throne, appropriately uncomfortable. The criminal joins the scoffing of the leaders and the mockery of the soldiers with the intent of finally bringing Jesus to an angry point of reprisal. "Are you not the Messiah?" carries the desperate hope that he is what he claims, and liberating violence is somehow at his command. "Save yourself AND US!" The ignorance of the leaders, soldiers, and the one criminal is the atmosphere of their actions. They don't know what they are doing.

"And the people stood by watching." The people do not share the consciousness of the rulers, soldiers, and the one criminal. They are not ignorant actors. They are observers. Their wickedness does not blind them, and they are not led astray. Just the opposite, their patient watching will bring them to revelation. After Jesus' death, "when all the crowds who had gathered there for this spectacle saw what had taken place, they returned home, beating their breasts" (Luke 23:48). They came for a spectacle, but they returned home in repentance. They repented because they saw the truth of what had taken place. They watched as Jesus forgave his enemies, offered paradise to the repentant criminal, handed his spirit over to the Father, and as the centurion affirmed that Jesus was righteous. They realized a wrong had been done. They did not yet know how God would turn it right.

> **But the other [criminal] rebuked him, saying, "Do you not fear God, since you are under the same sentence of condemnation? And we indeed have been condemned justly, for we are getting what we deserve for our deeds; but this man has done nothing wrong."**
>
> **Then he said, "Jesus, remember me when you come into your kingdom."**
>
> **He replied, "Truly I tell you, today you will be with me in Paradise."**

The rulers, soldiers, and the one criminal have berated Jesus for not saving himself. But he was not sent to save himself. In fact, it was his own salvation, his relationship of love with the Father, that energized his mission to save others. Jesus is the saved one who spends himself for others. This was the project that guided his life, and this is still the project to which he is faithful as he dies. The exchange with the criminal is a fitting culmination of the life of one who defined himself as a seeker after the lost (Luke 19:10).

This criminal is rightly disposed. He knows the sentence of death means he will stand, as all people will, before the judgment seat of God. He recognizes that his and his fellow criminal's sentence of execution is legitimate because they have done wrong. Acknowledgment of sinfulness is the initial move of repentance. He also recognizes that Jesus' sentence is not legitimate. Jesus is an innocent man; he has done nothing to deserve crucifixion. This criminal fears the judgment of God, repents of his wrongdoing, and recognizes that Jesus' death does not discredit him.

Knowing all this, the criminal who turns to Jesus rebukes his fellow criminal for joining the mockery and derision of the rulers and the soldiers. Even though the criminal derides Jesus for a quite different reason, he buys into the theology of test of the rulers and angrily begs Jesus to play fantasy Messiah and take him down from the cross. If the criminal who derided Jesus saw correctly, he should ask what the criminal who has turned to Jesus is about to ask: "Jesus, remember me when you come into your kingdom."

The rulers, soldiers, and the other criminal have tossed around titles. They thought they knew what the titles meant and they judged Jesus by those meanings. However, this criminal does not use titles. He simply says, "Jesus." The cultural meanings attached to titles do not rule over Jesus. The person of Jesus transforms the inherited meanings of titles. Jesus does not fit into preexisting categories. He breaks those categories to create something new. The criminal who turns to Jesus knows whom he is turning to. Unlike the persecutors, he does know what he is doing.

Jesus is waiting. He is eager for someone who engages in the inner work that is necessary for openness and turns to him with the one request he wants to hear. To request the kingdom galvanizes the kingdom-bringer into action. It is God's pleasure to give people the kingdom (Luke 12:32). It is not the divine duty, obligation, or burden. It is the Father's pleasure to pour God's self into the empty bowl of a person. Jesus knows this personally for he has experienced this pleasure (Luke 3:22). In fact, this pleasure is essential to his identity, alerting him to every possibility of passing it on to another. That possibility has just arrived. Is there any doubt about what will happen?

The moment of openness becomes the moment of fulfillment. Whenever the repentant sinner turns to the merciful God, it is "today," a time of actualization. There is a correct alignment between human receptivity and divine initiative. The receptivity did not produce the initiative. The initiative was always knocking; the receptivity merely opened the door (Luke 11:9-11). This divine initiative lives in the heart of Jesus, and the criminal has established a relationship with Jesus. "Remember me" is met by "you will be with me." As Paul summed it up, "In Christ God was reconciling the world to himself" (2 Cor 5:19).

In popular Catholic piety, the criminal who turns to Jesus is known as the Good Thief, the thief who stole heaven. If the criminal who derided Jesus wants Jesus to come down off the cross and take him with him, the criminal who turns to Jesus wants him to go into the kingdom of heaven and take him with him. The first criminal is betting on this life, and the second criminal is betting on the afterlife. This conversational exchange between Jesus and the criminal who turns to him may be about looking past their common deaths to a better post-death existence.

In the Christian tradition, paradise has become a euphemism for afterlife communion with God and others in heaven. But its primary referent is to an earthly condition that was disrupted by sin. Paradise is the condition of integrated unity among God, humans, animals, and the earth. In the Fall, this unity was splintered into alienation. What was once held together is now broken apart. We live in this brokenness, in a world where the one who wants to develop a reconciled unity is violently resisted and brought to his death. Sin rules.

However, in this most unlikely of places, the garden has suddenly returned. Paradise has emerged in the cross-bound conversation between two dying men, one a representative of sin reaching for wholeness and the other a Son of the fullness of God reaching toward what has been lost.

> For the LORD will comfort Zion;
> he will comfort all her waste places,
> and will make her wilderness like Eden,
> her desert like the garden of the LORD;
> joy and gladness will be found in her,
> thanksgiving and the voice of song (Isa 51:3).

This song may envision a before-and-after scenario—now waste place and later comfort, now wilderness and later paradise, now desert and later garden. But it may also mean a change in consciousness—comfort suffuses the waste places, paradise enters the wilderness, and a garden blooms in the desert. When the merciful God and the repentant sinner meet, the time of exile is over. We no longer live east of Eden; we are back in paradise. Jesus is doing what he was sent to do, even as he dies, even in his dying.

Teaching

The ancient world valued integrity. They were well aware that people who talked a noble game might not have a noble game in their heart. So there was a discrepancy between thinking and saying. But also, people who had a noble game in their heart and on their lips might actually play a villainous game. So there was a discrepancy between saying and doing. The way to unmask these possible hypocrisies was to bring onto the stage that great persuader of truth: death.

Take the case of Secundus the Silent. This philosopher had taken a vow of silence. But the emperor Hadrian decided to test him and demanded he speak. Secundus refused. The emperor sent him off with the executioner. But he had given the executioner these instructions: if he talks in an attempt to save his life, cut off his head; but if he remains silent in the face of death, spare him. Secundus remained silent and he was spared. He did not abandon his way of life in order to live. How he lived was how he was willing to die (see Charles H. Talbert, *Reading Luke: A Literary and Theological Commentary on the Third Gospel* [New York: Crossroad, 1982] 221–50).

The death of Jesus makes clear his integrity. What he said and what he did were of one piece. He did not seek out death; but he died as a martyr, one who valued God's will more highly than his own life. He taught and lived a nonviolent way of life, holding forgiveness and reconciliation to be absolute values that had to be followed at all costs. When pressure was brought against him to abandon those values and use whatever powers he had to protect himself and defeat his attackers, he refused to do so. He died as he lived. This simple yet profound integrity lifts him above others and recommends his revelation of a forgiving God as truthful.

This presentation of Jesus' dying has made martyrdom the supreme act of witnessing to the truth of Christian faith. It is assumed that people have been formed in the Christian vision of loving God and neighbor. They have brought these twin truths into their minds and hearts and committed themselves to living out these truths in whatever circumstances they find themselves. The ultimate circumstance would be if they gave their lives for this revelation, if they refused to compromise these teachings even though their refusal meant their own death. This witness is so powerful and, ultimately, so attractive that it is sanctioned by a traditional saying that every Christian child has heard: "The blood of martyrs is the seed of the church."

Although this path of martyrdom is essential to an authentic following of Jesus, most Christians will not be called upon to face this test. However, there is a contemporary form of testing life by dying that everyone faces from time to time. Rachael Remen tells a story about how it came up at a crowded party ("Beyond the American Way," in *My Grandfather's Blessings: Stories of Strength, Refuge and Belonging* [New York: Riverhead Books, 2000] 300–2). A woman in her thirties, who was told that Remen worked with the dying, confronted her, telling her she resented all this talk about death as something meaningful. Then she recounted the horrible death of her husband a number of years earlier. He had been diagnosed with cancer; and as therapy after therapy had failed, he became bitter, lashing out at everyone, rebuffing anyone who tried to comfort him. When he looked back at his young life, he regretted the choices he had made. He died angry and withdrawn. She ended her telling of this ordeal with, "I do not want to die this way."

Remen asked her, "So how do you need to live?" The woman looked puzzled. So Remen asked her again. "How do you need to live to be sure that you do not die this way?" This time she got it. "She looked past me for a moment, making eye contact with something intensely personal. Then she reached out and touched my hand and turned away into the crowd." Some months later, Remen receives a note from this woman. She realized she was not living as authentically as she wanted. There were many things left undone; many roads not taken. She began to revise her life in the light of her death. In her case, life was still tested in the dying, but in a reverse fashion. Contemplating her death started a process that led to her rearranging her life.

This is a path that spiritual traditions recommend. They ask us to move our death from sometime in the future to right now. In this position of nearness, death can test our lives and teach us what to do. And it has many lessons to contribute to our education. It weans us away from the illusion of immortality. It encourages us to prioritize our activities and focus on what is most important. It instills a sense of freedom, reaffirming our ability to lead a life of integrity. It awakens us to the dangers of procrastination, telling us to get out of our chair and deal with unfinished business. They are relationships that need reconciling and people who need to be thanked. Finally, it opens us to each moment, cherishing whatever arises in all its fragility. No one knows how they will die. So meditating on our death is not preparation for a future event. Rather, it tells us how to live so that whenever and however we die, our life will be fulfilled.

Scripture Index